Toward Social Hope

TOWARD SOCIAL HOPE

THEODORE CAPLOW

Basic Books, Inc., Publishers

NEW YORK

Library of Congress Cataloging in Publication Data

Caplow, Theodore.
  Toward social hope.

  Includes bibliographical references.
  1. Social change. 2. Planning. 3. Social
history. I. Title.
HM101.C24   301.24   74-79286
ISBN 0-465-08649-7

Contents

Preface

A S the title suggests, this is a moderately cheerful book. It began several years ago as an inquiry into the perfectibility of social institutions that covered a good deal of ground without making much progress. Slowly it dawned on me that although perfect social institutions are not possible or even desirable, a greatly improved society might be within our present grasp if projects of social improvement were undertaken in a more rational way.

In the following pages, I shall try to show that deliberate social change is easier to bring about than most people suppose, and that we already have most of the theoretical knowledge required for a competent social technology. But as we review the major projects of social improvement that have been undertaken in this country in recent years, we shall have to recognize that many of them were so poorly designed that they could not have achieved their stated goals under any conceivable circumstances.

The important question is whether the American style of social reform can be changed enough to make a difference; whether, in effect, the project of improving social improvement is feasible. I think it is. This book is presented in the hope that its proposals will be heeded by social reformers, and it is respectfully dedicated to them and to their success.

I am grateful to Philip Elsworth Allen, Howard M. Bahr, Jacques Barzun, Robert M. Bierstedt, Christine Caplow, David A. Shannon, and Erik Wensberg, who read and criticized the manuscript at various stages, to Katherine Reed and Mary Jane Ellsworth, who prepared it for publication, and to *The Columbia Forum* for permission to reproduce portions of Chapters 1 and 9–14, which appeared in the 1973 Winter and Spring issues.

THEODORE CAPLOW

Charlottesville, Virginia
September 1974

Toward Social Hope

CHAPTER 1

Is Social Improvement Feasible?

IT is conventional to say that the social sciences have not kept pace with the physical sciences, and to point out that while we know how to produce a steadily increasing quantity and variety of material goods, we do not yet have an adequate scientific basis for the solution of social problems. In this book I will try to show that the difficulty lies elsewhere, namely in our unwillingness to apply existing sociological knowledge to the real world in a serious and rational way.

The difference between physical technology and the contemporary version of social technology is a difference of orientation to the future. In physical technology, the present is part of a continuous span of time moving into the future at a constant rate. When necessary, the future is described in as much detail as the present and is treated as equally real. A task involves defining some future condition precisely enough to permit all the intermediate conditions separating it from the present to be described and measured with as much accuracy as the task demands. In other words, ordinary technology tells us how to get from where we are to where we want to be, how long it will take, how much it will cost, and where we will be at various points along the way. Such estimates have a margin of error and sometimes they fail entirely, but in a well-grounded technology most of them work most of the time.

Because making predictions is costly and time consuming, the operators of ordinary technology tend to restrict themselves to measuring those aspects of the future situation that are relevant to the success or failure of their own assignments. The measurements that they are most likely to omit, either innocently or intentionally, are those referring to larger systems; for example, the impact of an industrial process on the natural environment.

Social technology is applied in a quite different way. Its attention is focused on the present and particularly on those elements of an existing situation that make us uncomfortable because they embody either contradictory values held by the same citizens or conflicting values held by different citizens. Our social technology has had an uncertain grasp of the future. The conditions to be achieved are seldom described in any detail, seldom located at a particular point in the future, and almost never related to any larger system in the future. It is not customary to specify the intermediate conditions which must be traversed to go from where we are to where we want to be, or the costs involved, or the time required. Social technology, as we have known it so far, has had an aversion to simple arithmetic.

This aversion is not willful, nor is it chargeable to the lag between the physical and social sciences. Perhaps it can best be explained by the kind of assignment that social technology mistakenly accepts, which is to bring about a transition between a particular situation and something better but undefined somewhere in the future. The vagueness of the goal to be attained wraps the whole effort in a cloud of confusion, virtually guaranteeing its failure when the project is at all complex or ambitious.

But many of us are convinced that we already have enough sociological knowledge to improve our society beyond recognition if we can only learn to design feasible projects of social improvement in addition to the platforms and slogans to which we now pin our hopes.

A feasible project of social improvement resembles any other technological project, such as planning a bridge across a river. We start with the end-condition we want to achieve, describe it as accurately as we can, locate it in space and time, and then work back and forth between the future situation we want and the present situation we have until we have built up a detailed account of the intermediate stages through which we must pass to get from where we are to where we want to be. This sequential procedure implies continuous attention to the question of who must do what to move from each stage of the project to the next, how long it will take, how much it will cost, and what risks are to be anticipated at each stage. Following this procedure forces the social reformers to attend to matters they are otherwise tempted to overlook. It requires careful counting of time, money, people, and results at each stage of a project, forcing them to recognize the impossibility of many seemingly plausible projects that once begun cannot be successfully completed. Another advantage of the sequential procedure is that when we have described the intermediate stages which necessarily intervene between where we are and where we want to be, we are then able to estimate the success or failure of an ongoing project at each stage without waiting for its final outcome and to take corrective measures when a project begins to falter. We are also in a better position to study the unanticipated consequences that a successful project inevitably generates before they have gotten out of hand.

A project of this kind is similar to technological projects in having a number of essential parts, which are listed below. Another similarity is its inability to operate properly unless all of those parts are present and in working order.

A. An accurate description of the existing condition to be changed.
B. A careful and honest description of the end-condition to be achieved.
C. A division of the project into successive stages and description of the conditions to be achieved at each stage.
D. Practicable methods for getting from each stage to the next.
E. Estimates of the time, personnel, material resources and information required to get from each stage to the next.
F. Procedures for measuring goal-attainment at each stage.
G. Procedures for detecting unanticipated results at each stage.

The elementary character of this list cannot be sufficiently emphasized. In the simplest non-sociological project the same requirements would be respected as a matter of course. It would be unthinkable when building a shed for example, not to specify the size and appearance of the shed in advance. It would be quite insane not to inspect the shed continuously as it went up in order to detect deviations from the plan and to determine whether the work should be corrected or the plan modified in response to each deviation. It would be nearly impossible for a normal adult to embark on such a project without regulating the dimensions of his shed by the time, money, and materials available to him. Those who undertake feasible projects in any field of human activity must be continuously attentive to their chances of ultimate success or failure, and that is why they count their resources and measure their results at every stage of the project. The same preference for success over failure makes them reluctant to experiment with a new method on a large scale unless it has been successful on a small scale. Similar constraints imposed by the environment and verified by common experience force the shedbuilder to keep an eye out for the unanticipated events that almost always occur in any sequence of planned activities. If a large pool of water suddenly appears on his building site, he will not ignore the occurrence but will try to discover how it is connected with his own activities.

Such simple technological reflexes are often wanting in current programs of social improvement. Programs are designed and undertaken without any attempt to describe a desired end-condition, or to estimate the cost of reaching it. When these programs fail, as they inevitably must, given the loose linkage between their means and their ends, observers are likely to be confirmed in the superstition that modern society is too complex and mysterious to be manipulated by rational human effort. Some may find solace for their disappointment by turning to magical formulae that promise the resolution of all social problems.

These reactions are no more irrational than the failures of social intelligence that provoke them. The average citizen sees around him a multitude of massive and expensive programs for coping with social problems. When as often happens, these programs aggravate the problems they were intended to solve—when new forms of crime control seem to raise crime rates; when laws against drug abuse encourage the distribution of addictive drugs; when the prohibition of roadside billboards leads to the erection of giant billboards on the hilltops; when a treaty limiting nuclear weapons marks the beginning of an intensified contest in weapons development; when the desegregation of a public school system leads, after various redistributions, to sharper segregation than prevailed initially; the average citizen is entitled to his bewilderment, his cynicism, or his panacea.

In the course of this book, we shall have many occasions to distinguish between feasible projects of social improvement (which may or may not succeed) and defective projects which *cannot* succeed because they lack essential parts. Sometimes the desired end-condition is undefined, as in the Federal program of assistance to dependent children. Some programs, like the prohibition of international aggression by the United Nations, are purely rhetorical and cannot be reduced to concrete terms. Sometimes the end-condition is self-contradictory or impossible, as in the attempt to abolish poverty when poverty is defined by a standard that shifts from year to year.

In other programs, the end-condition can be visualized readily enough, but no socially acceptable methods are available for bringing it about. Many millions of dollars have been allocated in recent years to the rehabilitation of heroin addicts in treatment institutions, although the overwhelming majority of persons treated are known to resume their addiction at the first opportunity. The lack of practical methods fatally hampers all sorts of programs geared to the rehabilitation of alcoholics who do not want to be sobered up, delinquents who relish a life of crime, unemployed adolescents who can live comfortably without working and unwed mothers whose illegitimate children are their sole source of support.

Another type of defective project involves a painful disproportion between means and ends. For example, the end-condition of raising culturally disadvantaged but mentally competent children to a normal achievement level by means of intensive tutoring, a lengthened school year, and special incentives is feasible as to its purpose and its methods, but requires an enormous investment in teaching salaries and physical equipment and direct expenses. On the basis of available experience, the cost of such a program may run as high as $10,000 a year per pupil. This figure being unacceptably high, the program is launched at a much lower cost, say two or three hundred dollars per pupil, and accomplishes nothing.

Of the several essential parts of a feasible project of social improvement, the one most routinely omitted from contemporary programs is the continuous, concurrent measurement of results. This omission can almost be counted on in a governmental program created by an isolated legislative act so that it must persist in its errors until the next legislative occasion; but it also occurs in many private and informal

programs, since the prevailing ideology of social improvement emphasizes good intentions more than good results. A low-rent public-hous-
ing project, let us say, is intended to provide improved living conditions for slum-dwellers. When the rules for establishing the eligibility
of occupants turn out unexpectedly to select a population of unstable
families, it should not, in principle, be difficult to put the project back
on course by amending the rules to attract a more balanced population.
In the grim, real world of social improvement nothing like this happens, since there is no system for continuous measurement of results
and little obligation to match the outcome of a project with its original
purposes. Failures of administration and design may go unrecognized
for many years and the errors may accumulate until it is easier to abandon the program than to restore its original purposes.

The procedure of solving social problems by intermittent legislation,
often hastily drawn and heavily compromised before passage, leads to
all sorts of fascinating fiascos. The giant billboards are thick on the
hillsides long before the last of the little billboards have been removed
from the edge of the arterial highway and their owners duly compensated. Meanwhile, the legislature has moved on to other matters and
the giant billboards are outside the jurisdiction of the officials in charge
of removing the little billboards. There is no one to receive a report
that the program has broken down or to take timely corrective action.

If programs of social improvement often turn out to be useless or
silly, it is not so much because society resists reform as because social
reformers cling to bad habits and defective theories.

At the end of the nineteenth century, nearly everyone in the world
who could read was aware that the world was caught up in a powerful
trend of increasing human control over the physical environment. As
we shall presently see, many believed that technological progress led
directly or indirectly to moral progress. During the twentieth century
this faith has been sorely tried, and it has become more fashionable to
believe that technological progress leads to moral degeneration. I think
we have enough solid evidence to show that neither proposition provides us with a useful key to recent history. Some of the social consequences of modernization appear to be automatic and inevitable while
others do not. Not all social institutions are transformed by modernization. Some are left intact while some undergo changes that cannot be

directly attributed to technology. Contemporary nations do not seem to have much freedom with respect to modernization. None of them have been able to hold aloof from automobiles and radios, literacy and anti-biotics. At the same time, few nations have so far been able to speed up their own modernization sufficiently to overtake more advanced nations or to gain a significant advantage over their cultural neighbors. Technological progress has so far followed so definite a trajectory that short-range prediction presents no problem at all, and even long-term predictions have been quite accurate. By contrast, the political and social developments of the twentieth century have been shockingly different from the general expectations with which the century began. Hundreds of prophets foretold the growth of metropolitan cities and their suburbs in the twentieth century. No prophets foresaw the magnitude and duration of twentieth-century wars. Television was described with great accuracy fifty years before its invention, but nobody visualized the counterculture before it appeared. The bombing of railroad yards from the air was expected a hundred years before it happened; not a soul anticipated the chauvinistic hostility of communist states toward each other. The discovery of an infallible contraceptive came as no surprise to anyone; the concurrent rise in illegitimate births was astonishing.

After more than two centuries of modernization, there has been neither a clear trend of moral progress nor an unmistakable trend of moral degeneration. If man's relationship with his fellows is changing qualitatively, as some sociologists propose, the changes are too subtle or perhaps too slow to be measured objectively. Propensities to love and to hate, to cooperate and to fight, to obey and to rebel, seem to fluctuate as readily in one direction as the other. Cruelty and kindness, greed and generosity, snobbery and brotherhood, luxury and austerity, are all as conspicuous in the latter part of the twentieth century as in any preceding era. The incidences of marriage, murder, suicide, and mental breakdown have not changed in any consistent way. Mechanization made war more destructive and genocide more convenient but encouraged the abolition of slavery and child labor. Corporal punishment and cruelty to animals have been suppressed in countries that practice saturation bombing. The era is full of moral paradoxes but none of them suggest any fundamental change in the nature of man.

If we have read these trends correctly, modernization does not have a uniform and predetermined effect on social relationships, and, therefore, the choices open to us are much wider than commonly supposed. The improvement of society is not a forlorn hope—because many societies have been deliberately improved before; nor is it an apocalyptic triumph to be accomplished once and for all—human nature being what it is. But it is also not a matter out of our control, since modernization can proceed under a variety of institutional arrangements, and seems to be compatible with both despotism and freedom.

There is nothing very new or interesting about the idea that an effective social technology may be developed at some time in the future. That idea is commonplace and, in a lackadaisical way, universally accepted. The major point I want to make in this book is quite different and may be briefly summarized as follows: Social improvement—that is, social change in a desired direction—is entirely feasible under contemporary conditions. It is even fairly easy, provided that the social inventor respects the requirements of technology by specifying the existing conditions he desires to change, the end-condition he desires to reach, the means to be used in getting from one to the other, and the intermediate conditions to be traversed in the process.

Let us put this a little more concretely. What I shall try to show is that the social environment, like the physical environment, has become increasingly susceptible to rational manipulation in the course of the past two centuries, with the result that the continued survival of any social system is no longer guaranteed by its own resistance to change but must now be deliberately contrived.

The dominant American view of history, heavily influenced by social scientists and social philosophers, visualizes the past as a sequence of processes and patterns: industrialization, urbanization, immigration, the closing of the frontier, the rise of the middle class, the decline of regionalism, the changing family. These are useful categories for summing up innumerable discrete events but they are likely to lead us astray if we think of them as autonomous forces and lose sight of the human purposes and projects of which they are composed. In these big, cloudy forces, all the successful projects of men—the clearing in the wilderness, the better mousetrap that finds a market and turns a profit, the family transported from rural Poland to south Chicago, the rebellion that succeeds, the constitution that works, the ceremony that unrolls according to the printed schedule—are downgraded from purposive activities to historical accidents.

To think of a trend like urbanization as the result of a myriad of individual projects rather than as their cause requires a real effort of imagination but it is worth the trouble because it forces us to inquire why the project of migrating from country to city was so attractive to certain rural people and why it was so consistently successful. That kind of inquiry is more likely to yield useful knowledge than any attempt to explain urbanization in less concrete terms.

When we analyze social events in this realistic fashion we are immediately struck by the perennial scarcity of new and original types of feasible projects and the enormous impact they have on existing social institutions. The hallmarks of a feasible project, of course, are the familiar minimum elements of technology—the description of an existing condition and of a desired end-condition, the identification of practicable means of getting from one to the other, and the specification of intermediate stages in the sequence. Only a few of the innumerable proposals for social improvement that are brought forth have this character and most of those attract sufficient following for a fair trial of their feasibility.

Even highly implausible projects have a fair chance of being tried out if they have a formally sequential character, as the history of sectarian movements abundantly illustrates. Once the actual feasibility of a project has been demonstrated, it is almost certain to be imitated regardless of the ultimate desirability of its end-condition.

To explain why the malleability of modern social institutions has not permitted them to be more rapidly perfected, we will have to trace—at least briefly—the entire history of social improvement in modern times. If the line of argument seems to meander, and the reader finds himself asking what the Treaty of Versailles has to do with welfare reform, I ask his patience and hope to show him that there is indeed a connection.

We shall begin by describing the growth of a desire to improve social institutions that accompanied the process of modernization from its beginnings in the seventeenth century. We will follow the evolution of this desire with particular interest through the nineteenth century when the increasing momentum of modernization began to change the world in ways that no observer could overlook, since the increase of agricultural and industrial productivity, the expansion of population and the accumulation of knowledge outscaled anything in historical experience. When the social scientists of the nineteenth century became aware of these massive trends, some of them overgeneralized the experience of their own era and taught that progress was as inevitable in the development of social institutions as in the development of physical technology. Gripped by this illusion, they ignored the abundant evidence which suggested that social progress—unlike the progress of physical technology—was sporadic and subject to dramatic reversals. By the end of the nineteenth century nearly all educated men and women believed in the inevitability of social progress, holding either the liberal version of this belief, which taught that the improvement of social institutions was a continuous, self-activating process, or its radical version, which foresaw an inevitable revolution, followed by the abolition of private property and the establishment of a perfect society.

It ought by now to be obvious that both versions were founded on false premises and one hardly knows whether to laugh or weep at the realization that the same theories are not only widely held today but still provide the underpinnings of many social movements.

The defects of the theories of automatic progress are thrown into high relief when we examine, with the advantage of hindsight, the prophecies about the twentieth century which were based upon them. In Chapter 4 we will look at three sets of predictions made around 1890: Edward Bellamy's description of a postrevolutionary and perfected American society, Karl Kautsky's authoritative blueprint for a post-revolutionary Marxist society, and the somewhat abstract guideposts set up by Emile Durkheim to trace the future direction of social evolution. At this distance of time, the sharp differences that originally separated these prophecies pale into insignificance beside their common failure to foresee the importance of nationalism and war in the twentieth century.

It is instructive, however, to compare the perfect societies visualized by Bellamy and by Kautsky. Bellamy worked out his postrevolutionary utopia with a fine sensitivity to its technological possibilities, but he thought it unnecessary to specify the means by which the revolution itself was to be achieved. He counted upon self-interest and common sense to bring it about automatically. Kautsky's sketch of the "Socialist Commonwealth" was a much cruder plan but it contained, for the first time in the history of socialist doctrine, all of the essential elements for a sequential project of large-scale social transformation. The desired end-condition—the state as one big industrial firm—was clearly specified and based on a model whose feasibility had been fully demonstrated; the privately owned industrial firm. Not only was the existing condition to be changed described with much more objectivity than in previous revolutionary writings, but the methods to be used in the successive stages of the revolution were specified in considerable detail (at least for the early stages) and were copied after models of political action which had already been tested. It remained only for Lenin to fill in the tactics of the later stages for the project of founding a durable communist state to be complete. That state, with its harsh industrial discipline and its general subordination of the individual to the collectivity, was much less attractive, even on paper, than Kautsky's new order or Marx's original vision but its feasibility was immediately apparent to discerning eyes. It is the argument of this book that feasible projects of social improvement have an enormous power to shape events and indeed that such a project is almost irresistible, regardless of its intrinsic merits, when it is proposed as an alternative to a weakly defended *status quo*.

Our story will continue with the history of social change as it actually unfolded in the twentieth century. On the one hand, the great trend of modernization and the cornucopia of gifts it brought for the human race: more years of life, more varied entertainments, a vast array of comforts and ingenious devices for pleasure; on the other hand, the startling growth of nationalist sentiments and the powers of the national state, the multiplication of wars without apparent purpose or justification, and a dramatic increase in the number of successful revolutions.

In Chapter 6 we will examine a number of familiar projects undertaken by individuals and organizations in order to show that their consequences can account for much of recent social change without any help from inscrutable social forces. Such projects, for example, as the

migration of peasant families to a metropolitan city, the encouragement of industrial development by the governments of backward
countries, the creation of permanent strategical establishments by the
governments of advanced countries, or the liberation of colonies by indigenous movements.

Many of these projects were not only formally rational, but have
proven to be very sensible. The peasant families ate better, worked
shorter hours, enjoyed more cultural opportunities, had their health
better cared for, and gave their children a better chance to rise in the
world. Once the feasibility of this project had been demonstrated by a
relatively small number of pioneer families, the hundreds of thousands
who followed after had only to imitate the actions of their predeces-
sors. When the government of a backward country subsidizes the importation of foreign machinery and technicians to set up an electric
power plant, it expects benefits without any immediate disadvantages.
The project has been tried a hundred times before and has usually been
successful. The anthropologist or the tourist may deplore the changes
that occur in the fabric of village life when the soft light of oil lamps is
replaced by the harsh glare of electricity but the villagers—whose
wishes are more relevant—prefer electricity.

Another striking feature of successful projects is that the conditions
permitting them to be successful may develop rather suddenly. When
this happens, it may take no more than the success of one or two prototype projects to produce a great wave of imitation. Thus at the end
of World War II, although it was not immediately apparent, the
emergence of the United States and the Soviet Union as superpowers
deprived the British, French and Dutch colonial empires of their strategical usefulness and left little reason for their continued existence.
These new circumstances were not widely understood until they were
illuminated by the extraordinarily easy achievement of Indian independence. Within a few short years, similar projects of liberation succeeded in more than a hundred other colonies.

Two generations earlier a series of technological changes had
abruptly transformed the conditions for a successful war. The net effect of these changes was to require a successful war to be planned
long in advance necessitating that most of the preparations be completed before the outbreak of hostilities. To meet these new condi-

tions, each major power developed a permanent strategical establishment whose peacetime business was to prepare and plan for a war against every possible enemy, including the nation's current allies. The effects of this innovation were far-reaching. In their efforts to raise the probabilities of success, strategical establishments were forced to be single-minded in the pursuit of military opportunities and relatively indifferent to all of the effects of war except victory and defeat. The on-going projects of strategical establishments made it inevitable that great wars would be fought for no apparent purpose, without much regard for social and cultural consequences.

The threat this situation posed to the survival of civilization was widely recognized almost at once, as can be seen from the proceedings of the First Hague Peace Conference in 1899, but the design of feasible projects for achieving international peace or for lessening the damage of war proved unexpectedly difficult in the next three-quarters of a century. It is to that set of unsuccessful projects that we will turn in Chapter 7.

The leading projects in this category may be roughly labeled as world revolution, world conquest, the parliament of nations, and negotiated disarmament. I shall try to show that each of them has failed not because of irresistible social forces, or inherent human intolerance for peace and safety, but because of a technologically defective program. The defects in these projects will by now be familiar—they do not clearly visualize the desired end-condition or specify practical methods for achieving it or describe the successive stages to be traversed. The lack of a visualized end-condition is most remarkable in the case of the Marxist project of world revolution in view of the fact that the local successes of Marxist revolutionaries have been founded on a combination of social theory and practical action that conforms rather closely to the requirements of social technology. With respect to the world order previsaged by the international communist movement, however, this pattern broke down early in the history of the Comintern and has never been repaired. It seems to be a fair judgment that the communist world revolution has been so far averted as much by the indifference of its supposed partisans as by the resistance of its antagonists.

The project of peace by world conquest has appeared intermittently since Napoleon's time but has not yet been seriously pursued, if only because none of the potential conquerors—the French in 1809, the Germans in 1941, the Americans in 1946—had enough confidence in their ability to occupy and govern the whole world to spend time in considering how to go about it.

The project of world peace through negotiated disarmament has an equally long but less interesting history, having been pursued since its inception in a spirit of duplicity by negotiators who, with few exceptions, had neither a mandate nor a desire to achieve their ostensible purposes.

The story of these projects is admittedly a discouraging one, but nothing in it compels us to conclude that future projects of world peace will necessarily fail. The technical defects of the projects undertaken so far are sufficient to account for their failure without resorting to any hypotheses about blind social forces.

From these large matters, we will turn in the later chapters to the history of social problem solving in the United States, giving special attention to the problems of the Great Depression and the solutions proposed by the New Deal, and—three decades later—the problems of the Era of Protest and the solutions proposed by the War on Poverty.

There is a good deal of instruction and useful guidance to be found in this long series of social experiments and it is a pity that a society obsessed with social problems and their solutions has not tried harder to learn from its own experience. Again and again in recent years, the lessons of the past have been almost perversely disregarded. It is astounding, for example, that the results of the prohibition experiment were not used to warn legislators of the probable consequences of attempting to control drug abuse by criminal sanctions. It is almost incredible that the reasons the Civilian Conservation Corps was more successful than the Works Progress Administration in the 1930s were not reexamined when the Job Corps and the Neighborhood Youth Corps were established in the 1960s. It verges on lunacy that programs as unsuccessful as those of the Bureau of Indian Affairs have been periodically expanded. The record of federal, state, local and private agencies in the United States has not been impressive with respect to every social problem, but there have been many successful projects and even some brilliant successes such as the abolition of child labor, the unemployment insurance system, and the recent desegregation of higher education.

The elements that account for the success of some projects, the mixed results of others and the failure of still others are not at all mysterious. They are more often so painfully obvious that it is hard to understand why old failures are often repeated and old successes often forgotten until we remember that the habit of thinking about social improvement in technological terms is not yet widespread and that good intentions generally count as heavily as good results when a social program comes to be evaluated.

All of this of course adds up to an argument in favor of a more realistic and rigorous approach to social improvement than has heretofore been practiced in the United States, or for that matter, in the Western world. We can generally go from where we are to where we want to be, this argument runs, *if* we know where we are, *if* we can describe where we want to be without violating any principles of logic or sociology, *if* we have methods for effecting the transition, and *if* we are willing to attend to the feedback that every project begins to generate as soon as it is launched.

A difficult question that lurks behind this simple formulation is what persons compose the *we* who are expected to do so much? How do *we* agree on what *we* want and why are *we* entitled to impose our choices on *them,* whoever they may be? A perfect society, like the one imagined by Mr. Bellamy or the one founded by Chairman Mao, resolves these questions by stipulating that there is room for only one *we* and all of us had better join it or else. A good society, which is a much better thing than a perfect society, must allow for multiple and overlapping projects of social improvement as well as mutually incompatible projects. Under these familiar conditions, *we* who determine the shape of the future comprise only ourselves, our friends and relations, and others who can be peacefully persuaded to agree with us. This is more than a sufficient number for most of the essential projects in a good society as well as for many projects that are not essential at all, the improvement of one's habitat being so fundamental a human impulse that no project which holds forth a plausible offer of human betterment is likely to want supporters. What is scarce, and what needs to be sought out and encouraged in every possible way, is the ability to design the prototypes of new projects in a rapidly changing environment.

CHAPTER 2

❦

The Origins of Social Improvement

ABOUT three hundred years have elapsed since men in Western Europe began to attempt the improvement of their social institutions on the basis of sociological theories about human nature, collective behavior, the structure of social systems, and the direction of social change. The high civilizations of other eras and other places—with the significant exception of Attic Greece and the late Roman Republic—had not been aware of sociology as a realm of discourse and did not consider their social institutions to be artifacts that could be redesigned. Innovations in government and organizational structure were made from time to time in ancient China, medieval Europe, and eighteenth-century Japan, but in an *ad hoc* and untheoretical way. For St. Thomas and Martin Luther, as for Confucius and Mohammed, monarchical government, parental authority, female chastity, private property, social stratification, war, poverty and wealth, the solidarity of kindred, retaliation for injuries, and discrepancies between social merit and social reward were as much part of the natural environment as rocks, trees, and rivers. When they urged, as all of them did, the reform of some particular social arrangement, they did so in the same spirit as a farmer building a dam across a brook. The rest of creation remained unaffected, and the particular project did not provoke any theoretical questions that went beyond its immediate feasibility.

Getting back into the heads of pre-scientific men and seeing the world as they saw it is not easy. As their works testify, the best among them were not inferior to our best men in intelligence, insight, or ability but their relationships to the external world were different in two essential ways. First, their gods were as real to them as their wives and children. It was not a question of deciding whether to believe or not to believe in divinity. There could be controversy about their nature and what was due to them, just as we have contemporary controversies about human nature and human rights, but the belief in beings greater than man was spontaneous and inspired confidence in the social structures over which these gods presided. Second, the universe of pre-scientific man was beyond human scale and human control. The energies of natural forces could not be imitated except by symbols, not measured except by hyperbole, and not explained except by a causal scheme remote from the causalities of everyday experience. The earth was vast and full of mysteries and, considered as a whole, did not seem to have changed within the span of visible history or to be changing in the passage from the present into the future. The natural world and the social world were fixed constellations, their patterns hardly affected by the continuous stream of births and deaths occurring within them. Neither the one constellation nor the other appeared to have been made by humans. Men had a small recognized capability to improve their immediate surroundings by planting a garden or enacting a code of law and an undoubted capacity to do mischief by burning a city or encouraging vice, but the world was not theirs to destroy and nothing in their experience suggested that it could be fundamentally redesigned. The perfect world—the perfect society—utopia—lay either in a vanished golden age or on blessed isles outside of geography or in a heaven prepared for the souls of the just.

This ancient view of the world has been so transformed by a combination of new ideas and new facts that even saints and preachers now assume a human rather than a divine origin for social institutions. As for the natural environment, we now see it as so vulnerable to human intervention that it must be vigilantly protected against damage. When, in the present century, men acquired a demonstrable capacity to destroy social institutions by revolution and a credible capacity to change the natural environment out of recognition by means of explosives and chemicals, these developments put the finishing touches to a world view that first appeared in the seventeenth century and has been gaining ground ever since, spreading from modernized to backward countries and from educated to uneducated persons.

The origins of this world view are well known. The second half of the seventeenth century in England was marked by several inseparable aspects of the same social movement—the invention of power-operated machinery for mining coal and making cotton cloth; the expansion of scientific knowledge by Newton, Boyle, Hook, Huyghens, Halley, and their friends of the Royal Society; the rapid application of that knowledge to practical projects; and the emergence of the Royal Navy as the first bureaucracy of the modern type, with a carefully designed table of organization, a rational division of responsibility, and a research and development program which raised its technological capacity from year to year. Similar phenomena appeared almost concurrently in France and Prussia and elsewhere in Europe soon after. It was no mere coincidence that the same period developed doctrines which identified social institutions as human contrivances and began to discuss the question of how defective institutions might be reformed.

Thomas Hobbes's *Leviathan,* written in 1651, was the most fundamental of these writings and Hobbes considered himself, not entirely without reason, to be the first social scientist, ranking his own achievements with those of Copernicus and Galileo. Hobbes retained the ancient concept of natural law which implied that social institutions were immutable parts of God's creation; but he nullified it in two strokes, first by denying that natural law had any coercive power in itself, and second by deriving the state and all other social systems from the voluntary actions of men acting in their own biologically-based interests. The central idea in his theory of "the covenant that men make with one another" was that the state and all of its dependent institutions are mere mechanisms for the accomplishment of human purposes, whence it follows that "No sacred mystique veils *Leviathan,* the 'mortal God' created by human association to which men owe their peace and defense. The commonwealth is the work of men; its utility is its sole justification." [1]

This same theme was repeated with greater emphasis in the writings of John Locke a generation later. His second *Essay on Civil Government* begins by asserting "that Adam had not, either by natural right or fatherhood or by positive donation from God, any such authority over his children, or dominion over the world, as is pretended." [2] In other words, institutional authority cannot claim a divine or a natural origin—it must be explained in terms of the needs generated by human nature and the collective agreements that men make with each other in order to satisfy their needs. "And thus, that which begins and actually constitutes any political society is nothing but the consent of a number of free men capable of majority, to unite and incorporate into such a society. And this is that only, which did and could give beginning to any lawful government in the world." [3]

Locke was closer than Hobbes in several ways to the dilemmas of modern social science. Unlike Hobbes, he did not regard the social contract as irrevocable. He thought that men are entitled to unmake the agreement they have made with each other. The last chapter of *Civil Government* asserts a right of revolution on the ground that the Prince is only the deputy of his people and that as deputizers they are competent to decide whether he has acted according to the trust reposed in him and to discard him if he has failed to do so. Social institutions, for Locke, do not have any claim to respect because of their size or age or familiarity. In reasoning about social origins, he contrasted the state of nature prior to the Social Contract—in which human beings were free, equal, and without authority over each other—with their condition after they had formed organizations and consented to inequality in all its varied forms. Life in Hobbes's state of nature had been described as "nasty, brutish, and short," but Locke's state of nature was so attractive that the advantages procured by the social contract hardly seem worth the sacrifices they require.

These ideas were not long in taking practical effect. The social contract theories were part of a movement which ever since the seventeenth century has been pushing the world toward an unknown destination. Even before Locke's *Essay* appeared in print, the first political revolutions based on a social contract theory had occurred. The Convention of 1689 offered the throne of England to William and Mary on the basis of a resolution declaring that "King James the Second, having endeavored to subvert the constitution of the kingdom by breaking the original contract between the King and the people . . . the throne is thereby vacant.'' In the following century, the basic document of the American Revolution, the Declaration of Independence, contained an elegant synopsis of Locke's *Essay* in which "life, liberty, and bodily indolencey" was improved into "life, liberty, and the pursuit of happiness."

We hold these truths to be self-evident, that all men are created equal, that they are endowed by their Creator with certain unalienable rights, that among these are life, liberty, and the pursuit of happiness. That to secure these rights, governments are instituted among men, deriving their just powers from the consent of the governed, that, whenever any form of government becomes destructive of these ends, it is the right of the people to alter or to abolish it, and to institute a new government, laying its foundation on such principles and organizing its power in such form, as to them shall seem most likely to effect their safety and happiness.[4]

A few years later the French Revolution took Jean-Jacques Rousseau for its prophet.[5] Rousseau was the first modern writer to analyze how men are shaped by society, to identify human organizations as the ultimate source of morality and to describe human nature as the product of social interaction. His *Social Contract,* a brief essay published in 1762, was largely responsible for the significant shift from the "life, liberty, and the pursuit of happiness" of the American Revolution to the "liberty, equality and fraternity" of the French Revolution.

Rousseau modified the earlier versions of the social contract theory by asserting that in forming the social contract, each individual gives himself and everything that belongs to him not to a separate sovereign but to an association—of which he remains a member and an integral part—in whose "general will" he participates.

Each of us places in common his person and all his power under the supreme direction of the general will; and as one body we all receive each member as an indivisible part of the whole. . . . It appears from this formula that the active association contains a reciprocal engagement between the public and individuals, and that each individual, contracting, as it were, with himself, is engaged under a double character; that is, as a member of the sovereign engaging with individuals, and as a member of the state engaged with the sovereign.[6]

In Rousseau's view, the people do not agree to nominate a sovereign, as Hobbes supposed, or make an agreement with a sovereign, as Locke said; they are themselves the sovereign, regardless of what agents they employ to carry out the chores of government. Rousseau recognized that the whole body of citizens cannot function as a legislature in large nations; he thought that all states should be small, simple, and homogeneous, like his native Geneva.

It is on this point that Rousseau's doctrine is most ambiguous. Under the ideal conditions of direct democracy, there could be no conflict, he thought, between individual interests and the general will. Not only must the state be small enough for every individual's opinion to be directly expressed; it must have no cabals or associations, no blocs or parties, no sub-organizations whatever. "It is therefore of the utmost importance for obtaining the expression of the general will, that no partial society should be formed in the state, and that every citizen should speak his opinion entirely from himself." [7] In short, a perfect society. Rousseau was fully aware that these conditions could not be met in a complex society, and this was one of the reasons why he regarded European society as corrupt, degrading, and inimical to the development of the individual personality. But he was not very clear about what modifications would be necessary to adapt his concept of individual freedom under perfect consensus to the necessary conditions of a modern society. Hence, his theory has turned out to be double-edged in practice. It can be used to defend both tyranny and resistance to tyranny, private property and public ownership, free speech and censorship. In the twentieth century, Rousseau's doctrines that sovereignty resides in the people and that true freedom consists of obedience to the general will are proclaimed by nearly all states, regardless of the mode of government they practice.

The violence and confusion of the French Revolution has somewhat obscured its importance as a massive sociological experiment. The revolutionists did not stop with the redistribution of land, the abolition of nearly all existing organizations, revision of the legal system, and fundamental changes in government, but went on to experiment with a new calendar, a new type of family, a new state religion, a new system of weights and measures, and new subdivisions of the national territory. Some of these changes persisted for a little while; only the territorial subdivisions and the metric system proved to be permanent. For a time, an entire society enjoyed the illusion that institutions could be successfully redesigned overnight. Mr. Jefferson wrote to Mr.

Madison from Paris in September 1789, during the first flush of revolutionary enthusiasm that, "The question whether one generation of
men has a right to bind another, seems never to have been started, either on this or our side of the water. Yet it is a question of such consequences as not only to merit decision, but place also, among the fundamental principles of every government. The course of reflection in
which we are immersed here on the elementary principles of society
has presented this question to my mind." [8] Reflection led him to the
conclusion that the earth belongs in usufruct to the living, the dead
having neither power nor rights over it. Hence all titles to property,
hereditary distinctions, endowments and organizational charters could
be changed at will by the "legislation of the day."

That these principles did not prevail in the following century is only
partly attributable to the mishaps of the French Revolution. The old institutions demonstrated a resilience that appears as much a cause as an
effect of the political fluctuations which followed 1789. Within a
dozen years, Napoleon would be ruling France as First Consul, the
sovereignty of the people expressed by a referendum approving his
dictatorship, and the desire to redesign social institutions channeled
into administrative reports on the improvement of hospitals and the efficient collection of taxes. Another dozen years and Napoleon would
be on his way to Elba, while all Europe submitted to a policy of re-
storing traditional institutions and hereditary privileges. Speaking of
this period Sir Lewis Namier writes:

A cold shadow lay over Europe for 33 years, the active life of a generation,
and people connected it with the person of Metternich, and called it his "system" . . . the history of the French Revolution and of Napoleon had shown
once more the immense superiority which existing social forms have over
human movements and genius, and the poise and rest which there are in a spir-
itual inheritance, far superior to the thoughts, will or inventions of any single
generation. It was the greatness and strength of Metternich during these fateful
years to have foreseen that human contrivances, however clever and beneficial, would not endure, and to have understood the peculiar elasticity with
which men would finally revert to former habits. [9]

But examined in detail, the restoration of former habits was much less
thorough than it pretended to be. The faith in the unlimited elasticity
of institutions that Jefferson had expressed in 1789 was irretrievably

lost, but so too was the unquestioning acceptance of traditional forms that had prevailed earlier. The re-established Bourbon Monarchy could not, and did not try to, re-establish the institutions of 1789 in any literal way. From among the reforms of the Revolution, the Restoration preserved legal equality, private rights, the new territorial subdivisions, the National Guard, the tax system, the constitution of the judiciary and a considerable measure of religious freedom. Napoleon's Legion of Honor, his concordat with the Vatican, his codes of civil and criminal law, and his reorganized system of higher education were left intact, together with most of the titles, civil service positions and properties acquired by imperial functionaries.[10] There was no real return to absolutism. The new government was a constitutional monarchy with a parliament modeled after England's. Elsewhere in Western Europe, there were a variety of local patterns, but the net result was much the same: the legitimacy of traditional institutions was reasserted, but the institutions restored were a patchwork of traditional and innovative elements.

With respect to hereditary stratification, the countries of Western Europe would thenceforth and down to the present day accept two contradictory principles: on the one hand, the legal equality of all citizens; on the other hand, the official recognition of titles of nobility, manorial rights, hereditary membership in exclusive occupations and all sorts of other inequalities derived historically or symbolically from the *ancien régime*.

In Russia and the United States, both involved in the Napoleonic wars but never subjected to Napoleonic reforms, events followed somewhat different courses. In the Russian Empire there was a serious attempt to return to pre-revolutionary conditions. The attempt was not wholly successful, but it did endow Russian institutions with a rigidity that resisted reform until the whole structure was swept away by another revolution a century later. Well into the nineteenth century, a Russian landowner could still address his peasants in this remarkable language: "I am your master, and my master is the Emperor. The Emperor can issue his commands to me, and I must obey him; but he issues no commands to you. I am the Emperor upon my estate; I am your God in this world and I have to answer for you to the God above." [11] Russian industry, as it slowly developed, was organized in a unique way that combined state and private ownership and subjected factory workers to the same discipline as agricultural serfs. As far as government policy could manage it, industrialization in Russia involved a minimum of urbanization and minimum encouragement for the rise of a middle class or the spread of new ideas. Nevertheless, these tendencies could not be entirely repressed, and the effort to do so introduced elements of instability into the Czarist regime that pointed to its eventual downfall for nearly a century before it actually occurred.

In the United States, the revolution had come and gone before the European upheaval started. Although it involved a conscious rebellion against the past and a desire to sweep away dated institutions, the innovative effects of the American Revolution were essentially limited to the basic change from monarchical to republican government and the disestablishment of religion. Other institutions were nearly untouched. The old system of social stratification was so little changed that references to "the court" and "the aristocracy" abounded in the debates and correspondence of the 1790s, and John Adams could refer without embarrassment to the "noble families of Boston." [12] The Revolution probably accentuated social inequality in the United States because of the military and political distinctions it provided and the opportunities for speculation in land and government securities that followed. The English common law continued to regulate civil and criminal matters in the several states. The organization of trade, manufacturing, and other forms of enterprise; the forms for holding property and passing it on by inheritance; the institutions of public philanthropy and higher education; the manner of punishing criminals and providing for the poor; the powers and duties of local officials—were left virtually untouched. Family manners from infancy to courtship and from marriage to the grave, were not affected in any perceptible way. The relationships between the sexes and between the generations had already assumed a characteristic American form before the Revolution.[13] There was no disposition in the country to reform these relationships or put them within the purview of government. The Anglican Church was disestablished but where it had been strongest, as in Virginia, it had long since surrendered its claim to exclusivity and was able to continue in its traditional path with no more than a few minor revisions to the *Book of Common Prayer.* In New England, and particularly in Connecticut where the Congregational clergy had considerable secular power, disestablishment involved no spectacular change in religious institutions.

The "peculiar institution" of slavery showed perhaps the most surprising resistance to innovation. The theory on which the Revolution was founded, as embodied in the Declaration of Independence, plainly called for abolition, and nearly all the framers of the Constitution were unwilling to accept slavery as a permanent feature of American life. Yet the best they could achieve was a prohibition of the slave *trade,* and even that was deferred for twenty years and foredoomed to be ineffective.

One reason for the extraordinary resistance of eighteenth-century American institutions to the anti-traditional philosophy upon which the American Revolution was ostensibly based, is suggested by Boorstin:

Within these years the American people crammed an extraordinary intensity of negation. But the past against which they were rebelling was foreign, distant, and vague. The French Revolutionaries were forced into the arena of speculative thought because they were fighting an enemy that possessed an articulate and systematic philosophy: clerical and royal theorists forced them to devise their own theories and gave them a clue—if only by antithesis—to the dogmas which they should assert in reply. . . . On this continent there was no Bastille and no Versailles Palace to symbolize the enemy; nor was there a mature and outspoken conservative philosophy to require an outspoken answer.[14]

Other reasons why the Revolution left the non-political institutions of this country virtually intact may be sought in the exceptionally neat match between Locke's theory of government and the society to which the Founding Fathers applied it.

Government, for Locke, was a voluntary association for the protection of private property. "The great and chief end," he wrote, "of men uniting into commonwealth and putting themselves under government, is the preservation of their property." [15] In this perspective, government is a convenience, nothing more. It has no life of its own and no rights that are not voluntarily conferred upon it by individuals. It is not, and ought not, to be the object of a cult. It is a practical arrangement, not a Sacred Being. Both of the principal terms of Locke's definition were applicable to the American Republic in its early days.

A majority of citizens were property holders working their own land. The rich were not very rich—by eighteenth-century European standards—and the poor not very poor. The services rendered by the national government were useful rather than essential and were hardly noticed in the daily lives of the people. The several states, of fairly recent origin and with frequently changing boundaries, had never excited more than a casual patriotism, while the United States, which demanded only a share of the citizen's loyalty, was clearly a voluntary association at first and its permanence continued to be debated until the Civil War put the question to rest. The American of 1800 did not have to weigh the interests of the individual against the government's claim to absolute devotion; no government made such a claim on him and none would do so for a long time to come.

CHAPTER 3

Nineteenth-Century Trends

THERE was an extraordinary amount of social change throughout the world in the nineteenth century compared to any previous
hundred years, and it was accompanied by a turmoil of new ideas
about social, economic, and political institutions. The people of the
nineteenth century were continually surprised by the rapidity and extent of the social transformation taking place around them.

The great current of social change in which Europe and America
caught up in the nineteenth century was generally called *progress;*
perhaps a more neutral label might be *modernization.* By any name, it
included the growth of science and technology, the development of industry, the mechanization of transportation and agriculture, a rapid
increase of population, the movement of country people to the city,
the enlargement of metropolitan cities to a scale not previously known,
the extension of European control over colonies and protectorates, the
mechanization of warfare, the establishment of mass communications,
the discovery of new means for stimulating and recording public opinion, a spectacular growth in the scale of government, productive enterprises and voluntary associations, and the expansion of bureaucratic
procedures in large organizations.

The trends enumerated above, along with many others not enumerated, belong to a cluster in which each may be plausibly interpreted as a cause of any other. Was it the availability of an improved technology that made industrial development possible or was it industrial development that stimulated scientific discovery and practical inventions? Was it colonialism that called navies into existence, or naval power that led to the acquisition of colonies? Questions like these are intriguing but bootless. Modernization, as a world-wide phenomenon, is an event that has happened only once. There is nothing else in history with which it can be closely compared, not even the development of a different style of science and technology in China many centuries before.[1]

The first stage of modernization can be traced back to the seventeenth century, although there was not much awareness of the phenomenon even in the following century.[2] The improvement of technology, especially in shipbuilding and ordnance, was apparent; by 1750, European and North American ships were able to reach every inhabited seacoast in the remoter parts of the world and to dominate the people near the seacoast without much trouble. A few observers were aware of a slow but significant improvement of public health. The periodic famines that had ravaged Europe throughout its history ceased soon after 1700.[3] In the *Wealth of Nations,* Adam Smith assembled enough quantitative data to make us certain, with the advantage of hindsight, that modernization was well-advanced in Great Britain by 1776, but he himself did not grasp the full pattern. Eighteenth-century statistics were more rudimentary than we can readily imagine. Most cities and states did not have even rough estimates of their own populations. Even when social statistics began to be recorded regularly in a few places, the lack of baseline information from earlier periods made it difficult to discern certain developments. The population was increasing at an unprecedented rate due to a steady decline in infant mortality, towns and cities were growing very fast and large cities faster than small, the production of manufactured goods and the use of mechanical power were accelerating from year to year and travel time between almost any two places on earth was being reduced.

After 1800, these trends became more clearly visible from year to year. By 1850, after the work of the Napoleonic Commissions, after Quetelet and Humboldt, Malthus, and Doubleday, seven United States censuses, a hundred years of Swedish demography, and the development of statistical registers from Paraguay to Schleswig-Holstein, the information available to describe social trends in Europe and America was very much greater than it had been in 1800. Also, a sufficient number of series were available for long enough periods to show that the various trends involved in modernization were for the time being irreversible and non-cyclical, and tended to continue from year to year, at different rates but without important reversals.

Strictly speaking, most of these trends were not linear; that is, if the growth of higher education or of iron and steel production in a given country was plotted over a long period of time, the resulting graph was a curve of some kind rather than a straight line. But, whatever its shape, it moved continuously in an upward movement, the value for nearly every year being higher than the previous year. When this upward movement was interrupted, as occasionally happened, by wars, revolutions, or economic crises, it was almost immediately resumed. Furthermore, the thing was contagious. As soon as the remoter countries of the world came under European influence, they too began to display a tendency to expand from year to year in population, per capita production and consumption, urbanization, the circulation of symbols, the speed of transportation and communication, the functions of government, and all the other familiar indicators. The distance between the leading countries in the modernization parade and those at the tail of the procession was enormous, much greater than is generally realized, but once included, every country marched in the same direction as all the others and at pretty much the same rate.

The nineteenth century did not become aware of this parade all at once and nineteenth-century social scientists never obtained enough information to describe it very accurately. Working with inadequate data within an intellectual environment that for various reasons encouraged the oversimplification of social facts, they fell into monumental errors when they attempted to place the progress they observed in its historical context. Two of these errors deserve our closer attention.

First, they stretched the great trend backward and forward in time, back to the dawn of history and further, and forward into the remotest future. Second, they assumed that progress must apply to every aspect of human life, not merely to control of the physical environment. They looked also for modernization in public and private morality, in the quality of human relationships, in law and government, in religion and the family, in the resolution of conflict and the alleviation of boredom. Indeed, the gradual improvement of human nature itself seemed to many of them to be as inevitable as continued progress in metallurgy or medicine.

Their reluctance to circumscribe the phenomenon of modernization and their inability to distinguish between the social indicators that were directly affected by technological progress and those that were not induced the social scientists of the nineteenth century to identify all sorts of local and short-term trends as part of the inevitable march of progress and to project them inexorably forward. If wages fell for a time in the English textile industry—then all industrial wages must decline to starvation levels in the long run. Was Europe unusually free of war in the 1880s and 1890s—then war was obviously disappearing from the world. Did Victorian England adopt a fashion of sexual prudery—pornography and prostitution would soon vanish from human experience.

We ought not to be scornful of these quaint, archaic modes of thought. They are still very much with us and will probably remain with us for a long time to come. We now have incalculably more and better information about modernization than was available in the nineteenth century. The basic statistical series have been projected many years into the future, while painstaking research has pushed back the boundaries of ignorance for earlier periods as well so that we now know a good deal more about the distribution of population around 1850, for example, than anyone could possibly have known at the time. Yet with all this accretion of data, and all the new electronic and statistical machinery we have for handling it, it remains difficult to trace the limits of modernization in an exact way. Even when it has been done as well as possible, we are left with an open question: Will technological progress eventually affect some aspects of society that are now outside its scope? It is not inconceivable that some biological device might, one of these days, stretch the span of human life to a hundred and fifty years, and thus triple the duration of active adulthood. The social effects of such an innovation are literally incalculable in the present stage of sociological knowledge. We can hardly guess what effect such a change might have on the prevailing patterns of work, marriage, or politics. On the other hand, it is very easy to exaggerate the impact of technology on social institutions. The century of historical experience that gives us an undeserved advantage over the first modern sociologists testifies eloquently to the stubborn persistence of human nature under new conditions and the stubborn survival of traditional elements in social institutions that were modified in various ways during the nineteenth century by the major trends of modernization within an expanding territory. In 1800 China, Japan, most of Oceania, the whole interior of Africa, Central Asia, all of North America west of the Appalachians, and a large part of South America were outside the zone of European influence. The great majority of their inhabitants had never seen a printed page or heard a gun fired. Large sections of Europe itself—the Balkans, the Spanish mountains, the Russian steppes—were fully medieval; in some of the remoter regions Christianity still struggled for ascendancy with tribal cults. By 1900 the entire world, except for a few insignificant corners, had been opened up to European influence and control. There were guns and newspapers everywhere, together with steam engines, kerosene lamps, steel tools, postage stamps, and other implements of modernity.

Population poured into the cities from the country. There were more than ten times as many city dwellers in 1900 as there had been in 1800. In 1800, there was not a single metropolis in the entire world with a population over a million. In 1900 there were ten, led by London, New York, and Paris.[4]

As the proportion of the population in agriculture declined everywhere, urban occupations proliferated. The learned professions multiplied and subdivided. New trades sprang up while new industries and old trades were fragmented by specialization. In 1800, there were probably less than a hundred distinguishable occupations in the United States. The census of 1900 counted more than a thousand.

This proliferation of occupations was accompanied by a great increase in the number and variety of occupational associations. Professional societies, syndicates of workers and managers, labor unions, trade associations, workers' parties, and farm bureaus, were all social inventions of the nineteenth century.

Day schools, boarding schools, colleges and universities had long existed and did not have to be reinvented, but their scale and scope increased greatly. In 1800 schools were reserved for a small minority. By 1900 education was the normal occupation of children and adolescents. Its duration had been extended at one end by the invention of nursery schools and kindergartens, at the other end by the invention of graduate schools. Local schools were combined into district or national systems. The control of education largely shifted from private scholars and religious bodies to states and public corporations.

Similar tendencies—a great increase in scale and scope, and a shift from private to public control—affected all the other types of eleemosynary institutions: hospitals, almshouses, museums, laboratories, scientific institutes and charities.

Productive enterprises of all kinds grew in scale and scope throughout the nineteenth century. The largest factories expanded from a few hundred workers to many thousands. The stock corporation or the cartel combined many factories into a single enterprise. The department store, the mail order house, and the chain store were nineteenth-century inventions. Banks, publishing houses, shipping lines, communication systems, railroads and mining enterprises displayed parallel tendencies to grow larger, richer and more powerful from year to year. Of the United States at the end of the century, one critic wrote, "In 1800 we were a few millions of people, and we loved liberty. In 1900 we are nearly a hundred millions of people, and we love money. Most of this money is invested in what are called corporations. From a handful of individuals we have become a nation of institutions." [5]

Of all the large organizations that grew in size and scope during the nineteenth century, none was more impressive than the state itself. The governments of modernized countries generally claimed less power in 1900 than they had in 1800. The system of absolute monarchy, which the Congress of Vienna tried to restore, had disappeared from all of Europe by 1900 with the exception of the Balkan countries, which were still governed by the Ottoman Turks. [6]

However, the loss of absolute authority by national governments was accompanied by a vast extension of their activities. They often took on new functions and rarely, if ever, relinquished any old ones. At the end of the century they were operating railroads and telephone networks, making iron and steel, administering examinations in secondary schools, compensating the victims of industrial accidents, and doing many other things that had previously been done by local authorities or not done at all.

The independent, culturally-integrated nation, which was to become the universal model of social organization in the twentieth century, was, in effect, a nineteenth-century invention. When the Congress of Vienna adjourned, France, Spain and England were the only sizeable countries of Europe, and Japan the only sizeable country outside of Europe, in which a central authority ruled a large territory inhabited by people who spoke the same language, claimed a common identity and regarded the rest of the world's population as strangers. By 1900, the scattered states of Germany and Italy had assembled themselves into nations. The Russian Empire had begun to acquire a national character. The states of Scandinavia had divided along their linguistic boundaries. Spain was separated from Portugal. A civil war had made the United States an indissoluble nation. Hungary, Greece, and Serbia were more or less autonomous. Nationalist movements, marked by fanatical patriotism, were springing up from Ireland to Ceylon.

The mass political party was another important institution invented in the nineteenth century. Earlier parties, where they existed at all, were coteries of officials and would-be officials and their friends, supported on rare occasions by popular uprisings. The political party that developed in the nineteenth century was a permanent organization with a hierarchy of officials, a large dues-paying membership and a network of local and regional branches. It reflected a steadily expanding definition of citizenship and the extension of the suffrage from a small elite to most of the adult male population. By 1848 there were parties of this type in many countries, and nearly everywhere they had fallen into the familiar left-to-right configuration that has persisted ever since. They ran the gamut from anti-parliamentary socialists on the extreme left through moderate socialists, liberals, and moderate conservatives in the center, to anti-parliamentary conservatives on the extreme right.

Such were some of the principal transformations in social institutions that took place in the expanding province of modernization during the nineteenth century. It is equally important, however, to examine some institutional changes which did *not* occur, although they were repeatedly forecast by sociological writers, and sometimes prematurely announced.

The European type of family, not much changed since 1800, still flourished throughout the same territory in 1900 and had even been exported to some extent as the province of modernization expanded. There were numerous local trends but they did not point in a single direction and some of them turned out to be reversible. The great majority of adults in modernized countries contracted a monogamous marriage before the age of thirty and thereafter maintained a common household for themselves and their children, to which one or two servants or relatives might be added. The husband had considerable but not absolute authority over his wife; women of vigorous character often tyrannized their husbands. Parents had nearly absolute authority over their small children; this eroded imperceptibly as the child grew up and left the parental home when he or she married. The number of children born into the average family declined during the century but because of lessened infant mortality, the number surviving to maturity increased. Extended family relationships were important in upper-class families everywhere and in villages that remained isolated for one reason or another. Inheritance arrangements varied a good deal, but most property passed to spouses or direct descendants, excluding remoter kin.

Premarital chastity was everywhere valued, and nowhere completely enforced. Local patterns of licentiousness appeared from time to time, especially in aristocratic circles, urban slums and among the children of recent immigrants, but seldom persisted. In rural villages, marriage was often delayed until the bride was pregnant. Adultery was everywhere disapproved but nowhere unknown and the reaction of public opinion regarding a particular affair depended on the relative social status and the marital histories of the people involved. Divorce was rare but marital separation quite common. Widows and widowers remarried freely. None of these traditional patterns changed in the nineteenth century.

To look at the matter more broadly, there were few changes in the prevailing patterns of intimate relationships or in the sentiments attached to such relationships that could be attributed to modernization. Men still courted women, with either honorable or dishonorable intentions, while suspecting that the women might be taking more initiative than they pretended. The love songs and sentiments of 1800 still made sense in 1900. The rules of sexual morality, while apparently stricter in England in 1900 than they had been a century before, were probably more permissive in the United States. The double standard applied with unequal force in different places and groups. It was more conspicuous among Catholics than Protestants and more in middle-class than in upper- or lower-class circles. The roles of a suitor, a sweetheart, a courting couple, a mistress, an unfaithful wife, a jealous husband, a young man about town, a poor but respectable girl, or a lady of easy virtue were just about the same at the end of the century as they had been at the beginning, although the study of any particular milieu would disclose various fashions and fluctuations.

One has only to read family letters of the 1790s and compare them with family letters of the 1890s to see how firm the basic institutional pattern remained. The tone a man might take with his son-in-law, the option of cherishing or ignoring nephews and nieces, the importance of cousinship in wealthy families, the admiration that younger sisters sometimes reserved for older brothers and the special affection of grandparents for grandchildren all carried the same nuances in one epoch as in the other.

The institutions of religion suffered many vicissitudes during the nineteenth century. There is no evidence, however, of a general decline in religion. There had perhaps been a tendency towards the continued disengagement of church and state, as exemplified by the diminution of clerical influence in American politics, the conferring of civil rights on Catholics, Jews and non-conformists in England, the annexation of the papal territories to the Kingdom of Italy, and the rise of anti-clerical movements in several countries. There had been many exceptions to this disengagement, however. As of 1900, the political influence of the Catholic Church was still to be reckoned with in Austria, Belgium, Hungary, Italy, Spain, Portugal, Poland, Germany, and most of the Latin American countries. The established churches of Greece, Scandinavia, Serbia, Switzerland and the British and Russian Empires did not seem less influential than they had been a century before. In the United States, the available evidence shows that church attendance, church membership and the financial support of organized

religion increased dramatically around 1810 in response to the Great
Revival, again during the Evangelical movements of the 1850s and
then quite steadily from 1865 to 1900.

The world panorama of religion in the nineteenth century exhibited
all sorts of contradictory tendencies. As one Central American republic was expelling the Jesuits, another was placing all primary education in their hands. The debate between evolution and scripture in the
English-speaking world was won by the followers of Darwin and
Huxley, but in the parallel debate between atheism and faith, the athe-
ists were routed. The Church's control over marriages, funerals and
vital statistics was broken in some places but strengthened in others.
Along with the growth of secular education in the United States, there
was a vast growth of parochial schools, Sunday schools, denomina-
tional colleges, theological seminaries, and other centers of religious
instruction. An unprecedented number of missionaries went out to
bring Christianity to the remoter parts of the world and they made and
kept great numbers of converts.

Public morality was not uniformly affected by modernization. It is
impossible to determine from the available evidence whether crime
rates increased or decreased throughout the province of modernization
between 1800 and 1900. There is some reason to think that with the
advent of street lighting, rapid transit, and uniformed police, the
streets of large cities became considerably safer for life and property
than ever before, but improvements in the technology of crime tended
to cancel out improvements in the technology of law enforcement—as
every reader knows who has followed Sherlock Holmes in his contest
with the wicked Professor Moriarity.

Other forms of deviance seem to have been subject to inconsistent
influences. The improvement of living standards and the increase in
employment opportunities for single women probably tended to diminish prostitution but the growth of cities encouraged it. Drunkenness
and tobacco smoking seem to have increased pretty steadily with the
increase of disposable income but snuff-taking and opium smoking
went out of style toward 1900, and the widespread addiction to narcotics that followed the invention of morphine in the 1860s did not
elicit much social disapproval at the time.

Rioting and mob violence varied according to local custom and provocation. The Chartist riots of England, the New York draft riots during the Civil War and the disorders that accompanied the establishment and dissolution of the Paris Commune were bloodier, on the average, than similar upheavals in our own time but in the absence of television and air travel they did not propagate the waves of imitation that would be expected nowadays.

Some old forms of cruelty disappeared during the century but new ones were invented. Public executions were abandoned in most of the Western countries. The practice of castrating boy sopranos to preserve their voices was given up as inhumane. At about the same time, the custom of lynching was introduced and practiced with enthusiasm. The white slave trade flourished, hordes of homeless children wandered the streets of every great city, and savage punishments were inflicted on rebellious natives in colonial territories.

It is difficult to decipher the many changes that took place in the social stratification of modernized countries during the nineteenth century and to determine whether on balance there was a trend towards or away from social equality. There were many changes in the social hierarchy but they did not all point in the same direction. In the course of the century, slavery was abolished throughout the Western hemisphere and serfdom throughout Europe, but in each case, the living conditions of the liberated population remained more or less the same and numerous quasi-legal devices were invented to keep them in subjugation. At the other end of the status scale, the legal privileges of nobles and gentry disappeared almost completely in most of the modernized countries by the end of the nineteenth century, but the number of families with aristocratic pretensions increased considerably and the resources they had to support their pretensions were very much greater than those that had been available to the leading families of 1800. The ownership of land remained as important a source of social status as ever before. Newly gained industrial wealth was often used to purchase land and to support the life styles traditionally associated with land ownership.

The occupational specialization that accompanied modernization increased the number and complexity of status distinctions in the urban labor force, especially in what are now called white collar occupations. The expansion of the middle class, with its comfortable style of life and its strict standards of respectability, softened the previous sharp contrast between the privileged class of property owners and officials and those who worked with their hands. But from another standpoint, the differences in status and self-esteem *within* the new middle class were roughly comparable to those which prevailed within eighteenth-century society as a whole, involving about as many levels of status and about as much effort to preserve the distinctions among them.

The development of the arts in the nineteenth century was marked by another sort of ambiguity. The relative number of professional artists—musicians, singers, painters, sculptors, writers, architects—increased somewhat and their techniques were improved in peripheral ways by such inventions as the upright piano, synthetic pigments and the typewriter. The number and variety of artistic productions increased greatly while the diffusion of graphic works of art by photogravure, of music by the phonograph, and of literature by mass publications were all well advanced by 1900. But the widely-held expectation that technical progress would be paralleled by a comparable sort of aesthetic progress turned out to be ill-founded (or perhaps meaningless). The nineteenth century in Europe and America was a period of notable artistic achievement but there were probably more foolish and insincere works produced in 1900 than in 1800. It is hard to find any basis for characterizing the best work of 1900 as superior to the best work of 1800. Beethoven, Goethe, Shelley, and Goya cannot be placed on a lower level than Mahler, Proust, Rilke and Picasso. Nor has it been possible to demonstrate convincingly that modernization was responsible for the aesthetic fashions of the nineteenth century. Impressionism might conceivably have appeared about when it did if the steam engine had never been invented or developed. Debussy's shimmering music would have suited the pastoral mood of the late eighteenth century to perfection.

Something similar may be said about the household arts, as distinct from household technology. The comfortable town house of 1900 had central heat, running water, flush toilets, gas or electric light, and an efficient kitchen—all of which had been lacking in the equivalent house in 1800. But its chairs, tables, sofas, carpets, curtains, beds, desks, dishes, and decorations were not superior to those of 1800. Indeed, by the standards of current taste, they were markedly inferior. The same must be said when we compare the costumes, the cookery, the gardens, and the indoor sports of the two eras. What was new was not particularly good, and most of what was good predated modernization.

The last important non-trend that invites our attention concerns the stability of large social systems. To what extent, we may ask, did modernization promote or threaten social stability within and between nations? Once again, the trends are ambiguous and contradictory. To the people who lived in it, the nineteenth century seemed to be an era of turmoil and upheaval. The revolutionary spirit was abroad from the very beginning, and the opposition between socialism and property rights dominated the politics of every country. The century was punctuated by bloody and unsuccessful rebellions. The multiple uprisings of 1848 sent waves of restlessness all across Europe. Revolutionary and nationalist movements sometimes met at cross purposes, sometimes conspired together against the existing order. A continuous argument raged between those who supported and those who abhorred the idea of drastic social change. In the United States, the war over slavery and states' rights shook the Republic to its foundations and left it permanently divided in some respects. On the periphery of the province of modernization, in Latin America and Eastern Europe, attempts to establish representative government by *coups d'état* alternated with campaigns of repression.

It was, in sum, a period of revolutions that failed. By 1900, a hundred years of socialist agitation had failed to establish a single socialist regime, except for the Commune which had governed Paris for two months in 1871; scores of episodes of native resistance to European domination had not succeeded in establishing a single new government controlled by people of non-European origin. The province of modernization was still securely in the hands of its original founders. The nineteenth century had not witnessed an attempt to change the social institutions of any country in the sweeping style of the English Revolution of the seventeenth century or the American and French Revolutions of the eighteenth.

The trend in war was inconclusive. Sorokin assembled figures on the frequency of war, the size of the armies raised, and the number of casualties sustained by France, England, Austria-Hungary, and Russia for a period of more than 800 years.[7] His data show that these countries mobilized 17.9 million soldiers for various hostilities in the course of the nineteenth century, compared to 24.9 million in the eighteenth century, and only 15.9 million in the seventeenth. The average casualty rate remained stable (around 15%) from 1600 to 1900. It had been much lower before 1600 and would be much higher after 1900. In proportion to the population, the war losses of the nineteenth century were much *lower* than those of the preceding centuries and were concentrated in the Napoleonic wars of the first two decades. The three most destructive wars of the century, the American Civil War, the Taiping Rebellion in China, and the Lopez War in Paraguay, did not affect the European trend. By 1900, a good many European observers thought they were witnessing the gradual disappearance of international war as an institution, and some of them were at work on projects to facilitate the conduct of international affairs in a warless world.

The trends and non-trends we have just reviewed may be roughly summarized as follows: During the nineteenth century human control of the physical environment greatly increased, enabling many more people to survive. The instruments of this achievement were a cumulatively expanding fund of scientific knowledge and an increasingly complex division of labor which together constituted the unique technology of modernization. The province of its application expanded steadily; the population within that province multiplied; the stock of physical goods (and of symbols) increased without apparent limit; and the human organizations operating the new technology increased steadily in size and intricacy.

Modernization had no perceptible effect on human nature, however, or at least no effect that has been empirically verified. Men did not love or hate more after modernization than before; they were not more or less susceptible to envy, sloth, avarice, gluttony, lust, anger and treachery. They were as readily moved to heroic deeds and as easily distracted from their obligations. The final triumph of virtue over wickedness came not an hour closer.

The foregoing generalization applies interchangeably to human nature in general and to the particular patterns into which it is shaped within the cultural tradition of Western Europe. These patterns include stable values that have endured since the days of Mycenae and Crete and other values that pass with the seasons, but neither the stable nor the evanescent elements of the personality models prevalent in Europe and America seemed to be affected in any consistent way by modernization.[8] Despite much speculation on the subject, there is no evidence that the Englishman or Frenchman of 1800 was more or less sentimental or honest or quarrelsome or devoted to his family than his descendants of 1900.

The human tendency to form intimate relationships and the satisfactions sought in those relationships were not affected in any obvious way by modernization. The interplay of pain and pleasure within the family, and between lovers and friends, was not seriously affected by the growth of factories. The act of worship and the use of sacraments turned out to be no less feasible in the age of science than before it, after some initial confusion about cosmology. The human taste for games, contests, carnivals, theatrical performances, and ceremonies; the craving for artificial terrors and imaginary delights; the use of intoxicants; the expression of individuality and status by details of costume and tricks of speech; the tendency to convert all repetitive collective events into games with arbitrary rules; the tendency to develop a fixed hierarchy regulated by status etiquette in every permanent community, the whole realm of social conduct and morality was left essentially untouched by modernization.

At the end of the nineteenth century, however, the belief in the beneficent effect of modernization on all social institutions was widely held, either in its Spencerian version, which equated moral progress with technological progress, or its Marxist version, which anticipated the automatic perfecting of society as soon as the hindrance of private property had been removed. It is no wonder that the nineteenth century was rung out in an atmosphere of nearly universal self-congratulation. European and American conservatives anticipated that the European hegemony of the world would remain undisturbed, that conflict would become increasingly rare, and that industrial and moral progress would continue to heap new benefits on mankind. Their socialist contemporaries were sure that the revolution was imminent, that it would succeed with relative ease, and that moral progress would be automatic

thereafter. In the peripheral territories of modernization, young nation-
alists like Mohandas Gandhi and Sun Yat-sen dreamed of an independence that would liberate the energies of their people and set them on
the road to material equality with, and moral superiority to, the ubiqui-
tous Europeans.

Before we attempt to understand how and why these bright hopes
were blasted, it may be helpful to look at some of the pictures of the
twentieth century that were held just before 1900, and that helped to
mislead our grandfathers about the shape of things to come.

CHAPTER 4

The Twentieth-Century Viewed from the Nineteenth

IT would be a formidable job to catalog in any exhaustive way the multiple expectations aroused in advance by the twentieth century. The diversity of opinions on social issues was much greater at the end of the nineteenth century than at its beginning, and the forum of discussion much wider, so that a comprehensive reconstruction of the *fin-de siècle* attitude towards the future would be a large undertaking. It is more relevant, for our present purposes, to examine the work of three intellectually powerful writers—Edward Bellamy, Karl Kautsky, and Emile Durkheim—whose different images of the future illustrate the courses of social development that could be projected from approximately the same point in time.

Looking Backward at
Looking Backward

Edward Bellamy, a utopian socialist, was one of the founders of American populism and some of his ideas have remained current ever since the publication of *Looking Backward* in 1888 and *Equality* in 1897.[1]

It is slightly unfair to call Bellamy a utopian. His reasonable and well-informed approach to social problems is far removed from the looniness of Fourier or the Oneidans, and he had no aversion to practical politics. Encouraged by the popularity of *Looking Backward,* which sold more than a million copies, Bellamy founded a political journal called *The Nationalist* (which advocated nationalization of basic industry) and was active in the formation of a nationalist party which flourished for several years until, with other elements of the Populist movement, it was absorbed by the Democratic organization of William Jennings Bryan. *Equality* was intended as a political tract; only Bellamy's premature death in the year after its publication limited its influence.

Looking Backward and *Equality* masquerade as science fiction. Julian West is a rich young man living alone in his family mansion in Boston in 1887. Suffering from insomnia, he builds a stone sleeping room in his basement and when its silence and seclusion fail to put him to sleep, he calls in a professional hypnotist. One night, while he lies in hypnotic sleep, the house burns down, and his hideaway is not discovered until the year 2000 when a Boston doctor excavating in his garden finds the stone chamber in which Julian is still asleep and successfully resuscitates him. Few simpler and more elegant modes of time travel have ever been devised. The doctor who unearths Julian is a genteel Bostonian of his own ilk, although he lives in a completely transformed society. The slender plot turns on Julian's discovery that his benefactor's daughter, Edith, who nurses him back to full health, is the great granddaughter (as well as the mirror image) of his lost fiancée of 1887. But the point of the story is in the long dialogues in which the doctor and his daughter explain the workings of the new social order to Julian, and criticize the old social order he represents. Like Lemuel Gulliver among the Houyhnhnms, Julian is easily persuaded to apologize for his former associates.

As a technological seer, Bellamy was very gifted. His Boston of the year 2000 has credit cards and computerized accounting, closed-circuit television, interstate highways, community colleges, disposable paper clothing, pantsuits for women, natural childbirth, painless menstruation, giant earthmoving machinery, tape-recorded messages, and rental cars available at the airport. So sure was Bellamy's touch in these matters that even those of his predictions that have not come to pass, such as the generation of electricity by tidal power, still appear plausible.

There is nothing superficially absurd about the system he proposes for the distribution of wealth and the assignment of occupations. All productive wealth is nationalized and operated by the General Government. Every citizen receives the same annual stipend, adjusted from year to year according to the nation's resources. In the year 2000, the standard stipend is $4,000, which the individual receives in the form of a bank balance at the beginning of the year. Money has been abolished. All major expenditures are made by credit cards; vouchers serve as small change.

Education is universal and compulsory until the age of 21, when young men and women enter the industrial service for three years of trial employment during which they shift from job to job. At 24, they apply for a specialized occupation, which they pursue until they retire at 45. The annual distribution of persons into occupations is accomplished by an exchange system. The General Government publishes lists of positions to be filled, and individuals apply for them. If two applicants seek the same position, preference is given to the applicant with the better work record. The personnel rating system is passed over lightly but seems to include a permanent centralized record of an individual's productivity and conduct in every job he has ever held. Every citizen has an absolute right to employment in his home locality. People who are dissatisfied with their assignments of occupation or locality are allowed to arrange a private exchange of assignments if they are able to do so. Anyone who refuses industrial service was furnished with a collection of seeds and tools and turned loose on a special reservation to support himself by his own efforts.

In the year 2000 the education of girls and boys is identical; women follow the same occupations as men, including the whole range of jobs in heavy industry; sexual freedom is absolute; and athletic contests are cosexual. All food is prepared in computerized central kitchens (it is vegetarian but delicious). All clothing is disposable and daycare is universally available so that there is no housekeeping left to do. Women are liable for industrial service on the same terms as men, although under a separate chain of command.

Not only was Bellamy a nearly infallible prophet of future inventions, he was also prescient about the standard of living of twentieth-century America, correctly predicting the universalization of education, the increase of leisure, the improvement of health, the extended duration of active maturity, early retirement, increased personal mobility, the diminishing differentiation of women from men, the personalization of fashion, and the expansion of opportunities for recreation and entertainment.

By contrast, his prophecies about social institutions were about as wrong as they could be. He predicted the disappearance of the private household as a unit of social organization and the total disappearance of stratification by social class. He foresaw a process of de-urbanization whereby the great cities would lose most of their population. This de-urbanization would be made possible in part by the spontaneous cessation of population growth as the cultural level of the masses rose, and in part by migration towards the open country. He believed that organized religion was about to vanish, that war would spontaneously disappear, that crime would diminish together with poverty, making prisons and courts unnecessary, that labor-management relations would cease to be a problem, and that representative government would be replaced by direct democracy (the entire body of citizens voting directly on legislative propositions by means of a national telephone hookup).

What gives his "New Order" its most utopian aspect is Bellamy's confidence in automatic solutions. He counted on the abolition of private capitalism to solve all social problems, from international war to painful menstruation, and expected the Great Revolution to accomplish itself without definite leaders or a definite program. "Slow at First, but Fast at Last," is the title of the chapter which gives a hypothetical account of the Great Revolution, which was to have occurred in the twentieth century:

"A bitter minority of the Capitalist Party and its supporters seems indeed to have continued its outcry against the revolution until the end, but it was of little importance. The greater and all the better part of the Capitalists joined with the people in completing the installation of the New Order, which all had now come to see was to redound to the benefit of all alike."
"And there was no war?"
"War! Of course not. Who was there to fight on the other side?" [2]

The Socialist Commonwealth

Kautsky's *Class Struggle,* written in 1892 by the official theorist of German Marxism under the approving eye of Friedrich Engels, was the version of Marxism ultimately translated into the parliamentary platform of the Social Democrats and, with some further modification, into the revolutionary program of the Bolsheviks.[3]

Before we consider the way Kautsky modified the Marxist orientation towards the future we must digress long enough to recall what that orientation was.

Marx himself was never preoccupied with images of the post-revolutionary future. He scorned efforts to visualize the future in detail and on at least one occasion, he criticized his followers for "playing with fancy pictures of the future structures of society." [4] The force and persuasiveness of his own writings lay in their denunciation of existing institutions. The promise of a better world was made repeatedly but never spelled out. It is, therefore, somewhat difficult to determine how Marx himself visualized the desired end-condition of his revolution. The difficulty is compounded by the changes in his perspective that occurred between the 1840s and the 1870s, as well as by a persistent, but unstated, difference of opinion with Engels, who, unlike Marx, seems to have had a definite proclivity for practical programs. *The Communist Manifesto,* [5] in which Engels had a large share, contains a ten-point program for revolutionary movements in the advanced countries that has very little connection with any of the previous or later writings of Marx. It advocated the abolition of private property in land, a graduated income tax, the abolition of inheritance, confiscation of the property of "immigrants and rebels," a national bank with a monopoly of credit, a nationalized system of transportation and communication, some additional public ownership of industry, compulsory labor in industrial armies, a program of de-urbanization, universal public education, and the abolition of child labor.[6] This curious program was the closest Marx ever came to describing his objectives in concrete terms.

In his earlier writings he was fairly emphatic about the disappearance of the state after the Communist revolution. "Revolution" he wrote in 1844, "is a political act. Without revolution socialism cannot develop . . . but as soon as its organizing activity begins, as soon as its own purpose and spirit come to the fore, socialism sheds this political covering." Two years later, in *The German Ideology* he wrote that the proletariat "are in direct opposition to the State as the form in which the members of society have so far found their collective expression and in order to develop as persons they must overthrow the State." [7] Still in the same decade, the *Manifesto* predicts that "the public power will lose its political character when production has been concentrated in the hands of a vast association in which the free development of each is the condition of the free development of all."

During the 1850s and the 1860s, Marx was largely occupied with *Das Kapital,* which contains no reference at all to the future of the modern state. Not until 1875, in his *Critique of the Gotha Program,* did he seem to concede that the state in one form or another would survive the revolution. The state he said, must be transformed from an organ dominating society into one completely subordinate to it. Like a note of doom, we hear for the first time about the era of non-freedom that is to precede the advent of perfect freedom.

Between capitalist and communist society lies the period of the revolutionary transformation of the one into the other. There corresponds to this also a political transition period in which the State can be nothing but the revolutionary dictatorship of the proletariat. [8]

There is a famous passage in *The German Ideology* which illustrates the expected disappearance of the division of labor when society regulates production by saying that it will be possible to hunt in the morning, fish in the afternoon, raise cattle in the evening, and criticize literature after dinner according to one's choice without taking on the occupations of hunter, fisherman, shepherd or critic. The tone of the *Critique of the Gotha Program,* written almost thirty years later, is much grimmer. We learn that in a communist society, as it emerges from a capitalist society, it will still be necessary to pay workers in proportion to their productivity. Although surplus value will no longer be expropriated, there will still be inequality. Some men are mentally or physically inferior to others, and some have more dependents to support so that even with equal effort, some workers will still be relatively poor. Not until that remote stage of communism from which the division of labor has vanished entirely would it be possible to take from each according to his ability and give to each according to his needs, thought Marx in 1875. With respect to other social institutions, he had progressed in a similar way from a transcendental idealism that counted on a new era of socialized humanity above and beyond all previous human experience to a kind of irritable practicability impatient with details, but sensitive to social constraints. The early writings promise that the disappearance of *all* social institutions will follow the abolition of private property. In the *Economic and Philosophical Manuscripts of 1844,* we read that "religion, the family, the state, law, morality, science, art, etc. are only particular forms of production and come under its general laws. The positive abolition of private property as the appropriation of human life, *is thus the positive* abolition of all alienation and thus the return of man from religion, the family, the state, etc. to his *human, i.e., social life."* Marx's later writings seem to take for granted the survival of a considerable number of social institutions, and the persistence of some kind of authoritative state, by whatever name it is called, in which the proletariat will rule—at least for a while—until authority is no longer needed. But whether the dictatorship of the proletariat should be nationalist or anti-nationalist, whether it would sponsor sexual freedom or stricter monogamy, whether legal codes would be abandoned or elaborated, whether voluntary associations would be encouraged or prohibited, what form of religion would be permitted, and how socialist production was actually to be organized, are questions to which the later writings of Marx and Engels gave vague, and sometimes self-contradictory answers.[9]

Kautsky's *Class-Struggle* did not answer all of these questions but resolved the most important of them, becoming the blueprint which was eventually followed in the development of real communist societies.

The coming system of socialist production in Kautsky's view was not to be modeled after the primitive agricultural commune but after the privately-owned industrial company. The transition to socialism was to be accomplished by uniting all of the large-scale enterprises required to satisfy the wants of the commonwealth into *one giant firm.*

Since modernization had already expanded capitalist enterprises so
that their operations embraced whole nations and made a nation's industries interdependent, Kautsky concluded that a socialist commonwealth of appropriate size would be coextensive with an existing
modern state. He reasoned that since international trade and international conflicts were attributable to the insatiability of capitalism, international relationships would be much reduced under socialism,
although a loose federation of socialist commonwealths might be useful.

According to Kautsky, the family would not be threatened in any
way by a socialist system of production. Indeed it would be more
secure than under capitalism, which encourages prostitution, celibacy,
and the "abominable practice" of daycare.[10] In Kautsky's commonwealth, although women would have legal and occupational
equality with men, marriage would be strictly monogamic and traditional family relationships not deliberately modified. Whatever future
changes occurred in the traditional forms of family life would be attributable to modernization, not to socialism.

Socialism would not require the expropriation of personal property,
household goods, or savings. The revolution would not even involve
the expropriation of the small artisan and the small farmer. Their
antiquated methods of production would be allowed to disappear naturally as craftsmen were drawn into public employment by superior incentives. Production for use in agriculture would be permitted, but dis-
couraged by a policy of de-urbanization that would rapidly diminish
the contrasts between rural and urban life.

The distribution of income was to be regulated neither by a principle
of equality nor by a simple formula like "from each according to his
ability, to each according to his needs." As under any other regime,
the distribution of products would be determined by the prevailing system of production. Since Kautsky's socialist society was to be an enlargement of the private industrial enterprise, it became necessary to
examine the forms of payment for labor used in capitalist industry—
fixed salaries, piece wages, time wages, bonuses—to find the appropriate forms of payment for labor. "As today in a large industrial establishment, production and the payment of wages are carefully regulated, so in a socialist society, which is nothing more than a single
gigantic industrial concern, the same principle must prevail."[11] In his

commonwealth, Kautsky projects a long-term trend toward the equalization of income resulting from a spontaneous consequence of increased productivity and permanent full employment.

The other important point he makes about income distribution is that a much larger proportion of the national product would go into what is now called *the public sector* of public institutions and social services. Only the residue—the portion of the national product that remained after the needs of the public sector had been satisfied—was to be distributed for private consumption.

The description of the future commonwealth concludes with a discussion of socialism and freedom. Kautsky concedes that socialist production is "irreconcilable with the full freedom of labor" but suggests that the freedom of the laborer to work when, where, and how he chooses is irreconcilable with modern industrial organization. He also believed that the relative freedom of the small independent producer was being steadily curtailed by the advance of modernization. Freedom of labor has come to an end, he says, not only in the factory but also in all other bureaucracies; the hospital physician, the school teacher, the railroad employee or the newspaper man are as unfree as the factory worker.

The one freedom the worker enjoyed under capitalism was occupational mobility. If he disliked his job or employer he could change them. He would not have this right in a socialist commonwealth since there would be only one employer, says Kautsky, but the loss would be more than compensated by employment security and the removal of the conflict of interests that marred the employer-employee relationship. Moreover, "in a socialist community the lack of freedom in work would not only lose its depressive character, it would also become the foundation of the highest freedom possible to man." [12] Kautsky explains this apparent contradiction at length. In the pre-industrial age, he says, the full development of physical and mental powers was only possible among the leisure classes but modernization and an intensified division of labor deprived the rich of their leisure. Like mechanics and farmers the rich became wholly taken up with their business and their education had become a commodity oriented to practical ends. (Kautsky adds the abandonment of Greek and Latin studies in secondary schools to his indictment of capitalism.)

The modern proletariat, precisely because their labor was devoid of intellectual content, had a stronger craving for high culture than the upper classes:

> While all other classes kill their time with the most unintellectual diversions, the proletarian displays a passion for intellectual culture. Only one who has had an opportunity to associate with the proletariat, can fully realize the strength of the thirst after knowledge and enlightenment. But even the outsider may imagine it, if he compares the newspapers, magazines, and pamphlets of the workers with the literature that finds acceptance in other social circles.[13]

Socialism, by shortening hours and providing universal educational facilities, would make possible the gratification of these impulses toward science and art. Not freedom of labor but freedom *from* labor would enable the socialist commonwealth to "outshine the moral greatness of all previous societies."

As socialism developed, nationalism, founded as it was on capitalist competition, would gradually disappear. The workers of all nations would recognize their common interests and come to understand that the only way to remove the threat of cheap foreign labor would be to assist backward countries toward modernization.

Durkheim's Self-Steering Future

Emile Durkheim never wrote a detailed description of the future. He did not think it useful or even possible to do so.[14] He seldom separated the phenomenon of modernization in the nineteenth century from the more inclusive trends of social change that led from medieval to modern types of social organization. His picture of the twentieth century must be teased out of scattered references in the three major books he published between 1893 and 1897 (*The Division of Labor, The Rules of Sociological Method, Suicide*) and several minor works of the same period. Given Durkheim's limited interest in futurology, is the effort worthwhile?

The answer is *yes*. Durkheim had more influence than any other scholar on the direction taken by sociology in the twentieth century and it is the ineffectiveness of contemporary sociology in solving social problems that we are trying to explain and to overcome. He was a powerful, original, and subtle theorist.[15] If his influence on the development of modern sociology was baleful, as I believe, it was not because he reasoned falsely but because his conception of the world was excessively narrow. Unlike his great sociological contemporaries—Weber, Pareto, and Simmel—Durkheim never developed an interest in economics. His interest in history was limited to a desire to separate it from sociology. There are hardly any references to modern literature or art, sports or games, or to specific scientific discoveries in his works. He seems never to have conducted a field study or an experiment or a series of interviews. So far as we know, he had no direct experience of war, litigation, agriculture, or poverty. He was never arrested, and the record is silent as to whether he was ever in love.

Durkheim's mentors were Herbert Spencer and Auguste Comte. From Comte he inherited the project of making sociology an empirical science, as firmly grounded as physics or chemistry, but with a larger scope. From Comte also, he took the assumption that the morality of the future would be rationally constructed with materials furnished by the new science. From Spencer he took the idea of classifying human societies into species and attempting to trace the line of evolutionary descent that led from simple to complex societies.

But unlike Comte and Spencer, Durkheim tried whenever possible to replace the terms of social description in common use by new sociological terms stripped of all connotations. "In the present state of knowledge, we cannot be certain," he says, "of the exact nature of sovereignty, political liberty, democracy, socialism, communism, etc. Our method should, then, require our avoidance of all use of these concepts so long as they have not been scientifically established." [16] Of all the rules proposed by Durkheim for the guidance of his sociological successors, this one has probably had the most effect so that a considerable part of recent sociological research is directed to the elucidation of concepts, like *role conflict* or *anomie,* whose connections with the world of common experience are difficult to trace. The same bias against concepts drawn from everyday language may account in part for the omission from Durkheim's writings of references to contemporary organizations other than the state; he had almost nothing to say about public or private bureaucracies, political parties, social movements, or social classes.

We noted earlier that Durkheim did not recognize modernization—the nineteenth-century increase of human capacity in relation to the natural environment—as a unique or important phenomenon. On the one hand, he merged it into a vastly greater sequence of social change leading from the most primitive tribe to the most advanced modern society. On the other hand, he did not consider the continuation of technological progress to be inevitable. "If it were true," he wrote, "that we tend at present to seek our happiness in an industrial civilization, nothing assures that, in epochs to follow we shall not seek it elsewhere." [17] The indicator of social development that he selected for special study in *The Division of Labor* was the shift from predominantly punitive to predominantly restitutive laws. This is one of the slowest moving social indicators that can be devised, and since Durkheim's investigation was centered in a particular legal tradition, he found himself comparing nineteenth-century France more often with the Roman Empire than with eighteenth-century France. Perhaps by chance, the suicide rate—the only statistical index that he studied at close range—is one of the rare social indicators that can *not* be used as a measure of modernization.*

Nevertheless, it was in the concluding chapter of his study of suicide that Durkheim predicted the shape of the twentieth century as he foresaw it. Discussing the increase in the absolute number of suicides

*As the following table shows:

A Table from Durkheim's *Suicide* Brought Up to Date;
Suicides per Million Inhabitants, 1866–1966

Country	1866–1870	1871–1875	1874–1878	1965–1966
Italy	30	35	38	54
England	67	66	69	104
Norway	76	73	71	77
Austria	78	94	130	230
Sweden	85	81	91	201
Bavaria	90	91	100	—
France	135	150	160	150
Denmark	277	258	255	190
United States	—	—	—	109

Source: Based on Emile Durkheim, *Suicide* (New York: Free Press, 1951), Table III, p. 50; and *Demographic Yearbook of the United Nations*, 1967, Table 24.

recorded in a number of European countries during the nineteenth century, Durkheim proposed the hypothesis that European societies were no longer sufficiently integrated to keep their members under control. The remedy was, he said, to restore enough consistency to social groups for them to obtain a firmer grip on the individual, who would then develop a sense of solidarity with a collective existence which precedes him in time, survives him, and encompasses him at all points. "If this occurs, he will no longer find the only aim of his conduct in himself, and understanding that he is the instrument of a purpose greater than himself, he will see that he is not without significance. Life will resume meaning in his eyes. . . ." [18]

But what groups, asks Durkheim, can provide modern man with these wholesome sentiments of solidarity? One by one, he goes through the list of possibilities:

Not the modern state; Durkheim considered it too far removed from the individual to affect him very much except in times of crisis; most people, he felt, were unaware of their national citizenship most of the time.

Not religious institutions. "Religion modifies the inclination to suicide only to the extent that it prevents men from thinking freely." The progress of reason, he states, has been irresistible and it would be childish to expect this progress to be checked. Durkheim felt that traditional religious institutions had lost much of their influence, and although new sects might be founded, they were likely to be so liberal and anti-dogmatic that they would have no restraining effects on the suicide rate.

Not the local community. Although some people still preferred to live where they were born and reared, he asserted, local patriotism no longer existed and could not in any way be revived. The local community had become a mere label, without emotional significance.

Not the family. The conjugal family was becoming more and more impermanent and for most of its duration, consisted of the married couple alone.

To fill the gap left by the crumbling of all these traditional institutions, Durkheim proposed a new type of occupational syndicate "outside the state although subject to its action" which would regulate labor-management disputes, fix wages and working conditions, administer unemployment insurance and old-age pensions, and provide a focus of personal identification for egoistic and anomic individuals. The occupational syndicate should be more than an assemblage of individuals. It could fulfill its purpose only when it became a traditional type of institution with a collective personality and a sense of unity. "The great difficulty," says Durkheim, "is not to decree that representatives shall be selected by occupation and what each occupation shall be, but to make each syndicate become a moral individuality." Who is to do this and how, he does not say.

Although the occupational syndicate is discussed again in Durkheim's famous preface to the second edition of *The Division of Labor* and elsewhere in his writings, it remained very much a *pro forma* program. As far as I know, he never proposed any practical steps to bring it about. What it symbolized was Durkheim's conviction that traditional institutions, including the state and the nation, had lost most of their power over individuals and were about to lose whatever influence they retained. On the eve of the twentieth century, he came to the astonishing conclusion that political parties and social movements were incapable of arousing any intense sentiments of solidarity among their adherents and that class, caste, and ethnic affiliations would count for very little in twentieth-century society.

It does not really matter that Durkheim was a poor prophet. He was not much interested in prophecy and he specifically denied the possibility of accurate social prediction. What does matter is that his model of social reality, which was so widely adopted by sociologists, turned out to be so remarkably at variance with the course of contemporary events.

In his model of social reality, there are only two actors—the *individual* and *society*. Society is the more important of the two because it shapes the individual but the indivudal cannot expect to change society.

Durkheim's society does not exactly correspond to any concrete social system. It is bigger than any local organization and more extensive than any government. In his own writings, society sometimes resembles the French nation and at other times seems to be as large as Europe, but it does not have definite geographical boundaries or a countable population. Conceivably it expands or shrinks according to what is said about it.

Durkheim's society is essentially a state of mind shared by a large number of people; it consists of a collective conscience enforcing a set of social constraints. The collective conscience is not a mysterious supermind, but it is something more than a body of shared opinions. The constraints enforced by the collective conscience are not merely rules and customs; they include all the basic understandings that make human life possible—the grammar of every language and the irresistible consensus that gives money its value, or makes it possible to recognize a beautiful woman.

Spencer had developed an earlier version of this model in his *Social Statics,* visualizing society as a giant organism evolving toward material and moral perfection and man as a component organism evolving in the same direction but independently. But since Spencer conceived the social organism as an abstraction and the individual as real, he was led to assert the importance of individuals acting on their own behalf and to deny the possibility of anyone's acting on behalf of society. Spencer wanted the state restricted to the bare minimum of protective and service functions; he considered its involvement in education and public health, for example, as an intrusion on the natural freedom of individuals.

Durkheim, although he considered himself an individualist, undertook to show that Spencer's idea of individual freedom was illusory, that the very structure of human thought is derived from social constraint, that human nature is not universal but the product of a particular social heritage at a particular time and place, and that individual morality cannot be even partially detached from the collective conscience without injuring both the individual and the society. Like Spencer, Durkheim believed in moral progress, but for him it consisted of the individual's obedience to an increasingly complex network of norms and obligations as society became increasingly complex and the division of labor more intricate. Whether Durkheim believed that individuals could contribute in any direct way to the uplifting of the collective conscience is uncertain, but for the most part, he regarded individuals as helpless to deflect or resist the blind forces of social evolution. Since he had no serious misgivings about the direction that social evolution might take in the immediate future and assumed that ethical improvements would occur as naturally as improvements in machinery, the implications of this theory did not worry him at all.

CHAPTER 5

Twentieth-Century
Trends

AS we saw in Chapter 4, the prophets of socialism at the end of the nineteenth century anticipated that the national state would disappear when capitalism was overthrown or would be reduced to a mere unit of administration, while the prophets of liberalism anticipated that its activities would be increasingly limited and that it would be partly replaced by new types of organizations. Both bodies of opinion anticipated the imminent abolition of international war—the socialists, because they could not conceive of war between socialist states; the liberals because they thought war had been rendered obsolete by moral progress and the calculations of political rationality.

As we know, they could not have been more wrong. The national state turned out to be the dominant institution of the twentieth century. The powers it wielded over its citizens tended to increase rather than wither away. Its old functions grew in scale and scope, and it acquired a great many new functions. The number of independent national states in the world has increased from about forty in 1900 to more than two hundred at present. In many countries, the cult of nationalism developed an intensity that exceeded any previous manifestation of fanaticism. A new faith in national rights sprang up and was soon accepted by the majority of the people nearly everywhere. The principal points of this creed were that the nation is a living entity composed of people who share the same ancestry, the same culture, and the same collective values; that the nation is an actor with a continuous personality engaged in a drama that transcends the interests of individuals; that consequently the citizen must serve the state, not the state the citizen. It was not an entirely new creed of course, but it did acquire new force in the early decades of the twentieth century and came to command public opinion in parts of the world where the European idea of nationality had previously been unknown. Along with this ideology, Western Europe exported to the rest of the world a system of international relations that had originally been worked out to accommodate the interaction of the few large, and many petty, monarchical governments which had emerged from the Reformation, the Thirty Years' War, and the dissolution of the Holy Roman Empire. The basic elements of this system were these: the sovereign, for international purposes, embodied his people, so that, for example, his enemies were not required to make any distinction between his property and his subjects' property; all sovereigns were formally equivalent and entitled to the same courtesies regardless of their power; every sovereign was absolute in principle and consequently, no outsider was entitled to interfere with a sovereign's treatment of his subjects; every sovereign was entitled to raise armed forces and use them at will against other sovereigns and, at times, against his subjects. To prepare for these occasions, sovereigns were expected to make both open and secret alliances. This system was restored and strengthened by the Congress of Vienna after Napoleon's attempt to establish a federated Europe under French hegemony. It has been with us ever since, surviving the partial displacement of monarchical by republican government, and of both of these by peoples' democracies. Contemporary communist states exchange ambassadors and plenipotentiaries, fire twenty-one gun salutes for visiting heads of state, and acknowledge a distinction between *de facto* and *de jure* sovereignty.

Before modernization, the mythmaking apparatus of this system simplified the complex interaction among nations into an interplay of princely sentiments—"The King of Prussia is aggrieved by . . .", "The Queen is pleased to learn . . .", "The Grand Duke is becoming impatient." [1] When in due course these linguistic habits were transferred to nations ruled by parliaments and congresses, soviets and parties, juntas and cabinets, whole nations were credited with personal acts and emotions—"France has attempted to deceive us . . . Germany feels threatened by these developments . . . England is calm but determined . . . The Chinese people are indignant."

The idea of the integral nation—a people of common descent and culture who share the same values, speak the same language, and occupy an exclusive territory under a government of their own choosing—was a formula for the manufacture of troubles on a scale hitherto unknown. Wherever linguistic and cultural boundaries did not exactly coincide with political frontiers—which was nearly everywhere—it encouraged a movement for the redistribution of territory which was generally resisted with violence by some of the governments holding power in the disputed territory. Whenever two or more populations of different ancestry and/or culture shared the same territory—nearly everywhere again—the ideal of the integral nation encouraged the majority to remove the minority or reduce them to political impotence by force or chicanery. All existing national states, including the few that could be described as integral, had been built by combining and consolidating groups that differed ethnically, linguistically, and culturally. They were now provided with a recipe for the revival of old differences and for separatist movements of various kinds. Not only were political boundaries incongruent with ethnic, cultural, linguistic, and religious boundaries throughout the world, but these latter boundaries were frequently incongruent with each other, so that the ideal boundaries of any nation could be drawn in a number of different ways. Under the influence of such maps, most states claimed pieces of neighboring states and accepted the duty of liberating them if a suitable opportunity presented itself.

What made the ideal of the integral nation so universally seductive is not entirely clear, although the development occurred within the memory of men now living. Although nationalism had developed greatly in the nineteenth century and furnished the basis for the multiple revolutions of 1848, only a small minority of the world's inhabitants identified themselves as citizens of a nation by 1900. That minority was heavily concentrated in Western Europe and the Western hemisphere. Elsewhere, the question of "Who are you?" was likely to be answered with the name of a tribe, a racial stock, a religion, a political movement, an occupational group, or an overlord. There were no real nations in Africa or on the mainland of Asia or in Oceania. The peasants of Russia, Austria-Hungary, China, and India were not encouraged to think of themselves as citizens of their respective empires and did not, in many cases, have any conception of the way in which the world was organized outside of their districts.

By 1970, the great majority of the world's inhabitants were citizens, duly registered and enrolled, suitably indoctrinated with myths of a heroic past and visions of a glorious future. Even those who quarreled with the form of government under which they found them-selves—Czech students agitating for freedom of speech, American students preaching the wisdom of Mao—seldom rejected the role of citizen. Throughout the world, gigantic efforts were underway to bring cultural boundaries into better alignment with national boundaries by shifting populations from one place to another, teaching national lan-guages, replacing local laws and customs by national laws and cus-toms, and assimilating or dispersing ethnic minorities. Everywhere the new nations pursued programs of cultural homogenization as invaria-bly as they undertook programs to accelerate modernization.

The institutional patterns associated with the modern nation-state are surprisingly uniform. Each of them has a flag, a national anthem, a capital with grandiloquent public buildings, a currency and coinage, an armed force with distinctive uniforms, a diplomatic service some-what larger than it needs, a national broadcasting network, a written code of laws and a hierarchy of courts to enforce them, a set of prov-inces with subgovernments and subcapitals, a secret police force to protect the state against revolutionary and foreign agents, a customs service to regulate imports and exports, one or several political parties to nominate public officials, periodic elections or plebiscites, a na-tional census, a national record of vital statistics, a procedure for natu-ralization, a schedule of public holidays commemorating the gaining of independence and the installation of the present form of govern-ment, an official version of the national history, a set of allies, and a set of potential enemies,[2] sometimes overlapping. The nations of the world resemble each other in all these features because modern nation-alism is a single cultural pattern, originally developed in France and

England and thereafter imitated by a widening circle of new nations, liberated colonies or in a few instances, like Japan and Iceland, by old nations which adopted whatever features of the pattern they had formerly lacked.

Each of the two hundred or more nations organized on this model exists in a continuous tension between the theory of sovereignty on which the whole system is based and the facts of power which control its operation. According to the theory of sovereignty, each state is absolute master of its territory and the sole protector of its citizens. The facts of power, by contrast, compel most weak nations to put themselves under the protection of stronger allies, while even the most powerful nations must avoid isolation. From 1900 to the end of World War II, these necessities produced a shifting configuration of alliances which were supposed to lead to a balance of power but which twice split the world into warring camps. For about two decades after World War II, the balance of power was replaced by the semipermanent confrontation of the United States and the Soviet Union called the Cold War. In this confrontation, most of the world's nations were solidly aligned on one side or the other. A few nations, like South Korea, the Congo, and Indonesia, became theaters of active hostilities and a handful of others were able to maintain neutrality, either by offering points of contact to the superpowers or by precariously playing them off against each other. Under this arrangement, any international dispute—however trifling—between nations of the two blocs automatically embroiled the superpowers and risked setting off another world war. A revolutionary movement in any nation on either side was certain to attract open or clandestine support from the other side. Hence, the Cold War consisted of a nearly continuous series of crises scattered over the entire world. Although it was a rather dangerous method of keeping the peace, the danger was mitigated by two interesting innovations: first, each superpower announced from time to time that the boundaries of its bloc would be defended against the armed forces of the other side in exactly the same way as its own national frontier. Whenever this principle was tested, it was so strongly sustained by the defending party that the designated boundary—the line dividing Berlin, the Hungarian border, the Yalu River, the Carribean sea frontier—remained inviolate. The other innovation was the development of a system of limited war which permitted non-critical disputes to be settled by local wars in which the superpowers, although always furnishing the weapons and supplies and sometimes committing their own troops, placed definite limits on their own objectives and announced them clearly to the other side. Such were the wars in Africa, Indochina, and the Middle East during the 1950s and 1960s.

Concurrently, the two superpowers worked out rules for a subtle and intricate game called mutual deterrence. Mathematical strategists on each side explored its possibilities. Their explanations of the game, carefully studied by their opposite numbers in the other camp, enabled both sides to maintain a common perspective and avoid fatal mistakes. Each side in a game of mutual deterrence must maintain *first strike credibility;* in other words, it must convince the other side that under a designated degree of provocation, it will attack with the full force of its nuclear weapons regardless of the risk of nuclear reprisal. The other main objective of each side is to maintain its *second strike capability,* which means its capability to respond to a surprise attack with a counterattack that would be no less destructive. The theory of the game is that nuclear war can be prevented by signaling clearly to the opposing power what hostile gestures on its part would provoke a first strike, while at the same time persuading the opponent that an unprovoked first strike would amount to national suicide.

For this game to be successfully played the two opposing powers must stay in very close communication with each other; each must, in effect, make sure that the other's espionage is successful and that military information is routinely exchanged at several levels. Beginning in 1962, a direct telephone line between the White House and the Kremlin enabled the heads of the two governments to communicate directly in an emergency. The conferences on nuclear disarmament carried on for many years at Geneva and elsewhere did not, of course, bring about disarmament but did provide multiple channels for the exchange of strategic information. In 1972, the SALT talks culminated in a flexible agreement between the United States and the Soviet Union which went far beyond the exchange of information, by regulating the composition of each country's nuclear arsenal for five years in advance.

In the earlier stages of the game, it was feared that a technical breakdown might occur at any time and cause an unimaginably de-

structive war. The breakdowns most easily visualized would be either
the unauthorized firing of nuclear weapons by an irresponsible individual in the armed services of either side or an accidental firing due to
mechanical malfunction or a mistaken signal by one of the detection
systems designed to give advanced warning of an attack. Elaborate
precautions were taken on both sides to prevent such accidents from
occurring and they have so far succeeded, although not without some
nervous moments.

More recently, the game of mutual deterrence has been threatened
in ways that are much less subject to the control of the principal
players. During the 1960s, three nations beside the superpowers—
France, China, and Great Britain—developed nuclear weapons of their
own together with the means of delivering a limited number of them in
almost any direction. India detonated a nuclear device in 1974 and
several other countries were attempting to develop them. Although
each superpower had proposed to the nations in its own bloc that it
would be advantageous to retain a nuclear monopoly, the proposal
had been greeted with derision and had, in each case, hastened the
breaking up of the bloc.

The game of mutual deterrence is difficult to visualize with multiple
players. The carefully timed exchange of unequivocal signals which it
requires continues to be possible between any two players provided
that no third player interferes by, for example, launching a first strike
against one of them, deceptively camouflaged as coming from the
other, in the hope that they will proceed to mutual destruction.

Another threat to the stability of the game was the gradual weaken-
ing of each superpower's authority within its bloc. By the nineteen
seventies, the communist bloc no longer existed, having broken into
two hostile segments headed by the Soviet Union and China and a
number of countries not fully committed to either. The western bloc
was less sharply divided but the influence of the United States had
been severely eroded by its misadventures in Indochina and its domestic scandals.

The long confrontation led neither to a clash nor to a settlement, but
to a state of confusion. Neither side had any program except to defend
itself against the unlimited malice and ferocity of the other side, but
with the passage of time, this matched pair of paranoid visions gradu-

ally went out of focus. With Russia and China at each other's throats, the image of a monolithic communist force bent on the domination of the world became implausible, while viewed from the other side, the United States was no longer as terrifying as it had been before its ten years of humiliation at the hands of a comically weak opponent in Vietnam. Yet the great engines of destruction that had been built under the spell of the two paranoid visions were not ready to be dismantled. They were still being enlarged and improved. The threat of insanely cruel destruction that each side posed for the other had not been removed at all but only deprived of human significance.

Presently only two nuclear weapons have ever been fired in anger. Among the first ones made, they were dropped by the U.S. Air Force on the Japanese cities of Hiroshima and Nagasaki in August 1945; a great number of people were wounded, and about a hundred and five thousand were killed. Since that momentous massacre, more than thirty thousand nuclear warheads have been manufactured. Some of these weapons, vastly more powerful than those dropped on Japan, have an explosive force equivalent to a million tons of TNT.

Although the use of nuclear weapons was successfully averted in the period following 1945, there was an exceptional amount of conventional war compared to any previous historical period. According to the statistical tabulations of Wright [3] and Richardson,[4] there were between twenty-five and thirty large wars (each costing over a hundred thousand lives) between 1484 and 1945. The numbers are not precise because it is not always possible to determine when one war ended and another began or to count casualties accurately, but roughly speaking, a large war occurred every twenty years before 1945. Since 1945, a large war has occurred every two years: in India, Korea, French Indochina, Colombia, China, Algeria, the Congo, Nigeria, in Indochina again, and Bangladesh.

This period marked the culmination of certain trends in war that drastically changed its relation to social institutions. For many centuries, organized warfare fit in with and reinforced prevailing patterns of religion, social stratification, the family and the community. Wars were painful for the vanquished but advantageous for the victors. In the thousand years prior to 1900, only a few got out of hand and devastated the social structure throughout a large area. The twentieth-century wars which are as damaging for the victors as for the vanquished were only faintly portended by the big wars of the nineteenth century—the Napoleonic Wars and the American Civil War. Although their casualties were very heavy, these wars did not exhaust or demoralize their respective societies, and did not differ in their essential outlines from the wars of the previous five or six centuries. During that long period, wars were fought between bodies of armed men, enlisted or conscripted for short periods and led by professional officers of a higher social class. They included two types of important events: pitched battles and sieges of fortified towns. Battles were held by preference in spring or summer since soldiers could not keep the field in the winter, and were often needed at home for the harvest in the autumn. Selecting a suitable site in the country, two large bodies of foot soldiers, armed with single-shot weapons like crossbows or muskets and some kind of knife or pike, paraded in sight of each other until the more confident force charged forward for hand-to-hand combat. The large mass of foot soldiers were supported by much smaller groups of horsemen who engaged in reconnaissance and flanking attacks. The artillery was stationed in fixed positions behind the lines and used mostly for psychological effect.

The losing army often broke and ran before coming to grips with the enemy. Sometimes it melted away from the battlefield but more often it was formally surrendered and sent home. The outcome of a battle was largely determined by the confidence and coolness of the generals, who presided over the field in plain sight of their troops. Battles were often decided by the death or capture of a general.

Another type of military confrontation was the siege. Although sieges were sometimes drawn out for months or years to end in rape and pillage, few were carried to that extreme. Most fortified towns surrendered quickly when encircled, or were able to resist successfully until reinforcements arrived.

Naval warfare was an even more orderly affair. Engagements between single ships or between whole fleets were generally settled in a matter of hours as the loser sank, surrendered, or fled. Armed ships preyed on the merchant vessels of the enemy and often on neutral vessels trading with him, but the crew of an unarmed ship seldom resisted attack and were not supposed to be murdered when the ship was taken as a prize.

Only rarely did European warfare in its traditional form involve the wanton killing of combatants or the massacre or systematic mistreatment of civilians. The mechanization of war in the twentieth century changed all that. Armies were bigger than ever before: about thirty million men were under arms in the various theaters of war at the beginning of 1945. Thanks to the improvement of agriculture and transportation, systems of supply progressed to the point where armies could be kept in the field year around. The Battle of Flanders went on intermittently, winter and summer, throughout World War I. The Battle of Stalingrad, in World War II, was fought every day for nearly a year.

The weapons of personal combat were gradually displaced by weapons of enormous power fired almost at random in the general direction of the enemy. The rifle and the bayonet were still emphasized in military training for ceremonial reasons; but battlefields were saturated by high explosive shells, curtains of machinegun fire, clouds of poison gas, sheets of flame, and all sorts of projectiles delivered by machines placed far behind or above the lines.

The distinction between combatants and noncombatants was increasingly disregarded until, for all practical purposes, it disappeared. The factories, oil fields, railroad yards, and other facilities supplying an army came to be identified as legitimate military targets; but since high explosives could not discriminate them from the communities in which they were embedded, these soon came under equal or heavier bombardment, and once the sight of dead and wounded civilians was sufficiently familiar to soldiers, they no longer hesitated to turn their personal weapons on unarmed villagers who were presumed hostile. At the same time that civilians were losing their traditional immunity to attack, many soldiers were acquiring such an immunity for themselves. Either they avoided direct confrontation because they were engaged in support functions remote from the actual fighting or because, as leaders, their lives were considered too important to be risked. Also, some operated machinery that inflicted death at a distance without exposing them to reprisal.

Between World War I and World War II, there was much discussion of a fluctuating balance between offensive and defensive weapons. The machine gun, it was said, when entrenched and protected by barbed wire, had given a decisive advantage to the defense in any confrontation of reasonably equal forces. The development of the tank and other armored vehicles tipped the balance in favor of the offense. This was accurate as far as it went (until the invention of nuclear explosives tipped the balance permanently in favor of the offense), but did not give due weight to other aspects of the evolving technology of war: modern armies were suffering higher casualty rates than earlier armies; civilian populations were in some cases enduring more casualties than the armed forces protecting them; and the physical damage to the environment exceeded anything previously known. According to the figures compiled by Sorokin for four European countries—France, England, Austria-Hungary, and Russia—on the size of armies and the number of military casualties over a number of centuries, the casualty rate in the armies of these countries during the first quarter of the twentieth century was 40 percent; the figures for the previous three centuries ranged around 15 percent. The same calculation has not been repeated for the second quarter of the twentieth century, but the weapons of war are estimated to have caused about thirty million deaths in World War II (compared to about ten million in World War I), in addition to the millions accounted for by mass murder, hunger, and disease. The prolongation of the trend towards greater destructiveness may be clearly seen in the Vietnam War of 1962–72. The proportion of military casualties on both sides was higher than in any previous war involving the United States, but civilian casualties exceeded military casualties by a ratio estimated at 5 to 1. The tonnage of explosives used by the United States exceeded the total tonnage during World War II and is said to have cratered an appreciable fraction of the total land surface of the country so badly that it can no longer be cultivated.

The Vietnam War illustrates another significant feature of twentieth-century warfare. Although the majority of troops on both sides, even during the maximum American involvement, were Vietnamese, the weapons used on both sides were of foreign provenance, as was the case in all the other large wars fought after 1945. Only a few advanced countries have the capacity to mass-produce the basic implements of modern warfare. The United States (with some help from France and Belgium) must provide all of the countries in its bloc with weapons if—as American foreign policy proposes—they are to retain any serious war-making capacity. This is routinely done even when, as in some Latin American countries, the only conceivable enemy against whom the weapons can be directed is another country friendly to the United States. The Soviet Union (assisted by Czechoslovakia and East Germany) fills the same role of volunteer armorer to the countries in its bloc and to some other countries whose support it seeks.

The casualties sustained by the Allies in World War I were relatively higher than those of the Triple Alliance. In World War II, they varied from country to country, and comparison is complicated by the difficulty of ascertaining civilian casualties; but the heaviest losses seemed to have been sustained by the Russians and the next heaviest by the Germans. The brunt of some recent wars, like the civil war in Nigeria, has been borne by the losing side; but in other cases, like the war for the independence of Bangladesh, by the winning side. The typical situation is that both sides in any protracted war sustain losses that are out of scale with any material advantages they gain from the war and may or may not be disproportionate to their political gains. If the winning side emerges badly shaken from a large twentieth-century war, the losing side nearly always has a revolution or a series of revolutions which sweeps away the regime that conducted the war together with the political values sustaining it. Such was the aftermath of the Russian defeat in 1917, and of the defeat of Germany, Austria-Hungary, and Turkey in 1918. Revolutions occurred in France and China after their initial defeats in the early stages of World War II and later, in Italy, Germany, and Japan. Wars of colonial independence seem to follow a different pattern. They are almost invariably won by the rebels, but the demoralization and strain toward revolution occurs in the governing country *during* the war, rather than afterward.

If twentieth-century wars are so much greater in scale and scope than earlier wars as to be different from them in kind, the same may be said of twentieth-century revolutions. There have been many more of them; a larger proportion have been successful; and those that were successful have had more sweeping consequences than in any previous era known to history. Of the 70 major countries we have had occasion to mention before, only the United States, Switzerland, Sweden, and the Netherlands, and perhaps Yemen have not experienced a political revolution in this century. Most of the countries on the list experienced

more than one. These ranged from simple coups d'etat to convulsions
that lasted for years and took hundred of thousands of lives.

In ten of the 70 countries, with about forty percent of the world's
population, the most recent revolution established a communist
regime. Within the communist states, there have been frequent and
desperate palace intrigues and crises of succession. Furthermore, armed
uprisings have not been uncommon. As of this writing, however, there
have been no revolutions in communist states to restore private property or parliamentary government. The revolutionary thrust in the eastern European countries, where communism was established under Soviet protection at the end of World War II, has been toward the
achievement of national independence, not toward de-communiza-
tion. In China, the Great Cultural Revolution of the 1960s shook the
whole society profoundly but does not seem to have changed its fundamental character.

So far in this century, parliamentary government has not been
seriously disturbed in the United States, Great Britain, the former British dominions, Scandinavia, the Low Countries, or Switzerland. The
important revolutionary movements in these countries have been separatist rather than anti-democratic. In most of the rest of the world's
non-communist countries, there has been an uneasy alternation between parliamentary government and one of two forms of dictatorship—either the dictatorship of a charismatic leader at the head of
an armed party with an extensive mythology, or a military dictatorship
with a platform of law, order, and economic progress. The two forms
of dictatorship have some tendency to merge into each other. A long
established one-party dictatorship may shed most of its original ideology, as has happened in Spain, while a military dictatorship, like that
of Atatürk or Nasser, may develop an elaborate ideology and a pattern
of leader worship over the course of time.

The failure of parliamentary government to take deep root in Asia,
Africa, or Latin America (except in a few countries like India, Israel,
South Africa, and Japan where European influence has been especially strong) may be at least partly explained by the relative weakness
of all forms of voluntary association in those countries, compared to
the army (invariably supported and trained with the help of foreign
powers) or in relation to revolutionary workers' movements, similarly

supported by foreign powers. The governing majority in a stable parliamentary system is normally a coalition of center parties with adjacent parties of the left or of the right. Such a government falls when it moves so far in either direction that some of its components desert the coalition. The parties of the center represent professionals and white collar workers, civil servants, independent farmers, small-property owners, factory workers with accumulated savings, and pensioners. When this group is numerous and confident, governments with leftist and rightist tendencies will probably alternate in response to current events; but both the left and the right, realizing that they cannot govern without the center, will be committed to the maintenance of representative government, as has been the case so far in the United States and Great Britain. Where the center is somewhat weaker, or has been demoralized by inflation, unemployment, military defeat, or internal disorder, as has occurred at various times in Italy, Germany, and France during this century, parliamentary government is subject to sudden collapse, but is likely to be restored after the failure of the subsequent dictatorship. Where the center is not insignificant but always a minority, as in most of the Latin American nations, military dictatorships alternate regularly with intervals of parliamentary government. Where the center is weak because the people on whom it depends are a small minority in a population of agricultural laborers, primitive tribesmen, or urban slum dwellers, as in many of the African states, parliamentary government is almost impracticable because no governing coalition can count on a firm base of popular support. At the same time, communism is unattractive to the small educated elite of these countries because it offers much smaller rewards than those they expect if private property is preserved. Under these circumstances, the choice lies between the charismatic dictatorship of a Nkrumah or a Nyere and straightforward military dictatorship. Neither of these systems of government, however, is likely to remain stable, faced with the inevitable efforts of foreign agents to align the dictator with one bloc or the other and the inevitable efforts of other foreign agents to overthrow him after he has been aligned.

This hasty review of the three great patterns which dominate the social history of the twentieth century—nationalism, war, and revolution—has been conducted from the outside so far. We have looked at them from the standpoint of Martian observers, surveying a global panorama. From such a vantage point, every detail takes on a semblance of historical inevitability. We may deplore the resurgence of despotism in our time or applaud the victories of nationalism over imperialism, but we do not get much sense of being able to affect the outcome of the dramas played out on the world's vast stage.

This picture, or at least one's relationship to it, changes when we examine the same events from the standpoint of those who organize social movements and begin to ask ourselves the basic questions with which the development of any successful strategy must begin: What features of the situation we confront are we capable of changing? What means will it require? How much time will it take? What happens if we fail? What happens if we succeed?

One obvious approach to these questions is to analyze some of the strategies that have actually been applied to the major social problems of our time to see whether we can isolate their results, and to see what lessons we can draw from them.

CHAPTER 6

A Set of Successful Projects

BEFORE the rise of evolutionary theories of society, statements about social events generally attributed them to human agents with discernible motives. "King Louis," wrote Machiavelli, "was brought into Italy by the ambition of the Venetians, who desired to obtain half the state of Lombardy by his intervention. I will not blame the course taken by the King, because, wishing to get a foothold in Italy, and having no friends there—seeing rather that every door was shut to him owing to the conduct of Charles—he was forced to accept those friendships which he could get, and he would have succeeded very quickly in his design if in other matters he had not made some mistakes." [1]

The contemporary habit of attributing historical events to abstract and irresistible forces is not a mere trick of speech but reflects the widely held belief that the history of modern society is not much affected by the plans and projects of living men but follows a predestined course set by forces outside human control. This belief, as we saw, was a nineteenth-century reaction to the discovery of modernization and we find versions of it in the writings of Hegel, of Marx and Engels, of Comte and Spencer, of Durkheim and his followers, and of behaviorists from Pavlov to Skinner, often incongruously joined to a

clarion call for social action, as when Marx and Engels announced the
inevitability of a proletarian revolution and the necessity of an heroic
struggle to bring it to pass.[2]

There is nothing inherently absurd about this prevailing model of
social reality. It conforms in one way to the ordinary individual's experience of social phenomena as vast, surprising and inexorable. Nevertheless, it may not be the most useful model in which to study the
possibilities of social improvement or the best model for organizing
the information we obtain from empirical studies of projects of social
improvement. In the present chapter, I am going to examine some
twentieth-century phenomena with the object of separating what was
done on purpose from what occurred by accident and from what cannot be explained at all.

Before we undertake this, it may be helpful to remind ourselves of
certain features of the social landscape that are likely to be overlooked
when we view social change as a play of impersonal forces. The first
is that social technology, like physical technology, consists in part of a
relatively small number of blueprints, which tell us how to set up particular projects that will have a high probability of success. Such
blueprints do not rely exclusively on systematic knowledge. They
always contain an admixture of knowledge obtained by trial-and-error,
such as the information that one method works better than another for
unknown reasons or that some component whose function is not understood is essential. Whenever a successful method is devised for accomplishing a widely held purpose, it will be widely imitated and, at
least for a time, the discovery of alternative methods will be somewhat
hindered.

Nearly all serious projects of social improvement require the cooperation of an organized group of people with an established division of
labor. The table of organization which regulates their collective efforts
is part of the social technology available for the accomplishment of a
given purpose. When a particular type of organization has been consistently successful in a particular type of project, other types of organization that might serve the same purposes are neglected. Thus, as we
noted in the last chapter, modern nationstates, regardless of their cultural peculiarities, follow quite uniform institutional patterns in their
governments. It cannot be plausibly argued that the pattern followed,

for example in the exchange of diplomatic representatives, is the only possible arrangement or the best conceivable arrangement or in any other way dictated by necessity. On the contrary, we know that it developed in a particular part of the world at a certain point in time out of a mixture of old customs and rational innovations and was then imitated by newer nations when they began to develop foreign policies patterned after those of the European powers.

Another feature of social systems that needs to be kept in mind when examining the effectiveness of projects of social improvement is the possibility—and in some fields of action the certainty—of mutual interference between projects with similar purposes. The end-condition of one project may be incompatible with the end-condition of a similar project (this is conventionally called *competition*) or the end-condition of one project may include the failure of another project as a goal (this is called *conflict*). In such fields of action it is logically impossible for all projects to succeed.

In a previous chapter, we examined the previsions of the twentieth century that were held by competent observers just before 1900 and asked ourselves what went wrong with their generally hopeful expectations. Let us see now whether this question can be answered without resort to explanations involving impersonal, enigmatic forces, or to the familiar analogies that compare human society to an anthill or a space ship.

If we try to describe the world of 1900 without using metaphors, we discover it to be full of ongoing projects, on all levels from the world community down to the individual.

Migration Projects

Many of the projects of individuals and families involved migration, either from country to city or from older to newer settlements. When W. I. Thomas began to study the Polish peasants who had immigrated to the United States and settled in Chicago, several hundred thousand of them had already accomplished a project of that kind.[3] The desired end-condition—which included resettlement in a new country within a community of fellow-immigrants, a transfer from agricultural to factory work, the partial relaxation of paternal authority and the assumption of an urban life-style—were familiar to every village child in Poland. The methods—borrowing steamship fare from relatives, arranging transportation through an immigrant agency, finding a safe lodging on arrival and maintaining contact with family members left behind—were all standard. The migration of a family typically took place in stages with adult males going first, saving money to bring over their wives and children and eventually their parents and other relatives. The normal duration and the average costs of the project were known to everyone and, as the letters in Thomas's famous collection show, the members of a family, as they exchanged letters between Poland and Chicago, continually gauged their progress against norms derived from the experience of neighboring families involved in similar projects. Like all programs of social improvement, the migration of the Polish villagers had unanticipated consequences, notably the disorganization of families as the mutual dependence of wives and husbands was reduced by new work habits and the authority of parents over children was rendered ineffectual by the children's superior knowledge of the new culture.

Modernization Projects

National modernization provides us with another example of a type of project that was widely imitated and almost always successful. The important point, from our present standpoint, is that it did not happen by itself but had to be accomplished wherever it occurred—in Russia and Japan, Mexico and Italy, and many other countries where industrialization was consciously pursued as a national goal. The agencies that planned and carried it out were not the same in every country, but their modes of operation were fairly uniform. In every case, goals were set for the achievement of particular levels of production of iron and steel, machinery and textiles, with accompanying increases in steam or electric power, in railroad capacity, and in port facilities. The technology was bought or borrowed from one of the advanced countires—Great Britain, the United States, or Germany in most instances—and, as far as possible, was taken over intact with the help of engineers from those countries who supervised the installation of equipment. The foreign experts not only installed equipment, they also set up tables of organization, job classifications, training methods, operating records, and the other social apparatus that had developed along with the original technology. Not all these projects were equally successful. The industrial progress of Japan was far greater than the industrial progress of Russia; Italy moved ahead more rapidly than Mexico. To explain this by impersonal forces, we might say that the national culture of the Tsar's Russia was less receptive to industrial modes of production than the Mikado's Japan. But if we confine ourselves to the projects and their outcomes, we note that the Japanese campaign to industrialize was more amply supported by a government with greater authority and that the sub-project of recruiting and training managers was given much higher priority in Japan than in Russia. This kind of explanation has two advantages: it compels us to attend to the details of each project, which are highly instructive, and it avoids the absurdity of arguing that whatever happened was inevitable. In any case, although projects of modernization were not all equally successful, few of them failed entirely. Most were successful enough to provide a base for further projects and to contribute to that gradual extension of the province of modernization which we have already described.

Revolutionary Projects

Many of the revolutionary movements conducted in the Marxist style have undertaken feasible projects of limited scope. Such projects include a fairly complete description of the end-condition to be achieved, (customarily couched in highly rhetorical language), an outline of the stages to be traversed, and an estimate of the time required to reach the end-condition. Close attention is given to the recruitment of agents, and to the choice of effective methods for attaining a particular set of goals. In sum, a typical Marxist project includes all of the essential components of a feasible project of social change that I enumerated in the first chapter. It could hardly be otherwise seeing that the operators of these projects have been able to seize and maintain control of a large part of the inhabited world. If I am correct in proposing that the logic common to all technology imposes certain fixed requirements on projects of social technology, it must be the case that any series of projects which have been successful in their own terms must have included the essential components of a feasible project. Projects in the Marxist style, however, contain some distinctive elements which set them off from others. A Marxist project generally includes both a careful description of an initial condition and what might be called a mythological description of that same condition which places it in a larger historical context and emphasizes in one way or another the ascription of inevitability which is the hallmark of Marxist social theory. This may take several forms, the initial condition being described as a stage in an inevitable sequence, a crisis foreseen by the founders, or the outcome of a conspiracy already discovered and foiled. The function of this myth is to provide a kind of scriptural sanction for the strategy selected for the project. The selected strategy is never presented as the most promising of a number of possible strategies but as the *correct solution,* i.e., the only course of action that advances the revolution to its next inevitable stage. Another distinctive feature of Marxist projects is the denunciation of alternative strategies and of those who advocate them. Most formal statements of a Marxist project include *two* denunciations, one directed against external enemies—capitalist exploiters, imperialist war-mongers, fascist running dogs—and the other against real or fictional comrades—lackeys of the bourgeoisie, traitors to the working class, revisionist opportunists—who may disagree with the strategy proposed. The rhetoric of denunciation first displayed in the *Communist Manifesto* has been maintained with astonishing fidelity against the ravages of time and of translation into exotic languages. It relies heavily on pejorative adjectives ("greedy, shameless, despicable, rotten"), on metaphors of combat ("revisionism must be totally vanquished"), on the labeling of differing opinions as if they represented organized movements ("the conspiracy of the ivory tower intellectuals"), and on direct exhortations to punish ("smash, crush, eradicate, destroy") those who have been denounced.

Many Marxist projects specify two end-conditions, one of which defines the concrete purposes of the project while the other provides a long-range justification for it. The philosophy of dialectical materialism gives the procedure a certain legitimacy since it anticipates that a given social condition may lead to the opposite condition and hence provides a built-in justification for programs that seem to be moving directly away from a desired goal. Thus, for example, a project whose practical purpose is to increase the control of a Communist government over its citizens may claim, without apparent insincerity, that its ultimate purpose is to hasten the disappearance of the state.

Modern Communism is the work of bookish men; not only Marx and Engels, but Lenin and Trotsky, Stalin, Mao Tse-tung, and Fidel Castro won their places in history by writing social theory while engaged in political activity. All of them—even the morose and taciturn Stalin—were virtuosi in the application of Marxist social theory to the exigencies of current events.

That body of theory had the serious defect that its predictions about the matters with which it was centrally concerned were generally inaccurate. It predicted a steady decline in the living conditions of wage workers under capitalism; a steady improvement occurred instead and first became unmistakable in Germany, where the theory was most widely accepted. It proclaimed that "National differences and antagonisms between peoples are vanishing gradually from day to day, owing to the development of the bourgeoisie . . . the supremacy of the proletariat will cause them to vanish still faster"; [4] instead, nationalism flourished everywhere. It predicted that industrial and agricultural productivity would be greatly augmented by the abolition of private property; no such augmentation occurred. It proposed as a historical necessity that capitalism would first be overthrown in the most advanced industrial countries; nearly the reverse occurred. It predicted the concentration of capital in fewer and fewer hands; nothing of the sort took place. It anticipated that a successful proletarian revolution would be followed in the short run, if not immediately, by a decline in the exercise of coercion by the state. Instead, in every such case, the state became more coercive than ever before.

That the theory survived these successive blows to its credibility and is today perhaps the most influential body of social theory in the world testifies to the faith and ingenuity of the political leaders who took on the responsibility of reinterpreting it to fit events as they occurred. Lenin was the most important re-interpreter, and it is not surprising that he is equally venerated in Moscow and Peking. Beginning in 1902 with a book entitled *What is To Be Done?*, Lenin set about adapting Marxism to the revolutionary possibilities that he discerned in the crumbling Tsarist regime. Marx and Engels had been quite certain that the proletarian revolution would be a reaction to mature capitalism, and here Lenin had to take some liberties with the script, skipping the bourgeois revolution in Russia altogether and substituting a coalition of peasants and urban workers under the tight control of a highly disciplined cadre of professional revolutionaries for the proletarian majority who were to have made the revolution. With respect to the impact of the revolution on the state, the writings of Marx and Engels were much more ambiguous, including references to the ultimate disappearance of the state, its transformation into another kind of institution, the conversion of existing states to socialist purposes, and to some other possibilities. With exhaustive patience, Lenin sorted out the bits and pieces of these writings that mentioned the dictatorship of the proletariat and seemed to authorize the exercise of power on behalf of the proletariat rather than by them directly. The class struggle, instead of terminating with the overthrow of capitalism, was now extended for an indefinite term of years beyond the revolution, a conception which Mao was later to expand and embellish.

The project of turning the state into a giant enterprise and making it the sole employer within the boundaries of a former nation was introduced into Marxist theory before the end of the nineteenth century, as we saw in a previous chapter. The addition of a dictatorial government, operated by a tightly disciplined party with only minimum reference to public opinion, completed the constitutional design under which the Communist regime was established in Russia and has since persisted. The same fundamental constitution, with local variations, was introduced in all of the people's democracies founded later.

Imperial Projects

A similar uniformity characterized the various empire-building projects that were still active in the early twentieth century. By 1900, Europeans had been engaged in projects of exploration, conquest, and settlement overseas for more than 400 years. The series of successful projects that followed the rounding of the Cape of Good Hope by Dias in 1488 and the crossing of the Atlantic by Columbus in 1492 were unexampled in human history. Within thirty years after those events, all the settled parts of the Western hemisphere and all the important ports of Africa and India had been taken into secure possession by European expeditions of trivial size. The explorers had irresistible advantages—ships which could cross the sea and find their way back again, firearms which could be transported by sea and were incalculably superior to native weapons, and horses which could also be transported by sea and then taken some distance into the interior. The first expeditions were managed by the Portuguese, who benefited hugely although there were too few of them to occupy all the territories they acquired. The Spaniards came next and took title to half the world. They were followed by the English, Dutch, French, Swedes, and Danes, none of whom returned empty-handed. Their projects of settlement had various outcomes, but in the long-run, North America, Australia, and some smaller islands were densely settled by Europeans. Permanent European populations were established in Africa, South and Central America, Oceania, and Siberia. It would require a much larger book than this to give even the briefest description of the hundreds or thousands of projects that were launched to explore or settle unfamiliar territory between 1550 and 1850.[5] The end-condition of such a project was likely to include three related goals: wealth for the private promoters, prestige or tactical advantage for their sovereigns, and conversion of the indigenous population to Christianity. Only a few projects achieved all three goals but a great many were successful enough to encourage imitation and the movement was not brought to a halt until the supply of promising territory was exhausted. Toward the middle of the nineteenth century, sail was supplemented and then replaced by steam. A little later the wooden ship gave way to the iron ship. Later still, the direct control of distant fleets was made possible by cable and ultimately by radio communication. The new warships were much more specialized instruments than the old. They required a world-wide network of coal depots, repair docks, and signal stations to operate at any distance from home, and were quickly rendered obsolete by improvements in armament and armor. As late as 1860, both the Union and the Confederacy were able to raise substantial navies almost overnight, as navies had always been raised before. By 1890, the feat would have been technically impossible.

Large-scale war had come to require advance planning by a general staff, that is, by a permanent organization of military and naval experts responsible for developing the weapons and tactics of future wars and plans for using them in various contingencies. With some variation in style and nomenclature, every major power had developed such a strategical establishment by 1890, and has maintained one ever since.

General Staff

Projects

Taken one at a time, general staff projects are programs for winning a hypothetical future war against a given enemy power or coalition of powers at a given time and in given places. An efficient general staff attempts to prepare for all possible wars in which its nation might be involved in the foreseeable future, and thus must plan how to make war not only against opposing powers, but also against present allies and neutrals. This procedure, whenever it is simultaneously followed by two potential opponents, necessarily provokes an arms race between them.

When planning for a hypothetical war, a general staff must undertake to discover what the potential opponent's optimum strategy for winning that war would be in order to frustrate it point by point. To accomplish that purpose, each general staff develops a group of specialists whose full-time business it is to perfect the strategy of the potential opponent and to make innovations on his behalf. Meanwhile, a network of spies is employed to keep a running fix between the predicted program of the opponent and his real actions, by a combination of melodramatic and routine procedures. In this way, a sort of dialogue is established between every pair of potential opponents and the arms race may continue for many years before it breaks out into hot war or is terminated by the involvement of the parties in another of the potential wars in their repertory. The communication achieved by this dialogue is necessarily imperfect, since each party, for its own protection, must look for a hostile intent behind every innocuous action and must take steps to counter all sorts of threats that may be quite imaginary but cannot be dismissed without some risk. General staffs are constantly apprehensive about being lulled into a false security by underestimating an opponent's hostile intentions. Thus, each side responds to an exaggerated version of the opponent's program at each stage of the arms race and some degree of escalation is nearly inevitable as the two linked projects develop.

Usually, the two sides are unevenly matched, and the stronger hopes to win the potential war by maintaining its margin of superiority while the weaker endeavors to remove it. These incompatible goals direct the attention of both sides to the national assets on which the margin depends, such as population, energy resources, defensible frontiers, and bases within striking distance of the opponent's territory. When the apprehension generated by each general staff's exaggerated version of the opponent's project is communicated to its civilian supporters, they are effectively compelled to shape their transactions with other governments in accordance with the war projects of their strategical establishments lest they seem to neglect national security. Hence the overwhelming importance that statesmen in democratic countries, guided by the secret advice of their general staffs, attach to undefinable national intersts in remote and exotic places.

The arms race which inaugurated the twentieth century centered the concerns of the world's great powers in the unlikely neighborhood of the Sea of Japan. World War I began almost by accident when the reciprocal contingency plans of the Triple Alliance and the Triple Entente were activated by a dispute in the Balkans. In the giant Cold War between the United States and the Soviet Union that followed World War II, the strategically relevant territory included the entire world so that any shift of power in *any* country provoked some degree of mobilization on both sides.

Proper strategical planning includes the development of a war project for every nation capable of being warred against during a foreseeable future of ten to thirty years. The projects of a general staff are generally confined to preparing for and winning wars. Even in totalitarian states, such organizations are relatively indifferent to the social and political implications of a war, except as they influence projects for other future wars still in the files. Strategical planning does not normally take account of non-military war aims, except for their limited utility as propaganda, and it is ordinarily unconcerned with the social consequences of victory.

These peculiarities of modern strategical planning have a number of fascinating consequences. One of them is that the conclusion of any given war automatically reactivates for the victorious allies the projects of future war among themselves which they had shelved for the duration of hostilities. Another consequence is that bloody and costly wars have been waged in this century for no discernible political purpose at all or for purposes invented late in the conflict. It is not the mission of a general staff to reflect about just or unjust wars or to question the worth of a projected victory. American plans for winning a nuclear war in which more than half of the American population would be destroyed do not express either irony or cruelty but merely illustrate the function of a general staff (whose individual experts are as reasonable and compassionate as anybody else.) Really good strategical planning, although directed to winning future wars, also includes some provision for the contingency of losing. If the general staff remains intact or can be reconstituted, it may set about planning for a more successful repetition of the same war. The Germans were able to do so between the two world wars, as were the British after Dunkirk, and the U.S. after the Korean War.

The scenario of a major modern war reflects the intensive and logical strategic planning which made the war possible. Coherent events succeed one another in a comprehensible way; the whole vast sequence of events has a dramatic unity that persists from the first pre-dawn invasion to the signing of the last cease-fire. This unity is dissolved, however, in the events that follow the cease-fire, for they have an entirely different character. The wars of the twentieth century have generally been followed by revolutions in the losing countries, and by political and social disorders in the winning countries. These have been disorderly and inscrutable events, confusing to the participants and susceptible to all sorts of conflicting interpretations. The universal discomfort that has followed the wars of the twentieth century accounts for the popularity of post-war projects for achieving universal peace. These projects will be taken up in the following chapter.

CHAPTER 7

A Set of Unsuccessful Projects

AS we saw in preceding chapters, the great trend of modernization established in the nineteenth century continued without interruption into the twentieth, bringing to a large portion of humanity such undoubted benefits as a lower risk of death at every age, more and better food, literacy and multiple means of communication, easy travel, numerous and diverse entertainments, admirable tools, magical toys, and indigestible amounts of new information about the physical universe and human society. We have also seen that the twentieth century has been marked by profound disturbances that have quite undone the hopes which our grandfathers attached to modernization, particularly the hope that technological progress would be accompanied by moral progress. The hyperdevelopment of nationalism and war in this century is closely related to the frustration of these hopes, and we have examined some of the concrete projects which fostered nationalism and war. World War I, which broke out by accident and was waged with great ferocity for no particular purpose, transformed international war from a normal social institution into a social problem demanding a solution, and an enormous amount of collective effort has since been devoted to projects intended to reduce the frequency and severity of war, or to bring about a condition of universal peace. It is obvious that these projects have failed, but the reasons for their failure have not been as carefully studied or as much discussed as they ought to be. The proponents of these projects have generally elected to attribute their outcome to a mistake or a mischance and to insist on repeating them as soon as there was an opportunity to do so.

The principal projects for the attainment of universal peace that have been actively proposed and pursued during this century may be roughly labeled as world revolution, world conquest, the parliament of nations, and negotiated disarmament. We are not going to give the whole history of each effort here, but we will try to explain why each of them failed and to determine whether the failure was attributable to fate or to some flaw in the project's design.

The Project of
World Revolution

Lenin, as previously noted, was a designer of feasible projects, and this is nowhere more evident than in his approach to world revolution and world peace. On these matters, Marx and Engels had been not only quite clear but quite clearly mistaken. They believed that nationalist sentiments were being displaced as early as 1848 by sentiments of class solidarity and that as soon as the proletarians became self-conscious they would unite with their foreign comrades in common opposition to the exploiting classes. They took it for granted that armies could not be recruited against the opposition of a socialist majority or, if already recruited, would refuse to fight against fellow workers in the uniform of another country, so that national war would become impossible as socialism spread among the workers and would of course be out of the question between socialist nations, which would have no mutually hostile interests.

These happy expectations began to founder in 1914 when the caucus of the world's largest Marxist party, the German Social Democrats, voted to support the Kaiser's war budget in the Reichstag and the other socialist parties of Europe adopted comparable policies. (Kautsky's part in this decision provoked Lenin to attack him as a renegade.) During the uprisings that followed the surrender of Germany and Austria-Hungary, a soviet regime attempted, for a few months, to govern Hungary and communist seizures of power appeared imminent in Germany and Poland, and possible in Sweden and Italy. Lenin himself at first regarded the revolution in Russia as only a local phase of an onrushing world revolution. But the opportunity passed by. Nowhere outside of Russia was there another leader with Lenin's ability to formulate and carry out feasible projects within the limitations of Marxist doctrine.

The Russian revolution that began in 1917 followed a course remarkably parallel to that of the French revolution that began in 1789.[1] It was immediately challenged by counterrevolutionary armies within the country and supported by an expeditionary force representing former allies. In each case, the revolutionary government built a formidable military force which, stimulated by the patriotic sentiments aroused by invasion, was able to expel the foreign troops and then to suppress and extirpate the internal opposition. Early in this phase the Third International was founded under Russian auspices to promote world revolution along Bolshevik lines. Lenin's Twenty-One Points, endorsed by the new organization in 1920, established a characteristically authoritarian organizational structure which emphasized secrecy, discipline, the obedience of party members to their superiors and the subordination of national parties to the Comintern executive. Under this arrangement, no sharp distinction was made between the project of world revolution and the foreign policy of the Soviet Union on the grounds that the first priority of the former ought to be the protection of the revolution's sole base, encircled as it was by hostile capitalist powers. Although Communist parties were eventually established in most of the world's countries, the project of world revolution made no perceptible progress between 1919 and 1945. The prospect of a revolution under Russian sponsorship was not sufficiently attractive to gain the necessary support in any country. On the contrary, the presence of a communist party ostensibly bent on revolution provided the formal justification for the eventual seizure of power by right-wing extremists in a dozen countries.

Although the Comintern was founded to carry on the project of world revolution, it was almost immediately confronted by an inherent conflict between the goal of assuring the national security of the Soviet Union and the goal of sponsoring revolutions in other countries. This choice was one of the themes of controversy between Trotsky and Stalin, but the issue seems to have been resolved in favor of a predominantly Russian approach to world affairs several years before Trotsky was expelled in 1927 and Stalin took the reins of power. From then until the abolition of the Comintern in 1943, the world revolution was a *pro forma* project.

(In a *pro forma* project, all the parts of a feasible project are present but no real effort is made to connect them together because the commitment of the project's operators to their ostensible goals is only nominal. Their lack of enthusiasm may be traceable to other projects with higher priorities, or to a want of confidence in their ability to complete this *pro forma* project, or an unwillingness to bear its costs. When we examine a *pro forma* project more closely, we generally find that the collectivity which stands to benefit from it is not identical with the collectivity undertaking it and does not command the same passionate loyalty from the designated agents of the project. The interests of an organization in being will generally take priority over the interests of an unorganized collectivity and an existing organization is unlikely to sacrifice itself for a potential organization unless the latter is visualized as a literal continuation of the former.)

The explicit goal of Marxism was to unite the workers of the world into a single self-conscious collectivity, sufficiently organized to overthrow capitalism everywhere and then to rule the world harmoniously. As soon as the original doctrine began to be translated into practical politics, however, the parties that were organized to represent the proletariat in each country began—if we take the most sympathetic view of the matter—to identify the best interest of the workers with the immediate interests of the party. This identification was facilitated in countries where the communists were able to seize control of the state and to silence anyone who questioned the congruity of interest between the party and the constituency it purported to represent. In other countries, the claim of a communist party to speak and to act for the proletariat was always challenged by other parties claiming to represent the same constituency. This challenge became more effective as Russian control of the national parties in other countries became more obvious. The transition from the Comintern centered in the Soviet Union to a league of autonomous communist states was never clearly visualized and no plans were made to bring it about. The "world-wide communist conspiracy" had plenty of plotters but no plot. Between 1920 and 1945, it made no serious attempt to foment a revolution anywhere except in China, and even there the Comintern's support of the local revolutionists was withdrawn as early as 1927.

The Marxist project of world revolution suffered from some of the same defects as its capitalist counterpart, the parliament of nations. In both cases, the interests of the nominal constituency were disregarded when they inconvenienced the existing organizations which appointed the delegates and footed the bills. One is tempted to say that the broader interests were not even clearly formulated, but that is not entirely accurate. In some episodes, like the League of Nation's weak reaction to the Italian invasion of Abyssinia in 1935 and the sudden conversion of the French communists to neutrality after the signing of the Nazi-Soviet Pact of 1939, the incongruity between the ostensible goals of each movement and its actual policies was too plain to be overlooked. Neither the League of Nations nor the Comintern could visualize a line of continuous development connecting it with the future organization it was supposed to bring into existence, a parliament of nations in one case, a world federation of communist states in the other.

In the closing days of World War II, the Soviet armies came into control of Poland, Hungary, Rumania, Bulgaria, Czechoslovakia, and half of Germany. In each of these countries, the local communist leaders returned from exile and joined coalition governments which, after appropriate maneuvers under Soviet protection, became "peoples' democracies" with constitutions modeled on the Soviet pattern. Yugoslavia and Albania, liberated by the efforts of their own partisans, installed similar regimes without submitting to the same measure of Soviet control. In Greece, outside the area of Soviet occupation, the communists were defeated in a civil war; elsewhere in Europe they constituted minority parties engaged in parliamentary politics. In the Chinese civil war between the Kuomintang and communists, which had begun before the first Japanese invasion of China and which continued for about four years after the Japanese surrender, Soviet support of the communists was relatively unenthusiastic. Stalin provided the Yenan government with substantial military assistance but continued to recognize the nationalist government of China, as he had agreed to do at Yalta, until it was no longer realistic to do so. The establishment of the People's Republic of China and the outbreak of the Korean War was followed by a brief Sino-Soviet rapprochement, but when the Russians insisted on a type of relationship whereby communist governments, as well as communist parties in non-communist states, were expected to follow a party line promulgated under Russian auspices, the Chinese rejected these pretensions and nominated Chairman Mao as the authoritative spokesman of the world revolution. Of the two other successful communist revolutions that occurred in Asia, the revolution in North Korea was accomplished under the shadow of Soviet military power in the Eastern European fashion, while the one in North Vietnam proved to be more interesting.

Like the roughly contemporary Cuban revolution, the Vietnamese revolution was led by a talented theorist who was also a skillful enough guerrilla leader to win the support of the peasant population in a prosperous but underdeveloped country. Once their regimes were securely established, both Ho Chi Minh and Fidel Castro attempted to steer neutral courses between the Soviet Union and China, seeking military, technical, and economic assistance from both, while playing off the influence of one against that of the other, much as other small "Third World" nations had learned to balance off the Soviet Union and the United States so that benefits could be obtained from both of them without excessive submission to either.

Although it is easy to exaggerate the similarities of the four successful communist revolutions that occurred autonomously—Russia, China, North Vietnam, Cuba—it is difficult to ignore them. Each was led by a highly articulate intellectual who had studied the history of past revolutions attentively and who, long before coming to power, had developed a new version of Marxist theory to fit the local conditions of his country and circulated it in books, articles and speeches. Each leader continued to formulate his special theory of revolution after coming to power and then claimed a wider application for it. In all four cases, the revolution occurred in a country only slightly industrialized and found its principal support in a peasantry rather than in a proletariat. The consolidation of the regime was in each case preceded by a long, costly civil war with considerable foreign involvement and was followed by a massacre of political opponents, a massive emigration of non-sympathizers, and later by successive purges of the original revolutionary cadre. In each case, the leader came to embody and personify the revolution and was virtually deified during his lifetime. In each case, the effort to stimulate revolutions on the same model in neighboring countries met with indifferent success.

The limited exportability of these revolutionary models is something of a puzzle, particularly in the Latin American case, where conditions in at least a dozen countries somewhat resembled those which prevailed in Cuba before Castro's seizure of power and where there was already a cadre of experienced revolutionaries who enjoyed considerable popular support. Nevertheless, Castro's efforts to spread the Cuban revolution were conspicuously unfruitful.

It is still possible, of course, for communists of any persuasion to believe that the world revolution is gradually advancing and that its failures of the past half century are only temporary delays in an inexorable historical process. The most persuasive argument for this position is that no country, once communized, has reverted to parliamentary government or to private large-scale ownership. There have been innumerable fluctuations in the policies of communist regimes toward peasant proprietorship, retail trade, social stratification, private luxury, marriage laws, organized religion, freedom of opinion, industrial discipline and other matters. On two essential points, however, the monopoly of political power by a disciplined party and the monopoly of economic power by the state, these regimes have been uncompromising.

The principal argument against the supposed inevitability of a Marxist world revolution is that no highly modernized country, with the marginal exception of Czechoslovakia, has so far consented to a communist regime or come close to doing so. There is also some question as to whether any contemporary communist regime could maintain an adequate level of popular support if it were not able to point to the threat of foreign encirclement and call upon sentiments of national self-preservation. When the bordering foreign states are communist, rather than anti-communist, the same sentiments must still be invoked in order to maintain the necessary minimum support for an autocratic regime. Hence, each increase in the number of communist states tends to decrease their solidarity. Among the countries of eastern Europe and between the Soviet Union and the People's Republic of China, this divisive process is far advanced.

A more important reason for doubting the inevitability of a communist world revolution is that so far there has been no real effort to bring it about. No one has described the end-condition to be achieved in a plausible way, or seriously assessed the means for achieving it, or founded an organization capable of utilizing those means. If, as I am trying to show, revolutions are projects of social technology which succeed only when they are based on a rational selection of methods to achieve a desired end-condition, then, at least for the time being, the communist project of world revolution is more of a slogan than a project. The original Marxist project has been rendered obsolete by the rise of modern communist states in the peculiar form dictated by the revolutionary projects that led to their foundation. An international system composed exclusively of such states does not seem to be visualized or desired by those whose ostensible purpose is to bring it about.

World Conquest

The possibility of attaining universal peace by means of world revolution has been continuously present in the awareness of modernized peoples since 1848. The possibility of attaining it by world conquest has been only intermittently considered, but it merits attention.

In 1809 Napoleon came within striking distance of founding a world empire based on military conquest which involved a real commitment to a variety of social improvements: land reform, rational administration, social mobility and advancement by merit. Napoleon's system enjoyed considerable support in the countries he conquered or forced into alliance. Had he chosen to invade England instead of Russia or in some other way been able to complete the conquest of Europe it is not unthinkable that the world might have become a single political community early in the nineteenth century. The memory of that possibility has lingered on and was revived briefly in 1940 when Hitler controlled most of Europe and found his way to world domination blocked only by Britain and Russia.

In retrospect, the vision of a world owned and operated by the Thousand Year Reich is not totally implausible. Although the Nazi armies introduced no social reforms and made few friends in the countries they occupied, there was a working model of the relationship between a lesser and a greater fascist state in the Rome-Berlin axis which might have been imitated elsewhere. The fascist project of counter-revolution had proved to be exportable and adaptable to local conditions. It featured the monopoly of political power by a monolithic party under a charismatic leader who presented himself both as the heroic chief of the revolutionary struggle and as the author of an infallible social philosophy. Fascist regimes widened the economic power of the states they seized but did not abolish private property or private management. They were more likely to restore than to remove hereditary privileges and they advocated less social equality rather than more. The chauvinistic sentiments which communist regimes were always hard put to reconcile with the universalism of Marxist doctrine presented no problem at all for the theorists of fascism, who regarded national and personal aggrandizement at the expense of others—what the communists called exploitation—as legitimate and praiseworthy.

The project of world conquest made one more fitful appearance after World War II when the temporary monopoly of nuclear weapons by the United States led some Americans to speculate about the possibility of acquiring an overwhelming predominance of power that would enable America to act as a benevolent referee in all international disputes and maintain a permanent peace. This prospect disappeared almost before it could be evaluated when the Soviet Union broke the American nuclear monopoly more quickly than had been expected and proceeded to develop its own nuclear arsenal at a sprightly pace.

In the current state of military technology the probability of world conquest seems highly remote, but it is sometimes discussed by the theorists of nuclear deterrence as a possible sequel to a nuclear war, which might be so devastating that any surviving vestige of military power would be irresistible.

The Parliament

of Nations

The idea of an association of nations to keep peace in the world had been in the air since early in the nineteenth century, as Tennyson's famous lines, written in 1842, suggest.* It was launched, at least rhetorically, in the 1899 Hague Conference on International Warfare where the representatives of twenty-six nations worked out a set of rules for the conduct of international war, including among other amenities, a flat prohibition of aerial bombardment.

We do not lose much of the story, however, if we begin our examination of the project with the Fourteen Points that President Woodrow Wilson presented to a joint session of Congress in January 1918 as a summary of American war aims in World War I.[2] Eight of the points refer to particular territorial questions—the evacuation of Russia and Belgium by German forces, the return of Alsace-Lorraine to France, the independence of Rumania, Serbia, Montenegro, and Poland, new frontiers for Italy, Austria and Hungary, and the dismantling of the Turkish Empire—all described with sufficient ambiguity to lay the groundwork for future problems. Four of the remaining six points were concerned respectively with freedom of navigation in peace and in war, free international trade "so far as possible," the reduction of national armaments, and the adjustment of colonial claims. The project which concerns us here is described in points 1 and 14.

1. Open covenants of peace, openly arrived at, after which there shall be no private international understandings of any kind, but diplomacy shall proceed always frankly in the public view.
14. A general association of nations must be formed under specific covenants for the purpose of affording mutual guarantees of political independence and territorial integrity to great and small states alike.

As everyone knows, Wilson managed to have the Fourteen Points accepted as the basis for a peace settlement by both the surrendering Germans and the victorious Allies but was unable to have them respected in the drafting of the Treaty of Versailles. The one matter on

* *Locksley Hall,* published in 1842, predicts air warfare, followed by "the Parliament of Man, the Federation of the World" where ". . . the common sense of most shall hold a fretful realm in awe, and the kindly earth shall slumber rapt in universal law."

which he steadfastly refused to compromise was the 14th point, which concerned the establishment of a League of Nations. In the revulsion of sentiment that followed Versailles, the U.S. Senate refused, by a small margin, to ratify the treaty and the United States never joined the League, although Germany and Russia, originally excluded, eventually did so.

In 1924, Ramsay MacDonald proposed, in his Geneva Protocol, to amend the Constitution of the League so that international disputes would be subject to compulsory arbitration: a nation refusing to accept arbitration would by that act become an aggressor, exposed to joint military action by other members of the League. The proposal was abandoned by the succeeding British government in favor of a network of treaties signed at Locarno which, in effect, re-established the pre-war balance of power that had led Europe into World War I, although with some changes of detail that were considered significant at the time.

In 1931, after the Japanese invasion of Manchuria, the League responded to a Chinese appeal, appointed an investigative commission which found Japan at fault, and passed a complicated—and now inscrutable—series of resolutions that left the Japanese in comfortable possession of the invaded territory. In 1935, when Italy invaded Ethiopia, the League voted to label Italy as an aggressor and imposed a limited embargo on the exports of arms and raw materials to Italy, which was briefly maintained by some but not all of its members. The League debated Hitler's seizure of the Rhineland in 1936 and of Austria in 1938 and, of course, the dismemberment of Czechoslovakia in 1939. Its last significant action—taken in December 1940 before it quietly faded away—was to expel the Soviet Union for invading Finland.

It is startling to realize that only a few months elapsed between the last ineffectual sessions of the League of Nations and the meeting of Roosevelt and Churchill off the coast of Newfoundland in August 1941, where they drafted the Atlantic Charter to summarize the aims of a war the United States had not yet joined. The Charter had only eight points. Wisely omitting the references to specific territorial questions that had haunted Woodrow Wilson to his grave, the first three points proposed a general formula for the solution of territorial questions; no territorial or other aggrandizement for the signatory countries, no territorial changes that did not accord with the wishes of the people concerned and the right of all peoples to choose the form of government under which they will live.

The new formula of national self-determination, despite some difference in phraseology and emphasis, was essentially the same as the one proposed 23 years before. Although Wilson, in some of his public statements, advocated the universal adoption of parliamentary democracy, his sixth point, which assured Russia "of a sincere welcome into the society of free nations under institutions of her own choosing" had implied the right of a people to choose a nondemocratic government as clearly as the Atlantic Charter's more general statement.

The remaining five points of the Charter were concerned respectively with freedom of international trade, freedom of navigation, disarmament, and international economic cooperation. The language of the Charter was more vague on the whole than that of the Fourteen Points but the sense was unmistakably similar. Wilson's first point, however, was missing. There was no longer any objection to secret international agreements, as the conferences at Casablanca, Teheran and Yalta would soon demonstrate. The language in which the Charter seems to refer to a future international association is very vague indeed, "After the final destruction of the Nazi tyranny, they [the signatories] hope to see established a peace which will afford to all Nations the means of dwelling in safety within their own boundaries, and which will afford assurance that all the men in all the lands may live out their lives in freedom from fear and want." The ambiguity of the statement was intentional. Roosevelt's biographer says that:

Churchill asked the President if the charter could explicitly endorse some kind of 'effective international organization.' Roosevelt demurred; he said that he himself would not favor the creation of a new assembly of the League of Nations, at least until after a period of time during which a British-American police force maintained security. Churchill warned that a vague plank could arouse opposition from strong internationalists. Roosevelt agreed, but he felt that he had to be politically realistic. Churchill gave in, with the understanding that he could add some language that would strengthen the plank without uttering the dread words 'international organization' or invoking the ghost of Woodrow Wilson.[3]

The restoration of the missing language was not long in coming. On the first day of 1942, representatives of the 26 nations at war with the

Axis powers signed the Declaration of the United Nations which, in addition to its military clauses, pledged them to uphold the principles of the Atlantic Charter. In 1943 Congress, mindful of the congressional opposition that had prevented American participation in the League of Nations, passed by overwhelming majority the Fulbright-Connelly Resolutions committing the United States to join an international organization for the maintenance of peace. By October 1944, the tentative charter of the United Nations had been agreed upon at Dumbarton Oaks although the question of the veto was still being debated. In April 1945, the United Nations Conference on International Organization gathered the representatives of 50 nations at San Francisco to found a new organization consisting of four parts: a General Assembly with equal representation from all countries large and small; a Security Council composed of the grand coalition that had won the war—the United States, the Soviet Union, Great Britain, France and China—as permanent members and six temporary members elected by the Security Council for two-year terms; a Secretariat with uncertain powers and duties; and a cluster of specialized agencies dealing with subsidiary matters. The features of this constitution that made the United Nations look like something more than the League of Nations under a new name were the provisions for an international military force and for collective military action, but since decisions involving the use of force could be taken only by the Security Council in which each permanent member enjoyed an absolute veto, the new organization was in effect equipped to act only in international disputes so unimportant that the competing interests of the leading powers would not be involved. As matters turned out, there were some significant occasions for the raising of United Nations forces in the following three decades. In 1950, a Russian boycott of the Security Council in protest against the exclusion of Communist China enabled the remainder of that body, which was solidly anti-Soviet, to place the American and South Korean armies in South Korea under the flag of the United Nations and to recruit token forces from other countries. In 1957, after an unusual collaboration between the United States and the Soviet Union had put an end not only to the British-French attempt to secure control of the Suez Canal but also to the second Israeli-Arab war, a United Nations emergency force was sent to Egypt to supervise the armistice and remained there until Egypt requested its withdrawal ten years later. This incident touched off the third Israeli-Arab war. Another United Nations force was raised in 1960 when the United States and the Soviet Union agreed, for complicated and divergent reasons, to re-establish order in the former Belgian colony of the Congo. That same force, considerably augmented, was later used to defeat a secessionist movement in the Congolese province of Katanga. The cease-fire which ended the fourth Israeli-Arab war late in 1973, arranged under the joint auspices of the United States and the Soviet Union, was immediately followed by the dispatch of a United Nations force of about seven thousand troops to the cease-fire zone.

With the passage of time, the possibility that the United Nations would evolve spontaneously into a world government has become increasingly remote. The organization provides a useful diplomatic forum during international crises and it probably reduces the cost of maintaining international communication, especially for small, weak and backward countries, whose predominance in the General Assembly gives them more influence at its meetings than they could exercise elsewhere. The Secretary-General, because of his prominence and his official neutrality, has sometimes been able to serve as a mediator between opposed coalitions. Some of the subsidiary functions of the United Nations, like the collection and standardization of international statistics, are highly useful. But with respect to its primary function of keeping the peace, the failure of the United Nations has been nearly complete. As we noted in a previous chapter, there have been more large wars since the founding of the United Nations than in any like period in history. Although nuclear war has so far been averted, most of the significant confrontations between the superpowers have been resolved outside the framework of the United Nations by direct negotiation between the parties.

The failure of the League of Nations was always in the minds of those who framed the project of the United Nations. The ghost of Woodrow Wilson haunted the proceedings from the drafting of the Atlantic Charter early in 1941 to the ratification of the United Nations Charter late in 1945. It was evidenced by the care taken in the United States to guarantee bipartisan support and congressional ratification for the Charter and by the emphasis in public discussion on avoiding the mistakes of Versailles in the peace settlement. From Wendell Willkie to Bertrand Russell, from Norman Thomas to Colonel McCormick, the most discordant voices repeated the same hopes and the same warnings. How then, when armed with such hindsight and foresight, were the peacemakers of 1945 able to repeat so many of the errors of 1919? Minor errors such as the juggling of national boundaries in eastern Europe and of territorial concessions around the Sea of Japan without respect for the wishes of the people involved, were casually repeated, in addition to the major error of neglecting to provide peacekeeping machinery capable of keeping the peace.

One possible explanation is that the goal of international peace is not attainable because of some impediment in human nature or in the character of human institutions. Another—that the goal might be attainable at some other time but not under the conditions that prevailed in 1945. Or still another that the goal might have been attainable but the project was badly designed.

The project—with many circumlocutions and rhetorical flourishes— is described with a fair degree of precision in the Atlantic Charter. Its significant components were these:

Political. All people to choose the form of government under which they live; no territorial changes without consent of those concerned. The safety of nations within their own boundary.

Economic. Equal access by all states to the trade and raw materials of the world; international collaboration for the achievement of modernization and the improvement of social security.

Miscellaneous. Freedom of navigation, partial disarmament, abandonment of the use of force among nations.

Was this a feasible project at the time? Is it one now? The answer must be a qualified *No.* In numbers 15–20 of the *Federalist Papers,* Alexander Hamilton and James Madison combined a summary of the history of confederations with a theoretical analysis of their operation which cannot be faulted even today. Hamilton and Madison were able to show by numerous examples that history was full of confederations and that a few of them had succeeded very well. They were able to enumerate the necessary elements of a successful confederation, and, as we know, they joined in the founding of one. They concluded that a league or alliance without an effective government cannot permanently repress armed conflict among its members, but that a confederation—which has an effective government—can do so. To be effective, the government of a confederation must extend its authority beyond the constituent states and reach individual citizens:

Government implies the power of making laws. It is essential to the idea of a law, that it be attended with a sanction; or in other words, a penalty or punishment for disobedience. If there be no penalty annexed to disobedience, the resolutions or commands which pretend to be laws will, in fact, amount to nothing more than advice or recommendation. This penalty, whatever it may be, can only be inflicted in two ways: by the agency of the courts and ministers of justice, or by military force; by the *coercion* of the magistracy, or by the *coercion* of arms. The first kind can evidently apply only to men; the last kind must of necessity be employed against bodies politic, or communities, or States. It is evident that there is no process of the court by which the observance of the laws can, in the last resort, be enforced. Sentences may be denounced against them for violations of their duty; but these sentences can only be carried into execution by the sword. In an association where the general authority is confined to the collective bodies of the communities that compose it, every breach of the laws must involve a state of war; and military execution must become the only instrument of civil disobedience. Such a state of things can certainly not deserve the name of government, nor would any prudent man choose to commit his happiness to it.[4]

The initial project embodied in the Atlantic Charter did not even include the defective kind of confederation which the foregoing passage criticizes as unworkable. However, the Charter did refer to the eventual establishment of a "wider and permanent system of general security." We also know that Churchill at least had some kind of international organization in mind, and that he was prepared to consider the limitation of national sovereignty under certain conditions. Not many months before, on the eve of the French surrender to the Nazis, he had proposed an actual merger of France and Great Britain. In any case, surprisingly little effort was made during the war to design or even to consider the possible form a world confederation might take even when there was an overwhelming show of support for such a project, as when the Senate called on the United States to join an international organization having "the power to prevent aggression and preserve the peace of the world," with only five dissenting votes. There is no evidence in the proceedings of the conference that founded the United Nations of any serious intention to provide it with such power. The international organization that emerged could not even be described as a defective confederation; it was really no more than a voluntary association of sovereign states.

Why did an effective confederation appear so impracticable at that point in history that its possible forms were not seriously discussed? The answer must be sought in the Atlantic Charter's references to the right of peoples to choose their form of government and to live safely within inviolate boundaries. A confederation cannot offer less to states which join it voluntarily than a permanent guarantee of their mutual boundaries and of the forms of government with which they enter the confederation. In order to have founded a confederation in 1945, the Atlantic powers must have been prepared to guarantee *in perpetuity* the constitutions of the Eastern European regimes newly established under the wing of the Soviet armies. Even had they been willing to do so, which was quite unthinkable at the time, it is difficult to imagine the Soviet Union, whose conversion of these governments to people's republics had barely begun, consenting to freeze them all at some transitional stage while abandoning forever all hope of sponsoring revolutions in France or Italy or in any Latin American or African country. How could the existing forms of government have been guaranteed in all the colonial countries just beginning to move toward independence? Or in China, with its competing governments? How could the boundaries of divided Germany, which had been explicitly designated as temporary by all the parties concerned, be permanently guaranteed? And so on and so forth. In 1945, the world was unprepared for the general settlement of accounts and the tying up of international loose ends that the founding of a serious confederation would require. Yet we can speculate that the inexplicable chaos of 1945 was partly attributable to the failure of social inventiveness in 1941, when the embattled Allies would probably have been receptive to a well-designed project of confederation but were given only an updated version of the Fourteen Points. It is not difficult to imagine that the awareness of such a project by the people of the scores of countries whose forms of governments changed toward the end of the war or just afterward might have brought about an entirely different situation at the opening of the post-war era.

In the event, a world confederation to maintain international peace was not achieved in 1945. Whether it might be attainable now is another question. Today's world differs from the world of 1945 in a number of important respects: world conquest is unthinkable with the present military technology; the solidarity of the world revolutionary movement is broken beyond repair; nearly all nations are independent; and the diffusion of parliamentary democracy has come to nearly a full stop.

Hamilton and Madison were able to show by numerous examples that history was full of confederations and that a few of them had succeeded very well. They were able to enumerate the necessary elements of a successful confederation and, as we know, they were able to put their knowledge to use.

The *feasibility* of an effective world confederation has been questioned on two grounds: first, that a confederation cannot function unless its member states have uniform constitutions; second, that since a confederation is an organization for defense against common enemies, a world confederation would fail for want of external enemies.[5]

On both of these fundamental points, the historical evidence is inconclusive and sociological analysis does not provide much firmer guidance. Of the two ancient Greek confederations particularly considered by Hamilton and Madison, the Achaean League appears to have been composed of city-states with uniform laws and customs; the Amphictyonic Confederacy united a much larger number of cities with a variety of constitutions.[6] The Federalists much preferred the example of the Achaean League, but both confederations were ultimately ruined by ambitious alliances with foreign powers. Among other historic confederations, the Holy Roman Empire, which lasted the longest, was made up of a great number of unequal states, with a wide variety of constitutions ranging from democracy to feudalism. The United Provinces of the Netherlands had more uniform but not identical governments, as did the Swiss cantons. The principal weakness the Federalists found in all those confederations was not constitutional diversity or the absence of democracy, but the inability of the central government to exercise direct control over individual citizens in those activities for which it was directly responsible.

There is nothing contradictory about a system of government which is democratic at some levels but not at others; nearly every system of representative government works just that way. Michels's "iron law of oligarchy'' is one way of describing the condition. It is difficult to visualize *any* pyramidal process of representation in which oligarchical influence does not intervene to limit the electorate's freedom of choice.

On the other hand, even the most authoritarian method of selecting representatives—the designation of officers in an American corporation or of Praesidium members in a communist state—exhibits the rudiments of a democratic process at some level where the influence of competing factions is assessed. However, it cannot be denied that incompatible political attitudes might hamper a world confederation that had to accommodate not only the capitalist and communist powers but an assortment of Latin American dictatorships, Arab sheikdoms, and African tribal states.

The question of whether a confederation can survive without external enemies cannot be conclusively settled either by historical evidence or sociological analysis, and it is not limited to confederations. Could *any* state maintain its authority if there were no need to defend its frontiers? The examples which suggest themselves, like Japan and the Inca Empire before their first European contacts, are too remote and exotic to be very informative, but such diverse states as Guatemala, Switzerland, Canada, and Tibet have been preoccupied with internal affairs for long periods and there is no compelling evidence for the proposition that a state without foreign enemies would be ungovernable.

Restating the question, can a large-scale organization operate alone in its field when organizations of its type normally occur in sets? The answer is plainly yes, and examples are easily found. This is certainly true of industrial monopolies such as public utility companies. Although they do not operate in exactly the same way as enterprises in a competitive industry, the similarities are more conspicuous than the differences and there is no question about the viability of the arrangement. Many of the world's smaller countries have only a single university or airline, yet they seem to function as well as universities and airlines elsewhere. While an airline is not exactly analogous to world government, all large-scale bureaucracies have similar functional requirements.

I do not think that the available evidence tells us either that a world confederation is demonstrably feasible or that it is impracticable. The absence of a recognized plan[7] and of a social movement to support it are astonishing. Except for periodic conferences on World Peace Through Law and a feeble movement to revise the United Nations Charter, there has been practically no exploration of the possibility of world confederation in recent years. Mankind's most urgent social problem has elicited less intelligent effort than the problem of how to evaluate biddable hands in contract bridge.

A useful plan for a world confederation must include more than a bare listing of goals.[8] It also needs the other essential parts of a feasible project, namely, the specification of an existing condition, a practical method of getting from where we are to where we want to be, competent agents to apply the method, a division of the project into successive stages, estimates of the resources required to take the project from one stage to the next, and devices for measuring the project's progress at each stage. Putting the problem this way directs our attention to at least three alternative sequences (excluding world revolution and world conquest) which might lead to a world confederation: (a) the gradual assumption of new powers by existing international organizations, (b) the establishment of a confederation by a constitutional convention representing the entire world, (c) the initial federation of a few states, holding open to all other states an invitation to join on identical terms. I believe that the latter alternative would be the most promising provided that the founding members included both communist and parliamentary states.

Who shall bell this particular cat? It is absurd to suppose that the interests of nation-states can be brushed aside by well-meaning private persons. Such movements as world federalism and the Atlantic Union are harmless middle-class hobbies in Western Europe and the United States and are seldom heard of in countries with more authoritarian regimes. On the other hand, for reasons we have touched upon before, the primary task of a modern government is to plan for war, not for the abolition of war. The founding of a world confederation, if it ever occurs, will have to follow from the efforts of political parties working within their several nations to achieve a particular form of world confederation which has been convincingly described by a spokesman who has yet to appear.[9]

Disarmament

On the international scene of the twentieth century, disarmament is the homage that vice pays to virtue, an arrangement whereby nations agree to limit their preparations for hostilities against each other if they can gain a military advantage by doing so. The history of disarmament efforts is not really a fit subject for a book which purports to show how organized human effort can be efficacious in achieving social goals, but it provides some instructive lessons. The projects of disarmament that have preoccupied the world's powers ever since 1899, when twenty-six nations met at The Hague to discuss disarmament in response to an invitation from the Russian Tsar, have been monuments of foolish inefficacity. The powers met again at The Hague in 1907; among other things they banned the use of shot-guns in warfare as inhumane. In 1921, the nine-power Washington conference fixed a ratio of 5:5:3:1.67:1.67 for the capital ships of Great Britain, the United States, Japan, France and Italy respectively, agreed on a ten year holiday in the construction of capital ships, provided for the scrapping of obsolete capital ships; set limits on the tonnage of battleships and on the caliber of their guns; and restricted the construction of new naval bases. Naval competition promptly shifted to the unrestricted construction of cruisers, destroyers and submarines.

At the next major disarmament conference, the Geneva Conference of 1927, the points at issue were more explicitly technical:

The main controversy, between Britain and the United States, centered on cruisers. The Americans wanted to extend the ratio of 5:5:3 to cruisers and other smaller craft and to reduce the total tonnage of each class of ships. Since they did not have a world-wide network of bases, as the British did, they wished to concentrate their cruiser strength in ships of fairly long cruising radius displacing 10,000 tons and carrying eight-inch guns. The British were willing to extend the ratio to that extent but not immediately to the smaller warships they considered essential in guarding their trade routes and empire. They wanted a large number of lighter cruisers, above the limit set by the American naval experts, displacing 7500 tons and carrying six-inch guns. . . .[10]

At the London Conference of 1930, the principal dispute was between France and Italy, since both refused to sign that part of the

treaty setting naval ratios. The holiday in the construction of battleships was extended for another five years and the tonnage of cruisers
was limited to prevent their being constructed as large as battleships.
The new treaty contained what was called an "escalator clause,"
which allowed each power to exceed the limits to which it had agreed
if its security appeared to be endangered by an outside power. At the
next conference, in 1935, Japan, France, and Italy objected to the existing ratios; the representatives of Japan and Italy walked out. The
three remaining powers agreed upon a principle of "qualitative"
rather than quantitative limitations and upon an escape clause whereby
any signatory could release itself from the limitations to which it had
agreed. All parties then set about enlarging their fleets as rapidly as
possible, while the Germans—who had been working within a more
rigid set of limitations imposed by an earlier treaty—completed the
construction of a class of ships having the tonnage of cruisers but the
destructive capacity of battleships.

After World War II, disarmament conferences shifted their topic
from battleships to nuclear weapons. The first self-limiting agreement
was signed in 1963 by the United States, the Soviet Union and Great
Britain. It banned the testing of nuclear weapons in the atmosphere but
permitted the continuation of underground tests. France and China,
still in the early stages of developing their nuclear arsenals, refused to
participate. Nine more years of nearly continuous discussion between
the United States and the Soviet Union culminated in the Strategic
Limitation Treaty of 1972, which limited the number of intercontinental ballistic missiles each power might have for the following five
years and the number of warheads it might deploy in its missile system
but did not control the accumulation of submarines, bombers, and
short-range missiles. The parallel with the Washington Disarmament Treaty of 1922 was at once borne out by a massive effort on
both sides to increase the offensive capacity of the now limited store
of intercontinental missiles and to expand the strategic use of the
delivery vehicles not covered by the agreement.

All of these disarmament projects were spurious in a certain sense.
Although their short-term goals were explicit and attainable, the long-
term goal envisaged by public opinion and summed up in the word
"disarmament" could not be, and was not, taken seriously by the stra-

tegical planners who hammered out the terms of the agreement. They could not take it seriously because they were unable to imagine either the progressive reduction of heavy armaments to zero or the stabilization of heavy armaments at any sort of fixed ratio—given the highly dynamic technology under which such armaments are designed and the impossibility of predicting changes in other strategic factors.

There are perfectly good military motives for limiting armaments at certain points in time—for example, to halt the stockpiling of obsolescent weapons so that more effort can be concentrated on the development of new weapons and to reduce the domestic resistance generated by rising military expenditures in peacetime. Perhaps more important, an agreement to limit armaments requires the participants to exchange verified inventories of their existing arsenals, and this augmented flow of information facilitates the strategical planning of each party. The strategical objective can be changed from the attainment of superiority over potential enemies under all possible contingencies to the more elegant and practicable objective of attaining superiority within the limits that purport to establish a parity of forces. If these projects succeed, as some of them inevitably must, the agreement is certain to be rejected (or secretly violated) by the disadvantaged party, for whom the re-establishment of parity becomes too urgent a goal to be left to negotiation. The terms of modern disarmament treaties provide no defense against this escalating mechanism and it is not surprising that escalation begins even before the treaty is ratified and continues unabated until the agreement breaks down and a full-scale arms race is resumed.

It does not, however, follow from these considerations that a world confederation would need to be as heavily armed as a contemporary superpower. A military establishment designed only to maintain internal order would not confront, even in case of a rebellion, the kind of long-established and strategically sophisticated general staff that even medium-sized powers maintain today. A reasonable stock of weapons and widespread public support should be more than sufficient to maintain its authority.

CHAPTER 8

❧❧

Some Vintage American Projects

In this and the several following chapters, we shall selectively review some specific American experiences in social problem-solving, looking always for the useful lessons which can be extracted from that experience.

In the first few decades after 1789, there was a great deal of political controversy, but Americans never ceased to congratulate themselves on the general superiority of their society to the corrupt monarchies which contended for power in Europe. In the 1830s, slavery and emancipation became the predominant social problem and for almost half a century overshadowed all other public issues in this country. The anti-slavery movement was soon joined by a women's rights movement, an anti-immigration movement, and organized movements for the reform of insane asylums, and the improvement of education, criminal justice, and city planning. Like later reform movements, these were interconnected. The Seneca Falls Convention on women's rights was called because a group of American women delegates, finding themselves excluded from the World Anti-Slavery Convention held in London in 1840, "determined that the cause of emancipation affected them as well as slaves."

The distinctive American approach to social problems was already apparent in these early movements, especially in their dependence on private initiative, their close ties to organized religion, the vehemence of their rhetoric, their use of the private investigative exposé to mobilize public support, and the sentiments they attempted to arouse.

The sentiments aroused by social problems vary within a fairly limited range and depend on the orientation of the observer toward a particular problem. Compassion is an appropriate sentiment for an observer who is not responsible for a problem but has the ability to help some of the problem's victims. Shame can be aroused in those who acknowledge responsibility for creating a problem or allowing it to persist. Indignation is expected of an audience which is emotionally stirred by a problem for which they are not responsible and have no power to resolve. Resentment is the response of people who come to perceive themselves as the victims of a social problem. At the risk of gross oversimplification, it may be said that until recently American social movements concentrated on the arousal of compassion and indignation, while European social movements were more usually fueled by resentment or shame.

The principal method that has been used to arouse compassion and indignation about American social problems is the private investigative exposé—a convincingly documented investigation of a social condition by a volunteer investigator who undertakes the work in order to arouse public sentiment sufficiently to bring about ameliorative action. Dorothea Dix's 1843 memorial to the legislature of Massachusetts on the condition of insane and mentally retarded persons in public institutions was the first of a long line of exposés that fulfilled their author's objectives.

The desired end-condition of an exposé is a state of public opinion which defines a social problem in the author's terms, assigns it a high priority, and leads directly to projects for solving it. From Dorothea Dix to Ralph Nader, the authors of exposés have on occasion been able to generate an extraordinary amount of social action from a relatively small investment of investigative effort. The method is distinctively American. In other countries, social problems are more likely to be investigated by public agencies or governmental commissions, and there is much less opportunity for moral entrepreneurs.

It is largely because of this pattern that the United States sometimes seems to have had more—if not more serious—social problems than other modernized countries, and to have developed more—if not more effective—projects of social improvement. Out of the almost unlimited array of projects that might be picked out of the past for closer examination, I have selected three vintage projects—the movement for the abolition of slavery, the settlement house, and the prohibition experiment—in order to show that the requirements of social technology were the same in the past as they are now, and to illustrate how technical defects in projects of social improvement create new social problems.

The Abolition
Movement

The project of the abolitionists was set forth with remarkable clarity in the Declaration of Sentiments[1] drawn up by William Lloyd Garrison for the founding convention of the American Anti-Slavery Society in 1833. The end-condition to be achieved was the abrogation of all laws admitting the right of slavery, the emancipation of all slaves *without compensation to their masters,* and without relocation, and full social equality for "all persons of color, who possess the qualifications which are demanded of others."

The intermediate stages were specified also. First, the suppression by Congress of the interstate movement of slaves, and the abolition by Congress of slavery in the District of Columbia; second, the abolition of slavery throughout the disputed territories before their admission as states; third, "moral and political action" by the people of the free states to abolish slavery in the South, eventually by constitutional amendment. If this last step was rather vaguely described, it was because Garrison did not clearly visualize how such an amendment could be passed.

The means to be used are specified with reasonable clarity. The Society "shall aim to convince all our fellow citizens, by arguments addressed to their understandings and consciences, that Slave holding is a heinous crime in the sight of God, and that the duty, safety, and best interests of all concerned require its *immediate abandonment, without expatriation.*'' As to the slaves themselves, "This Society shall aim to elevate the character and condition of people of color, by encouraging their intellectual, moral and religious improvement . . .'', a clause which the opponents of abolition took to mean political agitation among the slaves.

Like so many straightforward and comprehensible projects of social improvement, this one eventually achieved its stated end-condition, although the project cost much more than anyone anticipated and was completed by men who were not fully devoted to it. "If I could save the Union without freeing *any* slaves," Lincoln wrote in 1862, "I would do it, and if I could save it by freeing *all* the slaves, I would do it; and if I could do it by freeing some and leaving others alone, I would also do that.'' ² Most of the leaders on both sides followed him in asserting that secession—not slavery—was the primary issue. Later historians tried to show that differences of economic interests between the capitalist North and the agrarian South were sufficient to account for the conflict. The common sense of the public, then and now, identified the real issue as slavery, as Lincoln himself came to do. In the marvelous language of his Second Inaugural, he expressed his somber amazement at the cost of resolving it.

In a narrow sense, the project of abolition was successful; its desired end-condition, the total abolition of slavery by constitutional amendment without compensation or relocation was eventually achieved. In a wider view, it was a partial, and probably unnecessary, failure. That failure, whose after-effects are still very much with us, is attributable to major defects in the original project: the unwillingness to consider concrete goals beyond emancipation and the insistence on no compensation for slave property as a moral principle. "If compensation is to be given at all," wrote Garrison, "it should be given to the guilt-ridden and outraged slaves, and not to those who have plundered and abused them.''

The contrast between British and American abolitionism is instructive. Both movements began at about the same time and took the abolition of the slave trade as a first stage objective. The two movements had a common vocabulary and a great deal of direct contact, but William Wilberforce, the principal spokesman of the English branch, was as conciliatory as Garrison was intransigent, and in the British version of the emancipation, considerable attention was given to the problems of adjustment that might be expected after emancipation, and compensation to the slave owners was taken for granted. When 700,000 West Indian slaves were emancipated by Parliament in 1833, 20 million pounds were appropriated as compensation to the planters, and elaborate arrangements were made for the transition from slavery to freedom. The differences between the West Indies and the Southern states do not permit the flat conclusion that this was a better way of accomplishing the purpose, but it is notable that although the abolitionist movement at first evoked the same violent hostility in England as in the United States, it did not stimulate the development of a counter-ideology glorifying slavery. By contrast, the American version of abolitionism seemed to threaten economic ruin to the planters and personal danger to the whole white population, and thereby put an effective stop to the anti-slavery sentiments which had long been current in the South. The rhetoric that bloomed in response to these threats struck nearly as jarring a note in the mid-nineteenth century as it does today. "This, our new government," said Alexander Stephens, the vice president of the Confederacy, "is the first in the history of the world based upon this great physical, philosophical, and moral truth . . . that the negro is not equal to the white man." This bizarre philosophy did not disappear with emancipation, but lingered on to work mischief for another 100 years.

That the abolitionists' project went no further than emancipation had equally grave consequences. Garrison, although never the undisputed representative of the movement, again expressed its central tendency when he declared in 1865 that since slavery was ended his career as an abolitionist was over. He then advised the American Anti-Slavery Society to dissolve and discontinued publication of *The Liberator*. A few abolitionists turned their energies to the cause of the freed slaves, but that movement was amorphous and feeble. The Freedman's Bureau did a valiant job of providing relief and assistance to the black population in the immediate aftermath of the war, but its long-term program never amounted to much more than the slogan which promised forty acres and a mule to every freedman, and the comfortable hope that after a short period of adjustment black workers would be able to shift for themselves in a country that still enjoyed a perennial shortage of labor. Most of the former slaves, as it turned out, stayed where they were and went back to doing much the same work they had formerly done as slaves. Their legal and social statuses were less radically transformed than had been expected, and with the passage of time, and the restoration of local autonomy to the South, a code of racial etiquette developed that excluded blacks from economic and social opportunities. The franchise guaranteed to them by the Fifteenth Amendment was gradually withdrawn by such transparent devices as the white primaries, grandfather clauses, and literacy tests administered with arbitrary discretion; while their collective subordination to whites was insured by an almost endless array of Jim Crow statutes. Slavery had indeed been abolished, and on the abolitionists' inflexible terms, but the net result was not equality but a new form of bondage.

The Settlement
House

Meanwhile, national concern shifted to another set of social problems, mainly urban, and variously interconnected: the demoralization of slum dwellers, organized vice and crime, and political corruption. The number of people living in American cities of more than half a million shot up from 1.4 million in 1860 to 3.1 million in 1880 to 8.1 million in 1900,[3] almost all in the North. In 1865, the majority of immigrants entering the United States spoke English. This had been the case since immigration began but was never to occur again. By 1900, only one in ten immigrants came from an English-speaking country.[4] In the 1880s, sentiments of indignation and compassion began to be aroused by the living conditions of immigrant families in tenement districts, their apparent alienation from the main currents of national life, the delinquency of their children, their exploitation by sweatshop employers, their excessively large families, the squalor of their neighborhoods, their overcrowded lodgings, and the high incidence of illegitimacy, intoxication, and violence among them.

Jacob Riis, a talented and adventurous journalist born in Denmark, had nearly the same message for the American public of the 1880s as Michael Harrington, author of *The Other America,* had for the public of the 1960s. Both of them set out to arouse concern in the comfortable sector of the population about the misery of the poor and the squalor of their living conditions. Both insisted that the poor were much more numerous than they appeared to be and both made a deliberate attempt to remove some of the barriers which rendered the poor invisible to their affluent neighbors.

(Riis was a talented photographer as well as a writer. Working with primitive lighting equipment, he was able to get astonishingly good pictures of indoor and night scenes in the New York slums of ninety years ago. It is instructive to compare his pictures of skid row derelicts and their lodgings with pictures of similar subjects taken recently, for they illustrate that the physical conditions under which these derelicts lived were much worse then. The cheapest Bowery lodging houses of today are well-heated dormitories with beds in separate cubicles. In the 1880s they were cellar rooms barely heated by a Franklin stove in the corner and the lodgers slept in their clothes on the damp floor. But I have the impression that the skid row faces of the 1880s showed more self-respect and less despair than the skid row faces of the 1970s. This may, of course, be only the effect of a slower camera shutter.)

The urban social problems that aroused public concern from 1870 onward generated a vast number of ameliorative projects, some of which are still visible on the contemporary scene. Among these, the settlement house invites special attention, because of the wide range of problems it touched and its influence on subsequent programs of social work, social service, and community action.

Although the first American settlement house, Hull House, founded in Chicago by Jane Addams in 1888, was modeled upon English prototypes, the settlement house came in time to be regarded as a distinctive American device for establishing contact between the inhabitants of ethnic slums and sympathetic, disinterested representatives of the majority culture, for their *mutual benefit.* This mutuality was the key to the project, but as settlement houses multiplied, and social work became a profession, the original model was discarded and replaced by a cruder model in which benefits supposedly flow from social workers to their clients even when, as is often the case, most of an agency's budget goes to the support of social workers rather than clients.

Jane Addams and Ellen Starr, the two educated young women who founded Hull House in a rundown mansion on South Halstead Street, were more clear-sighted. In an early paper on the "Subjective Necessity for Social Settlements," Miss Addams wrote that

We have in America a fast-growing number of cultivated young people who have no recognized outlet for their active faculties. They hear constantly of the great social maladjustment but no way is provided for them to change it, and their uselessness hangs about them heavily. . . . These young people have had advantages of college, of European travel, and of economic study, but they are sustaining the shock of inaction. . . . They tell their elders, with all the bitterness of youth, that if they expect success from them in business or in politics or in whatever lines their ambition for them has run, they must let them consult all of humanity; that they must let them find out what the young people want and how they want it. . . .

The Settlement, then, is an experimental effort to aid in the solution of the social and industrial problems which are engendered by the modern conditions of life in a great city. . . . It is an attempt to relieve, at the same time, the overaccumulation at one end of society and the destitution at the other . . . Its residents . . . must be content to live quietly side by side with their neighbors, until they grow into a sense of relationship and mutual interest.[5]

Hull House itself seems to have reached its peak after about ten years of operation when it had 25 residents, both women and men, and had added a dozen buildings to the original structure. Its activities were multifarious and developed more or less spontaneously according to the interests of the residents and the people they attracted from the surrounding Italian, German, Irish, Polish, Greek, Russian-Jewish, and Bohemian population. Programs were launched quickly and spontaneously on the initiative of individual residents, and continued as long as they attracted participants. Failures were cheerfully accepted. Among the more important activities were a kindergarten, a day nursery, domestic science classes, a visiting nurse service, literary readings, voluntary babysitting, a coffee house, nutritional surveys, young people's dances, art exhibits, a cooperative coal yard, a dormitory for working girls, a community gymnasium, lodging for homeless women, a branch post office for the protection of immigrant remittances, legal aid services, public lectures, the provision of space for weddings, parties, and public meetings, the founding of several women's labor unions, a popular social science association that met weekly for seven years, a folk art collection, a textile museum, and a large summer camp.

Hull House operated until 1961, when its neighborhood was cleared to make room for the Chicago campus of the University of Illinois. Long before that time, however, the original program had been transformed by the extensive involvement of its leading members in national and international movements, in state and federal lobbying, and in governmental positions. Collectively, the alumnae of Hull House accumulated an extraordinary number of public distinctions. An equally important change was the widespread acceptance of many of the programs with which Hull House had experimented—for example, kindergartens, visiting nurse services and legal aid, and the rapid professionalization and specialization of the people involved in them. The settlement house was the seedbed of many projects, but its own decline can be read between the lines of *The Second Twenty Years at Hull House*,[6] which contains chapters on the Progressive Party campaign of 1912, the Women's Movement, the Peace Ship, the campaign for the federal child labor amendment, the growth of organized social work, prohibition, national immigration policy, the World Court and Gandhi's campaign against the Indian caste system, but practically nothing about new programs at Hull House.

The distinctive feature of the original settlement house, in my opinion, was that it did not aim at the solution of the numerous social problems in the midst of which it was set down. Its desired end-condition was the establishment of warm and satisfactory relationships between the volunteers who came to live in the settlement house and the slum dwellers with whom they made contact, as well as among the volunteers themselves, who shared their adventures in a communal atmosphere. The stages of such a project consist of a series of individual programs whose success is measured by the enthusiasm generated among both clients and volunteers, rather than by external results. The measurement of program effectiveness under such an arrangement is simple and straightforward and the cost of failure is low, so long as the volunteers retain their solidarity and can find other programs to try. A program that goes beyond these modest objectives and begins to assume instrumental importance, like the visiting nurse and legal aid services at Hull House, can be counted as technically successful but, from the standpoint of the volunteers, is roughly equivalent to a failure, since as it becomes specialized and bureaucratized it will cease to provide much emotional satisfaction for participants.

There are many other social service projects that conform to a similar model, such as the Peace Corps, and programs of volunteer work in prisons and mental institutions. Like almsgiving in traditional societies, volunteer social service can benefit both the helpers and the helped, but the helpers to a greater extent. The designers of successful volunteer projects are seldom confused about this point. "I gradually became convinced," wrote Miss Addams, "that it would be a good thing to rent a house in a part of the city where many primitive and actual needs are found, in which young women who have been given over too exclusively to study, might restore a balance of activity along traditional lines and learn of life from life itself." [7] But as the settlement house matured, as its activities became institutionalized, and as the leaders of the movement were lured away by wider opportunities for social improvement, most of the life went out of the project. Social work became a "profession" at the instigation of former Hull House volunteers like the Abbott sisters and Sophonisba Breckinridge, and in the process, volunteers without a professional commitment became ineligible for full participation. The range of innovation was progressively narrowed by the institutionalization of earlier programs. It was no longer possible for a volunteer to start a kindergarten or a nutritional program overnight, or to do so at all without standardized equipment and training. In time, the residential idea was forgotten and no one except the night watchman was expected to settle at a settlement house.

The loss of spontaneity and enthusiasm among the volunteers had a discouraging effect upon the clients. It became easier to obtain contributions of funds for settlement house programs than to attract beneficiaries to them, and as patterns of imitation crystalized and large amounts of public funds became available, the purposes of the settlement houses became increasingly obscure. Some turned into recreation centers, offering a schedule of free entertainment; others evolved into specialized agencies handling such matters as the supervision of juvenile delinquents on probation, or vocational education for the handicapped. Others developed a mystique of individual counseling, related to psychotherapy, which made it possible for them to operate with a very small number of clients. The goals of the movement became increasingly obscure until the mission of the neighborhood service center, one of the newer variants of the settlement house, could be defined in an official publication as ''to perform outreach and referral and follow-up functions, and promote decentralization of social services.''

The Prohibition Experiment

It is not easy to capture the national mood that permitted the passage of the Eighteenth Amendment in 1919, but numerous states and localities had enacted temperance legislation in the previous decade, almost invariably by very narrow majorities. The amendment provided that ''After one year from ratification of this article, the manufacture, sale, or transportation of intoxicating liquors within, the importation thereof into, or the exportation thereof from the United States and all territory subject to the jurisdiction thereof for beverage purposes is hereby prohibited.'' This project, ''noble in motive and far-reaching in purpose'' as Herbert Hoover called it, was a real experiment in social improvement and its results still deserve careful study.

American men were hard drinkers in 1919, as they had been since the country was first settled. Women and children were expected to abstain from public drinking, and generally did so. The saloon was a major institution and the center of working class sociability. Whiskey and beer were the staple beverages, but every ethnic group had its own recognized drinking customs.

Alcoholism was a common ailment although its incidence was significantly lower than it is today.[8] The adverse effects attributed to alcoholism were loss of earnings, neglect of family obligations, immorality, and injury to the drinker's health. The destructive consequences of drunken driving were not yet recognized.

In 1919, the temperance movement was more than a century old and had a solid permanent base in several Protestant denominations. It was largely a women's movement but did not lack charismatic leaders of both sexes. In the two decades preceding the passage of the Eighteenth Amendment, such organizations as the Women's Christian Temperance Union and the Anti-Saloon League flourished as never before and obtained the enactment of bans against liquor in a number of states and counties, a few of which are "dry" to this day. In general, local prohibition worked—and still works—well enough since drinkers were merely put to the inconvenience of crossing a county or a state line to obtain their supplies.

Prohibition could also be traced back to another institutional pattern of long standing—the American practice of regulating morally-disapproved activities by first prohibiting them entirely and then allowing them to be carried on in a clandestine way with the connivance of law-enforcement agents. The penalties for violating these prohibitions are almost invariably levied on the seller of such pleasures, and almost never on the buyers. Prostitution and illegal gambling had been regulated in this fashion in American cities since the early 1800s as, of course, they still are. Urban political machines have always been partly supported by income from these enterprises.

It is not at all clear in retrospect what the millions of serious drinkers in the United States expected would happen after the ratification of the Eighteenth Amendment. Perhaps they thought it to be a dead letter, like the statutes and ordinances in every locality that prohibited fornication, or perhaps they took comfort in the text of the amendment, which did not forbid either the possession or consumption of alcoholic beverages, but only their manufacture, sale, and transportation. The traditionally ineffective prohibition of gambling and prostitution had overwhelming majority support; the norms of the period regarded a measure of hypocrisy on these topics as fit and proper and held the public defense of sin to be a graver breach of decorum than sinning.

There were two new elements in the prohibition experiment that would not disappear with repeal—a touching belief in the omnipotence of the federal government and the willingness of that same government to undertake assignments unrelated to its principal functions.

At the risk of laboring the obvious, it may be instructive to consider why national prohibition was not a feasible project. The desired end-condition, total abstinence for the entire population, was clearly visualized. Existing conditions had been closely studied. The method of enforcing the ban by a special police force working cooperatively with the regular police was superficially reasonable. The unlimited resources of the federal treasury guaranteed that the project would be adequately funded. No intermediate stages were provided between the existing condition and the desired end-condition, but that was because the plan called for a nearly instantaneous transition.

The flaw in the project must be sought in the relationship between the government conducting the experiment and the citizens whose behavior was to be changed. Governments, Jefferson had written, derived their just powers from the consent of the governed. The implications of that principle are easily confused with the procedure of majority rule. A majority can properly decide a controversial issue for the whole body of citizens, but it cannot give the necessary consent on their behalf. With respect to normal political issues, the minority consents after the majority has decided, and that is the end of the matter; the government then has its just powers. But when a minority is the subject of the enactment and its interests are disregarded rather than compromised, there is little likelihood that the minority's consent will be given. When such a minority is numerically weak, it can sometimes be overridden and the law enforced against it without its consent. If the minority is numerous and concentrated, and if it insists, for example, on preserving the institution of slavery, it may be possible for the majority to impose its decision by force, but the cost of doing so will be extremely high and the chances are that even afterward, the majority's decision will be effectively resisted in one way or another.

If the minority is numerous and dispersed through the population in such a way that it cannot be attacked as a body, the majority decision from which the minority withholds consent becomes unenforceable; the government discovers sooner or later that it lacks the necessary power. Since acquiescence to authority is routine and habitual in a stable community, this is not likely to happen unless the decision touches the minority more closely than the majority and requires sacrifices by the former that are not demanded of the latter.

By the time the experiment was terminated in 1933, it had become a fixed article of popular belief that prohibition, instead of curtailing the consumption of alcoholic beverages, had greatly increased it. The empirical evidence, although inconclusive, does not support this view. Warburton's estimates, based on such indirect indicators as the diversion of industrial alcohol, production of corn syrup, and the incidence of cirrhosis of the liver, suggest a substantial decline in per capita consumption during the prohibition years.[9] Jellinek estimated that the per capita consumption of alcohol by the population of drinking age during the prohibition years was about half of what the average consumption had been in 1915–1919. In other words, it could be, and has been, argued that the experiment was in some measure successful. The spokesmen of the temperance movement maintain to this day that it was never given a fair chance but was, in effect, sabotaged by half-hearted enforcement.

A somewhat parallel argument is advanced by Joseph Gusfield, whose *Symbolic Crusade*[10] is the only full-length sociological analysis of the American temperance movement. Gusfield views prohibition as the symbolic triumph of the Protestant middle classes over other status groups in the American population and regards the instrumental objective—the suppression of drinking—as secondary. The Drys, he suggests, were satisfied with the official recognition of their culture as entitled to greater worth or respect than the culture of other groups, and were content to settle for this recognition instead of provoking their opponents to more active resistance. Moreover, a serious attempt at enforcement might have undermined their symbolic triumph in another way. "The Drys were in the common dilemma of those who support a law which a significant minority oppose and which is illegitimate to them. The Temperance forces had claimed that they represented the legitimate position of most citizens. To maintain that the law was not enforceable without great sums of money and much police action was to deny the legitimacy claimed for it."[11]

There is a good deal to be said for approaching social problem solving in symbolic terms, and a similar position might be taken with regard to some of the other projects of social improvement analyzed in this book, that is, they might be said to have had more symbolic than practical significance. I would maintain, however, that even if a project is undertaken largely for symbolic reasons, its instrumental feasibility must still be established and, further, that neglecting to do so risks, as in the case of the advocates of prohibition, a severe symbolic defeat.

From an instrumental standpoint, prohibition was rendered intolerable not by its relative inefficiency in suppressing the consumption of alcoholic beverages, but by unanticipated results which were perceived as socially damaging by Wets and Drys alike, among them the following: (1) The quality and reliability of alcoholic beverages deteriorated so badly that their use involved an appreciable risk of death or permanent disability; (2) the public drinking hall declined from being merely disreputable and became a criminal institution controlled by the underworld; (3) heavy drinking by women and by adolescents increased sharply; (4) the price of alcoholic beverages and the profitability of their trade rose spectacularly as the quality of the product declined; (5) a network of illicit and violent business organizations sprang up in response to the economic opportunity; (6) the protection of this activity involved the corruption of law enforcement agents and agencies on a scale previously unknown.[12]

Although the bootleggers were able to obtain a measure of immunity from police action through political channels, they could not ordinarily call upon the police to protect them from their competitors or from federal agents with roving assignments. The organizations that emerged from the resulting anarchy were those which were most successful in the tactical use of murder and violence. When the prohibition amendment was repealed, they refused to disband and discovered or invented other forms of illegal enterprise in which they continue to flourish to this day. A parallel development occurred among the special agents recruited by the Treasury Department to pursue bootleggers and illegal brewers. Once assembled, they formed a cadre which never dispersed and later they became the principal entrepreneurs of the federal government's experiment with the prohibition of euphoriant drugs.

It is debatable whether we ought to add to the outcomes listed above what contemporary observers called "a loss of moral fiber" or "a growing disrespect for the law." Prohibition stimulated the growth of all sorts of underworld institutions, although an underworld had existed in various forms before the great experiment. The laws concerning alcohol were openly flouted by self-consciously law-abiding people and this necessarily involved them in friendly relationships with criminal types whom they would have avoided under other circumstances. Public morality, however, is not something that can be gained or lost once and for all. It, too, rests upon the consent of the governed and although it tends to deteriorate when many people disagree with the laws that are made for them, it seems to be re-established rather easily whenever a wide consensus is regained. The persistence of the criminal and anti-criminal organizations created by the prohibition experiment appears to be a much more serious social problem and to date, at least, no appreciable progress has been made toward resolving it.

The discussion of domestic social problems in the United States during the 1920s was not wholly dominated by prohibition and its side-effects. The Lynds' [13] remarkable study of Middletown, carried out in 1924–1925, reports public concern about the changes in values and life-styles associated with the automobile, the rise of the mass media, a decline of parental authority, suburbanization, inflation, immigration, the rise of divorce, the emancipation of women, disarmament, and many other matters. Nevertheless, the United States of the 1920s was regarded as an admirably organized society by most of its inhabitants. Probe as they would, the skeptical Lynds were not able to find evidence that either the business class or working class of Middletown were disposed to challenge the status quo. The descent from this peak of social confidence was to be extraordinarily abrupt.

CHAPTER 9

*The Projects of
the New Deal*

WHEN the stock market crashed on Black Friday in October 1929, the extent of the disaster was not apparent. The business cycle was an old, perennial social problem and market panics had occurred from time to time as long as there had been a financial market. The Great Depression developed gradually over the next three years. By March 1933, when Franklin Roosevelt took office, the stock market had lost more than eighty percent of its 1929 value, nearly a third of the labor force was unemployed, and many sectors of the economy were at a standstill.

The Great Depression was much more severe than any earlier or later economic crisis in American history, and lasted much longer. Its shadow was not lifted from the land until the upsurge of war production in 1942 and not until then was national confidence regained.

One of the most significant effects of the Great Depression was that the federal government assumed a permanent and continuous responsibility for social problems which it had not previously acknowledged. The Constitution was reinterpreted to give it jurisdiction over the banking system, the stock market, and labor-management relations, and subsequent reinterpretations expanded the government's responsibility to include supporting old people and cripples, clearing slums, resettling indigent farmers, regulating farm prices, finding jobs for the unemployed, and many other tasks that had formerly been outside its sphere.

The catholicity of the New Deal with respect to projects of social improvement makes it difficult to draw up a balance sheet of its successes or failures. To my knowledge, the job has never been attempted in any serious way although we have some excellent studies of individual projects and their outcomes. One way to approach this vast, disorderly experiment in social improvement is to take up in turn each of the principal devices upon which the New Deal relied: regulation, mediation, social insurance, direct subsidies, indirect subsidies, public employment, social services, community and regional development, executive advocacy.

Regulation

The American regulatory commission is a relatively old social invention. The prototype was the Interstate Commerce Commission, established by Congress in 1887 to control various abuses that the railroads had been practicing on their customers and the general public. The regulatory commissions established under the New Deal, the Securities and Exchange Commission, the Federal Trade Commission, the Federal Communications Commission, and the Civil Aeronautics Board, had broadly similar purposes, i.e., to prevent specific abuses in sectors of business where customers were particularly liable to be abused.

At the risk of some over-simplification, it is not unreasonable to evaluate the outcome of all these projects together, since they all turned out about the same way. In each case, the regulatory commission was fairly successful in putting a stop to the abuses it was designed to prevent and, with some lag, was able to cope with the new abuses that sprang up under its own rules. In each case, the adversary position which the regulatory commission was supposed to maintain vis-à-vis the businesses it regulated gave way, in time, to a close and comfortable working relationship whereby the commission became a spokesman for its industry. In each case, the procedures of the commission became so intricate and expensive that they constituted a barrier to the entry of new firms and a screen that prevented public scrutiny of the regulatory process. The net effect in each case was to increase the stability of the regulated industry at some cost in flexibility and innovativeness.

The overall success of these projects is suggested by the more recent creation of additional regulatory agencies (such as the Atomic Energy Commission and the Federal Power Commission), and the survival and growth of all of the older commissions. The desired end-condition—the continuation of an established system of business minus the practices that exposed it to serious public criticism—was undoubtedly accomplished. Until the bankruptcy of the Penn Central Railroad in 1973 revealed the perilous state of the railroad industry, the only serious critics of the regulatory commissions had been those who did not like the system of business that regulation maintained, who disapproved, for example, of the railroads' neglect of passenger service or the low cultural standards of television broadcasting—and correctly perceived the regulatory commission as a buffer against change.

Mediation

The mediation board was a New Deal invention confined to the resolution of labor-management conflict, although theoretically it seems suitable for other types of group conflict as well. In 1933, large-scale unionism in the United States had nearly seventy years of experience behind it but its legality was still doubtful. A single sentence in the National Recovery Act of 1933 legitimized collective bargaining and committed the federal government to protect the organizing of labor unions from management interference. Subsequent enactments spelled out this encouragement in more detail and the number of union members increased from 2.9 million in 1933 to 10.5 million in 1941.[1]

The jurisdiction of the federal government in this field was based—somewhat implausibly—on its constitutional right to regulate interstate commerce. By means of successively more elastic interpretations of "interstate commerce," nearly all labor disputes were eventually brought within this jurisdiction.

Collective bargaining means that a union has the right to bargain about wages, hours, working conditions, and related matters on behalf of all the workers in a particular bargaining unit (which may be an occupation, a workshop, enterprise or an industry), including those who do not belong to the union. The mediation board acts as a tribunal to determine the boundaries of bargaining units and to force reluctant parties to the bargaining table when necessary. It conducts elections to settle which union has the support of the majority of workers in a given bargaining unit and certifies (and uncertifies) bargaining agents in conformity with the results. It also enforces an elaborate set of rules that spell out the circumstances under which strikes, lockouts, and boycotts are permissible, what sorts of aggressive action may accompany them, and what countermoves are permitted to the other side. It attempts to turn industrial conflict into a regulated game played by more or less equal sides under reasonable rules, and serves as an impartial umpire in the periodic contests which ensue.

By and large, the project must be reckoned successful, although it has had some unanticipated consequences, such as the inflationary pressure created by the periodic renegotiation of union contracts under rules that virtually compel wage rates to rise at each renegotiation and prevent them from falling under any circumstances and the discouragement of technological progress in industries, like construction and railroading, where the jurisdictional divisions among unions reflect an outmoded technology. But these problems are minor compared to the bitter industrial warfare that mediation was designed to stop, and did stop.

Social Insurance

Social insurance resembles private insurance in its basic procedure of collecting money from a large number of persons exposed to a risk and paying money out to those for whom the risk becomes a reality. It differs from ordinary insurance in being obligatory, and in the absence of a fixed relationship between the payments made by an individual and the benefits he may receive.

The two major types of social insurance established under the New Deal were old age insurance and unemployment compensation, both included in the Social Security Act of 1935. The former program, which eventually expanded to include survivors, dependents, disability, and health insurance, was and is purely federal. Unemployment compensation was and is a joint program, administered by the states but largely financed by the federal government. The coverage of both programs was at first limited to employees in industry and commerce but has been progressively expanded until it now covers more than nine out of ten persons in the labor force.

Old age insurance provides an insured worker with a monthly income for life, beginning at age 65, on condition that he retire from the labor force (or that his earnings do not exceed a small amount). These payments are financed by a payroll tax imposed on both workers and employers. To be eligible for full benefits, the worker is required to have been covered for a certain number of calendar quarters equivalent to about ten years of regular employment.

Unemployment compensation provides weekly cash payments to normally employed workers during limited periods of involuntary unemployment. The right to benefits is based on the individual's employment and earnings during a recent base period, for example, during four out of the five past calendar quarters. The benefits paid average about half of the weekly wage earned by a claimant during the base period but are always subject to a fairly low ceiling. Most states provide somewhere between a half year and a full year of benefits. In normal periods, only a fourth or a fifth of the recipients exhaust their benefits before returning to work. In 1970, 16 million claimants were paid $4 billion in unemployment benefits, with an average payment of about $50 a week for about five weeks.

The unemployment insurance system has been clearly successful in alleviating the misery caused by layoffs during business fluctuations and in reducing the dependence of employed workers on a particular job or employer. The discrepancy between earnings and unemployment benefits is not so large in the average case as to cause great hardship or so small as to encourage people in well-paid occupations to work intermittently, although the system does have that effect for casual occupations. After paying out more that $50 billion in benefits between 1940 and 1970, the unemployment compensation system was still in financial balance and on practically the same contribution rate with which it had started.

The rate of contribution to the social security system for the financing of old age insurance has risen steadily over the years but the benefits paid have not increased quite as much as labor force earnings. The average monthly benefit paid to retired workers in 1972 was only $161.97.[2] More than 85 percent of the total population over 65 years old received some income from the social security system in that year.[3]

The tendency of social security payments to lag behind the rate of increase of earnings of the active labor force and somewhat behind the cost of living too, is attributable to two principles followed in its management: the relatively short period of employment required to qualify for full benefits, and the extension of coverage to more and more classes of dependents and survivors. By 1972, benefits were being paid to more than 28 million retired or disabled workers and their dependents and survivors. The cost of administering the old age insurance program was almost negligible: administrative expenses amounted to less than 0.2 percent of the annual receipts.[4] All in all, the system is fulfilling the purposes for which it was originally established. (Its health insurance programs, which were introduced much later, have been less successful.)

In addition to social insurance, the federal government in its multiplicity manages a number of ordinary insurance schemes; life insurance for members and veterans of the armed forces, casualty insurance for certain categories of growing crops, liability insurance on government vehicles, and so forth. Most of these programs fulfill their purposes without much fuss.

Financial Risk
Insurance

Two of the most spectacularly influential projects of the New Deal involved a type of insurance whereby the government guaranteed the participants in a private transaction against financial loss: the guarantee of bank deposits by the Federal Deposit Insurance Corporation and of home mortgages by the Federal Housing Authority. The Great Depression, like all previous troughs in the business cycle, was marked by waves of bank failures and foreclosures.

The typical bank failure was generated by a run on the bank resulting in a sudden loss of confidence which created the insolvency it imagined. Deposit insurance eliminated this self-fulfilling type of panic from the American scene, and made it possible for people of moderate means to keep an unprecedented volume of savings through good times and bad, without the hoarding that had previously been a factor in the business cycle.

The National Housing Act of 1934 guaranteed long-term, low-rate mortgage loans to be made by private banks to persons purchasing single-family homes. This provision was repeatedly modifed and liberalized until it was possible for moderate income families to buy new houses with only a nominal down payment and with monthly payments of interest, principal and taxes that approximated a fair rent. The purposes of the program were to promote home ownership while reducing its risks and stimulating new construction. By and large, these purposes were achieved. The number of owner-occupied dwelling units rose from 14 million in 1930, to 40 million in 1970, and the foreclosure rate for 1970 was lower than for 1930 or any intermediate year. The original act also provided for the guarantee of private mortgage loans on new apartment houses and other multi-family dwellings. This part of the program was inactive until the 1960s, when it became an important vehicle for speculative real estate ventures in metropolitan cities.

The program clearly achieved its original goals, but some of its unanticipated results were of dubious social benefit. The type of neighborhood fostered by Federal Housing Authority regulations and procedures was the suburban residential subdivision, composed of single-family homes on landscaped lots of moderate size with a tightly zoned pattern that provided adequately for schools, recreation, centralized shopping, and other necessary facilities, but mandated a life-style based on automobile transportation. Although the subdivision excluded nuisances, it also excluded diversity. In addition, the movement of large numbers of middle- and upper-income families out of the corporate limits of the cities to which they belonged undermined those cities economically and politically.

Direct Subsidies

Direct subsidies paid by the government to individuals and organizations were not unknown in the United States before the New Deal. They included relief payments to the indigent from local sources, the pensions eventually awarded to the veterans of all wars and their survivors; grants of public land to homesteading settlers and agricultural colleges and interstate railroads to encourage the settlement of frontier territories; bounties for carrying mail, capturing outlaws, and killing predatory animals. Under the New Deal many new kinds of direct subsidy were devised. Bonuses were paid to all living war veterans over and above their pensions, the shipping and aviation industries were placed on a subsidy basis, a variety of ingenious programs paid farmers a subsidy over the market price for the crops they produced, and beginning with the Social Security Act of 1935, regular cash subsidies were provided for the aged poor, the permanently and totally disabled, and families with dependent children.

Some of these programs, notably Aid to the Blind and Disabled and Old Age Assistance, have operated quietly and auspiciously ever since, alleviating the hardships of these groups. The problems associated with them have been essentially administrative. The joint federal-state pattern of operation was clumsy, complex, and full of meaningless inequities because the requirements for eligibility and the amounts paid in benefits varied from state to state and from program to program without rhyme or reason. In 1974, these problems were partially overcome by federalizing Old Age Assistance, Aid to the Blind, and Aid to the Disabled in a new Supplementary Security Income program, but some variability from state to state still remains. Despite administrative problems, these programs may be characterized as successful in meeting their objectives.

The case is different for those types of subsidy where the need is variable and the subsidy serves as an incentive to increase the need. Such programs recede from, instead of approaching, their desired end-conditions and the more vigorously the program is administered, the more it aggravates the problem which it intends to resolve. At the time that the shipping industry was subsidized, its basic problem was that American ships were operated in the same way as foreign ships and required crews of the same size, but since these crews were drawn from the labor force of a more advanced economy paying higher wages, American ships were unable to transport a ton of merchandise between two ports as cheaply as their foreign competitors. In addition, the shipping companies labored under numerous restrictions that did not apply to foreign competitors; they were, for example, prohibited by law from using foreign-built vessels in the coastal trade and were required to carry relatively expensive insurance. The subsidy program was intended to prevent the American merchant fleet from being driven out of business, and was justified in the name of national security. Its effect was to widen the gap in ton-mile cost between American and foreign shippers rather than reduce it since claims for higher wages and profits could be mutually conceded by labor and management without jeopardizing the jobs of one side or the equities of the other.

Direct subsidies to farmers—through support payments, crop loans, and conservation payments of various kinds—were introduced to cope with the basic problem that the great majority of farmers in the 1930s faced. They were not able to obtain a sufficient income from the sale of their crops to support themselves and their families in reasonable comfort. The fundamental reason for this condition was that the productivity of agriculture had been for some time greater than the demand for agricultural products, and by the time of the Great Depression large proportions of the agricultural labor force and of the acreage it cultivated were redundant. The less efficient farmers, working the less productive land and using obsolete equipment, were intended as the principal beneficiaries of the subsidy programs. However, since farm subsidies were generally added to the price received for marketable crops, and the poorer farmers had much less to market, the principal benefits of these subsidies were reaped by those who least needed them, namely, the large-scale, adequately capitalized farmers. In time, the farm subsidy program was able to prevent the reduced production that would otherwise have inevitably followed from the low market price of farm products and thus to transform a temporary crisis of overproduction into a chronic condition that persisted until the 1970s, when the opening of the communist countries to American farm exports finally absorbed the remaining surpluses. Meanwhile, the size of the farm population diminished from nearly 40 million in 1930 to fewer than 9 million in 1974, while the average size of American farms increased from barely 100 acres to more than 400 acres during the same period.

A classic example of a subsidy program that aggravates the problem it intends to resolve is the Aid to Families with Dependent Children (AFDC) included in the Social Security Act of 1935. Like the provisions for Old Age Assistance and Aid to the Blind in the same act, AFDC was originally intended to help the states support persons who were in need because they were unable to work and had no one capable of supporting them. In the first decade of the AFDC program, the number of cases grew only a little faster than the number of cases in the other two categories, but after 1945, it began to forge ahead impressively. The number of persons receiving Old Age Assistance in 1945 was 2,056,000; in 1970 it was virtually the same, 2,081,000, presumably because the increasing number of aged persons in the population had been balanced by an increase in social security, private pensions, and other resources.[5] The number of recipients of Aid to the Blind also increased very moderately during this period—from 72,000 in 1945 to 104,000 in 1970. But the number of children and mothers receiving Aid to Families with Dependent Children increased by more than 900 percent—from 943,000 in 1945 to 9,657,000 in 1970.[6] A 1969 study showed the father to be dead, incapacitated, unemployable or unknown in fewer than 25 percent of the recipient families; in all the remaining cases, he was living and employable but had in effect transferred the responsibility of supporting his children to the public. The AFDC program had become a mechanism for the large-scale production of orphans, mostly non-white, mostly in the central cities of metropolitan areas, mostly in families with three or more children, and mostly destined to be raised without paternal supervision.

Another type of direct subsidy to needy families first authorized in 1935 was the distribution to them of surplus food; somewhat later, this was supplemented by a food stamp program which allowed the recipients a wider choice of food items. Both programs followed very complex procedures, which have been repeatedly revised, and it is difficult to get any overall view of their outcomes. A substantial amount of food has been and is still being distributed in this fashion, but the

clients of the program have always complained about the public stigma
it imposes upon them and about the type and palatability of the products received. Considerable quantities seem to be thrown away, resold
to speculators, or otherwise diverted.

Public Housing

Indirect subsidies were used by the New Deal to provide low-rent
public housing in conjunction with slum clearance in metropolitan cities. A few low-rent public housing projects were built under the National Recovery Act of 1933. The Wagner-Steagall Act of 1937 authorized the establishment of local housing authorities in localities
choosing to participate in the federal housing program. There have
been repeated changes in organization, procedures, and benefit provisions over the course of the years, but for the most part, the local
housing authorities have devoted themselves to the construction of
safe, sanitary, and grimly functional apartment complexes which accommodate 50 to 500 low-income families. The plans of local authorities have greatly exceeded their ability to find sites and to undertake
construction. The grand total of low-rent public housing units occupied or available for occupancy in 1970 was only 1,037,000,[7] of
which 143,000 had been specially designed for the elderly.

The subsidy in low-rent public housing originally took the form of
the payment of construction costs by the federal government; it was
subsequently reduced to a share of construction costs and in some circumstances, to the payment of a subsidy per room or per apartment to
make up the difference between an economic rent and what the tenant
was able to pay. In exchange for the subsidy, the successive federal
agencies in charge of the program have always held the local housing
authorities on a very tight rein, as indeed they are required to do by
the enabling legislation, which provides that the complexes are to be
constructed without unnecessary architectural embellishment, that applicants for apartments are not eligible unless their incomes are below
a stated ceiling, and must be evicted if their incomes later rise above a
somewhat higher ceiling, that occupancy is on a month-to-month basis

without a lease, and that tenants are subject to managerial discipline.

The original program was coupled with a vigorous program of slum clearance. As originally conceived, the idea was to remove slum dwellers from their dilapidated, dirty, and overcrowded tenements to bright, new, clean apartments located on the same sites, thus simultaneously rehabilitating the family and the neighborhood. This turned out to be impractical if only because of the interval of several years that necessarily elapsed between the time that the original inhabitants vacated the site and the time that the new buildings were ready for occupancy. Since most of the early projects began by *reducing* the supply of housing locally available to low income families, they had a tendency to promote the formation of new slums even when, as was not always the case, the low-rent units eventually constructed were as numerous as those demolished. The income ceiling precluded any possibility that, with the passage of time, a public housing complex would become a normal neighborhood. Indeed, by stipulating that families who were able to escape from poverty—as the program intended them to do—would be promptly evicted the program ultimately selected a population predominantly composed of the clients with whom it had failed.

There were some other problems generated by low-rent public housing that only became apparent with sufficient experience. The gist of this experience was that the new neighborhoods were often less stable and well-integrated than the slum neighborhoods they replaced, in part because of architectural designs which kept the housewife in her apartment out of touch with the surrounding street life and the activities of her children, in part because of the absence of neighborhood stores and small retail services, in part because of the difficulty of establishing relations of mutual dependence in an excessively problem-ridden community.[8] Juvenile delinquency rates are likely to be higher and race relations more hostile in a public housing complex than in a conventional slum area. Many complexes had a blighting effect on the neighborhoods surrounding them, either because of the apprehension they inspired in their neighbors or because of the barriers they interposed to the normal movement of pedestrian traffic. Studies of public housing residents show that they seldom ascribe any social or psychological advantages to their neighborhoods; the sole inducement to occupy public housing is the substantially lower rent at which apartments are offered. The typical disadvantages perceived by residents include the stigma of a public housing address, a high incidence of crime and vandalism, and their helplessness vis-à-vis the project management. It is a tribute to the hopefulness of the American temperament that low-rent public housing projects continued to be built and operated in the same fashion for at least 25 years after their defects became evident. Although the number of units is small in relation to the national housing supply, they make up a considerable proportion of the available housing in the black urban ghettos of the largest metropolitan areas, where public housing seems to impose additional stresses on families already suffering from many social and economic disabilities.

Public Employment

The public service corps was another of the New Deal's institutional innovations. It took two very different forms in the Works Progress Administration (WPA) and the Civilian Conservation Corps (CCC). The former organization (with its predecessor, the Civil Works Administration) operated from 1933 to 1941 and was phased out with the advent of wartime full employment in 1942. At its point of maximum activity in 1937, the WPA had more than three million employees, amounting to 7 percent of the national labor force. The CCC was active during exactly the same period; its maximum enrollment, achieved in 1935, was 459,000.

The WPA was an employer of last resort for experienced workers who were unable to find regular private or public employment and had exhausted their other financial resources. WPA jobs were intended to be temporary, wages were set below the level of the private labor market, eligibility could be withdrawn for refusal to accept other employment, and workers were laid off in order of seniority if funds ran low toward the end of a fiscal period. The WPA was principally engaged in the construction and maintenance of such public structures as bridges, roads, culverts, post offices and county jails. The whole enterprise was greatly undercapitalized. There was little provision for heavy equipment and even hand tools were often lacking. An aura of inefficiency and laziness grew up around the program; the popular stereotype of the WPA worker pictured him leaning motionless on his shovel. There were, in fact, considerable difficulties in the allocation of manpower since the workers the WPA hired because they were eligible were not necessarily qualified for the positions it wanted to fill. A few projects in the larger cities were able to employ specialists in a more rational way. One of the WPA projects was a highly successful public theater, and the WPA Writers' Project produced, among other works, the first comprehensive guidebook for the United States.

The Civilian Conservation Corps was an organization which recruited unemployed boys and young men for work in reforestation, erosion control, and land improvement. The CCC built levees, irrigation systems, fire breaks, forest trails, national park facilities and other rural improvements, leaving a mark on the country that has never been effaced. It was organized on semi-military lines, using army clothing, kitchens and barracks, and a simplified military table of organization, but no attempt was made to institute military discipline, and the corpsman was always free to quit.

The work assigned, which was in effect voluntarily chosen by CCC applicants, was well-suited to their abilities and to the tools available, and it seems to have provided much more satisfaction than similar work imposed on WPA workers who lacked construction experience. In contrast to the WPA, the CCC operated without much public notice and without generating any new social problems at all, until it was put out of business by mobilization for World War II.

Social Services

Social services did not occupy nearly as large a place in the arsenal of the New Deal as they were later given in Lyndon Johnson's War on Poverty. Only one entirely new program, the United States Employment Service, was introduced. The existing programs of the Indian Bureau, the Children's Bureau and the Veterans Administration were considerably expanded, however.

The United States Employment Service was established by the Wagner-Peyser Act of 1933. By an offer of matching grants, it encouraged the states to establish state-administered employment offices. The purposes of the act were expressed in such thick rhetoric as to be incomprehensible at this distance, but the two functions envisaged for the new network of local employment offices seem to have been to obtain and exchange information about local job opportunities and to serve as free employment agencies for unemployed workers who, under the conditions then existing, were not adequately served by private employment agencies. Records of the initial performance of the public employment offices are scanty and scattered, but they seem to have taken over the responsibility of job placement for unskilled laborers, farm hands, casual and itinerant workers, and factory operators in low-paid industries, leaving to the private employment agencies the function of referring applicants to vacancies in more favored occupations. As might have been expected, the private employment agencies profited under this division of labor and some further specialization occurred during the following decade as union hiring halls became increasingly active in the placement of semi-skilled and skilled workers, both in artisanal industries like construction and in mass production industries like steel.

In 1937, the Employment Service was given responsibility for the administration of the unemployment insurance program previously described. The assumption of this responsibility coincided with the sharp recession of 1938–38 and for some time thereafter, the local offices were so heavily engaged in taking claims and processing papers for unemployment benefits that their employment activities were necessarily limited.[9] A distinctive feature of the agency's new relationship to its clients was its power to withhold unemployment benefits from anyone who refused to accept a suitable job offer. There was also a vast increase in the number of job applicants since every applicant for unemployment benefits was automatically required to become a job applicant at the same time. The increase in traffic generated by this arrangement established a pattern of long waiting lines and cursory interviews which precluded any close matching of individuals and employment opportunities or any exploration of individual job problems. As Blau's study shows, the disparity between the ostensible social service functions of an employment agency and its rough and ready processing of unemployment claims, dissatisfied both the officials and their clients and generated considerable hostility between them. This problem was temporarily resolved during World War II when the local employment offices were "federalized" and given wide powers to allocate and distribute manpower in accordance with the requirements of war production. After the war, they fell back into their former situation, which still persists today, despite a multiplicity of new responsibilities, youth opportunity centers, labor mobility demonstration projects, the Job Corps, the Neighborhood Youth Corps and community action agencies. Recent proposals for legislative reform have stressed the need for "identifying the role and mission of the employment service" which, after more than 40 years of continuous operation, appear to be still undetermined.

The modest activities in support of child welfare which had been carried on by the Children's Bureau since 1912, were expanded by Title IV of the Social Security Act of 1935, which provided for federal grants to the states—according to a complicated formula—for "public social services which supplement, or substitute for, parental care and supervision for the purpose of (1) preventing or remedying, or assisting in the solution of problems which may result in neglect, abuse, exploitation of delinquency of children; (2) protecting and caring for homeless, dependent, or neglected children; (3) protecting and promoting the welfare of children of working mothers; (4) otherwise protecting and promoting the welfare of children including the strengthening of their own homes where possible, or where needed, the provision of adequate care of children away from their homes in foster family homes or day care or other child care facilities." Title V of the same act provides grants for maternal and child health care services; for services for crippled children; for maternity and infant care projects; for school health programs; for training child-health personnel and for research relating to all these matters.

The most interesting thing about these programs, which have grown and ramified, is that no part of the money appropriated for them goes to the intended beneficiaries in cash, and only a minute fraction of it reaches them in the form of tangible benefits. Most of the money is paid to full-time public officials who provide services for the intended beneficiaries. Considerable amounts go to the support of institutions for training persons for these official positions. Other sums are allocated to private social agencies to enable them to support their own functionaries who provide similar services. Considerable sums are allocated to universities and research institutes for studies of the beneficiary population, their needs, and the services provided to them.

Of what do these services consist? A recent authoritative list of child-welfare services mentions:

> *Adoptions:* Counseling and study of child and natural and adoptive parents: placement of a child and follow-up.
> *Foster Care:* Counseling real parents and child, training and supervising foster parents, licensing children's institutions.
> *Protective Services:* Directed at parents who abuse or neglect their children with a view of protection of the child, taking action to remove child when he is in danger.
> *Daycare:* Licensing and supervision of day-care facilities.
> *Services:* To unmarried parents and their children.

The activities implied by the list consist for the most part of investigating children who are in trouble of some kind by interviewing them and the adults connected with them, giving them advice, helping them to fill out official papers, approving or disapproving the performance of adults who are in charge of children under various circumstances, and calling the police when an emergency threatens. The giving of advice is the core activity. It is sometimes solicited by the client but more often unsolicited and incidental to an official procedure of one kind or another. In contrast to some other fields of social work practice, much of the advice given by child-welfare workers is backed by sanctions. The client can be penalized if he fails to follow the advice and will certainly be penalized for any open resistance to it. Much of the advice has to do with how to comply with administrative procedures set up by the advisors to regulate their own relationships among themselves. The most standardized form of advice is a *referral*. This consists of advising the client to go to another office where he will receive further advice.

Some of these activities are useful and necessary but they tend to expand beyond all reason if, as is normally the case, the usefulness of a service is evaluated exclusively by the functionaries who provide it without giving their clients any opportunity for evaluation or even conceding their right to have opinions on the subject. The proliferation of services and of the full-paid functionaries who perform them is cumulative. As their number increases, a considerable population of supervisors, trainers, technicians, and analysts appears, many of whom have no contact at all with the clientele they are employed to benefit.

In the absence of any serious evaluation of the results obtained by social service programs, the technology of advice-giving has remained nearly stationary, while the volume of advice has grown in a spectacular way. In 1970, for example, the federal government alone spent $589 million on the services listed above at a cost of $960.00 per child involved,[10] but no one in the world has any effective way of determining what results were obtained for this money. Requests for additional child-welfare funds are almost invariably supported by showing that the problem to which the program is addressed has worsened since the last appropriation.

The oldest and most unsuccessful social service program maintained by the federal government is administered by the Bureau of Indian Affairs. It offers special education, employment assistance, health assistance, family planning, and housing assistance to about half a million Indians, Eskimos, and Aleuts who live on reservations or are listed in tribal registers.

Prior to the New Deal, the Indian Bureau, as it was then called, attempted to suppress tribal cultures by educating Indian children in boarding schools. It refused to acknowledge the legitimacy of tribal religion or authority. A New Deal reform reversed this policy and emphasized respect for the Indian heritage and the preservation of tribal autonomy. In the long run, however, this change of direction turned out to make relatively little difference. The beneficiary population continued to be highly disadvantaged compared to similarly situated populations that did not enjoy the special protection of the government. By 1970, the project had achieved an unparalleled pitch of absurdity in that the federal government was spending about one thousand dollars per capita per year to provide social services for an Indian, Eskimo and Aleut population whose annual incomes were only about five hundred dollars per capita per year.

The assumption behind every program of social services is that the advantages procured to the beneficiaries by the services provided them are more valuable, at least in the long run, than the same amount would be if given to them as a direct subsidy. In the case of the Indian program, the long run has lengthened out to nearly a century without producing any evidence for this assumption.

Community and
Regional Development

Local projects, intended to solve whole clusters of social problems, occupied an important place in the early stages of the New Deal. The most interesting examples were the rural cooperative settlements established by the Farm Security Administration, somewhat in the style of utopian colonies of the nineteenth century, although without any attempted modification of family structure or religious beliefs.[11]

Somewhat more viable were the two new commuter suburbs built under government auspices in accordance with the Greenbelt principles of Patrick Geddes and the English Garden City movement. Since the same principles were coming to be widely accepted by private developers in the same period, the new towns ceased, after a comparatively short time, to stand out distinctively from neighboring communities and the federal government, which found the management of company towns inconvenient, was able to divest itself of them painlessly.

The Tennessee Valley Authority was a comprehensive effort to solve the problems of an entire impoverished region by combining a giant hydroelectric project with public works of various kinds, a regional master plan, and an assortment of indirect subsidies to farmers, businesses, and communities within the region. The experiment was counted as successful [12] but has not since been repeated in the United States and hardly figures at all in the subsequent history of social problem-solving.

Executive Advocacy

This was virtually the only device employed by the New Deal in favor of the minority rights which figured so largely in its ideology. Not until the end of the era was this advocacy expressed by an explicit rule against racial discrimination; Executive Order No. 9 of 1941, which prohibited defense contractors and subcontractors from discriminating against minorities in hiring or promotion. Considering the limited character of this order, it was surprisingly effective under the special conditions of wartime and it may be said to have opened the federal government's long campaign to obtain equal opportunity for blacks against the stubborn resistance of local authorities, private organizations, and a large part of the white population. Judicial advocacy, which later became the primary instrument of desegregation, was not yet a factor. At the close of the New Deal, the authority of the courts still supported the system of legalized discrimination that prevailed in the United States wherever there was a large non-white population.

The Lessons Learned

1. The regulation of private persons or organizations by a public authority tends to stabilize and reinforce the existing hierarchy among the persons or organizations who are regulated, to protect their interests vis-à-vis third parties, and in general, to conserve the status quo among the regulated. Regulatory authorities are generally effective in enforcing specific roles and prohibitions but generally ineffective in adapting to new situations and conditions. For this reason, the ability of a regulatory authority to achieve its stated objectives tends to deteriorate with the passage of time.

Every regulatory authority needs to be reviewed and reformed by outsiders at frequent intervals. Unlike most other organizations, which require stable conditions to operate well, regulatory authorities, which tend to excessive stability, need to be shaken up often to keep them from settling into a mold of connivance with those whom they regulate.

2. Social conflicts that arise out of substantial differences of interest can sometimes be tamed and rendered innocuous to the larger society by converting them into contests conducted according to stated rules under the supervision of impartial referees. The necessary conditions are first, that the parties are roughly equal in strength (or can be equalized) so that each side has a realistic chance of winning when a confrontation occurs; second, that the referees are sufficiently impartial to be regarded as unsympathetic by both parties; third, that each party has viable alternatives to confrontation which it may elect after weighing the risks.

The ordinary courts satisfy these conditions to some extent, but are not the most suitable agencies for resolving the types of conflict that arise in connection with labor relations, the management of monopolies, zoning and land use, employee grievances, prison administration, pension and welfare claims, price controls, the determination of utility rates, acreage limitations, jurisdictional disputes between government agencies, and other conflicts that can be resolved more expeditiously and economically by tribunals specially designed and qualified for each sort of work.

3. Social insurance appears to be the most effective method by which a government can redistribute income according to need. The essentials of an effective insurance program are first, that payments are calculated automatically and do not depend on an interviewer's discretion; second, that the table of benefits is simple enough to enable the ordinary recipient to estimate his benefits in advance; third, that all payments are made directly to the beneficiary, and no payments are made to third parties on his behalf; fourth, that the grounds for entitlement are objective, explicit, and not subject to administrative discretion.

In general, the insurance schemes most likely to achieve their stated purposes, are those in which benefits are drawn from a fund made up of the beneficiaries' prior contributions, but this feature, although highly desirable, is not essential in government insurance plans. The other features *are* essential if payments are not calculated automatically since the costs of administration rise until—as in programs for compensating the victims of crime—they greatly exceed the payments to beneficiaries. If the table of benefits is not simple enough for the beneficiary to calculate his benefits in advance, as in some pension schemes, he is deprived of the opportunity to plan his own affairs in a rational way; if payments are made to third parties as they are to physicians and hospitals under many health insurance plans, the costs will spiral perpetually upward but the beneficiaries will often be insufficiently covered; if the grounds for entitlement are subject to administrative discretion, the beneficiary will be subject to discourtesy, stigma, inconvenience, and injustice, while the administrators come to despise their clients.

4. The guarantee of private transactions against the risk of collective panic is perhaps the most economical way for a government to confer benefits upon its citizens. The mere existence of the guarantee removes most of the risk, since depositors have no urgent motive to join a run on the bank and mortgagees have no reason to hurry to foreclosure. At the same time, covered transactions remain fairly responsive to market factors. Banks compete vigorously for customers. Interest rates for guaranteed mortgages rise and fall, with only a moderate lag, in response to fluctuations in supply and demand.

Precisely because these projects are so successful, they tend to have extensive social consequences, which ought to be appraised and discussed more often than they have been in the past.

5. Direct subsidies are an effective method of redistributing income provided that there is a fixed number of recipients who receive more or less uniform amounts. When the first of these conditions is not met, as in subsidies to families with dependent children, the subsidy program has the ultimate effect

of greatly enlarging the population requiring assistance. When the second condition is not met, as in crop subsidies, payments are automatically proportioned so that those who need the subsidy most get the least benefit from it. Programs of both these defective types are more likely to aggravate than to alleviate the problems they address.

6. The low-rent public housing program in the United States has suffered from the endemic malady of American social movements: the failure to specify or visualize a desired end-condition, with regard to the demographic and social characteristics of tenants, their relationships to their neighbors, or the place of public housing in the whole urban pattern.

The project of providing satisfactory new housing for the urban poor by means of governmental subsidies is entirely feasible, as can be shown by the successful experience of England, the Netherlands, Spain, Italy, Yugoslavia, Brazil, and a score of other countries. But the American legislation frustrates its own goals by the requirement that families admitted to public housing remain poor on pain of eviction.

As so often happens in a flawed project, secondary defects have developed to the extent that the basic trouble is obscured. In the sad history of low-rent public housing these secondary defects include the familiar aversion to arithmetic, whereby a program designed to increase the supply of housing for the poor, is allowed to demolish more dwelling units than it constructs; the failure to visualize intermediate stages, so that inadequate provision is made for relocating the population initially displaced; and the total absence, in most areas, of any provision for continuous measurement of project results.

Because of the way the enabling statutes were written (to avoid any shadow of competition with private real estate operators), the rules under which the local housing authorities operate aim to prevent departures from standard practice in response to local conditions. Hence, the tendency of public housing to be ugly, out of scale, and uncoordinated with its surroundings.

Doing it right would require the government to do much less. The local housing authority, upon presentation of a reasonable plan for construction, would be eligible for a lump-sum grant and/or a guaranteed loan at low interest. The authority would be legally bound to restrict admissions to eligible poor families, impartially selected. And there the intervention of the federal government should cease. A formula almost identical to this has in fact been used with notable success in the federal program for expanding local hospitals.

7. The lessons that can be drawn from the New Deal's experience with its two public service corps are equally plain. Such an organization can operate successfully as an employer of last resort for an otherwise unemployable segment of the labor force if it acts in other respects like a normal employer and orients its planning and administration toward the maximum productivity that can be achieved in its special circumstances. The success of a public employment project is properly measured by welfare criteria—including the workers' morale, and a high rate of transfer into ordinary employment—but these objec-

tives can only be achieved by a program in which the results of work visibly justify the effort. To achieve its welfare goals, a public employment project must be adequately capitalized, equipped and administered; must train and assign its workers with great care, must pay wages somehow related to skill and effort, and must enforce reasonable standards of industrial discipline.

8. A potentially effective program of social service, like employment counseling, can be distinguished from an intrinsically ineffective program, like that of the Indian Bureau, by noting whether the assistance offered is or is not wanted by the program's clients; whether, in other words, they would actively seek advice from the same counselors in the absence of external threats or inducements. As a general principle, the efficacy of unwanted advice is nearly nil.

9. When the advice *is* wanted, as in job referral services, considerable management is required to cope with two intrinsic problems: a tendency for the counselors to put their own interests before those of their clients, which leads, among other things, to the habit of perpetuating the client's status as a client instead of attempting to resolve his problems expeditiously, and a tendency for systematic hostility to develop between clients and counselors because neither is able to conform to the other's expectations.

An effective social service program should give the tangible benefits at its disposal to clients with as little interrogation and delay as possible, should terminate each client relationship as quickly as possible and should limit its counseling services to clients who actively and voluntarily seek advice. It is difficult for a public social agency to follow these directives over the long term but by no means impossible, if its activities are kept under close scrutiny by outsiders.

10. Community development under the aegis of the federal government seems not to be a feasible project because such projects imply a long-term stability of administrative goals and procedures which federal agencies, with their frequent reorganizations, fluctuating budgets, and rapid turnover of personnel, cannot provide.

CHAPTER 10

The Coming of the Era of Protest

FOR long stretches of its history, the United States—solitary, proud of its past, confident of its future—has held itself up as an example to benighted peoples. For other long stretches—not quite as many in aggregate years—the same proud society has wilted in the face of social problems it could neither ignore nor solve, from slavery to drug abuse. In these gloomy intervals, the number of social problems always rises without apparent limit, as dissatisfaction spreads from one institutional sector to another and public confidence in the entire social structure is shaken by the failure to cope with one or two urgent problems. In these troughs, our past is reinterpreted as a history of futility and failure. The records are searched for significant accounts of hypocrisy and aggression. Industrial progress is viewed as no more than a greedy despoliation, the settlement of the West as a mere excuse for cruelty to the Indians.

The Great Depression was accompanied by just such a "crisis of confidence" (as it was in fact called at the time). That crisis was met by the launching of multiple projects designed to change American society in fundamental ways. Peculiarly bitter divisions appeared between those who resisted each of these innovations and those who wanted many of them carried much further. But all things considered, most well-articulated viewpoints in the 1930s in literature, politics, or social science in the United States were essentially critical of existing institutions.

World War II fully restored the national confidence that had been lost in 1929. There was practically no domestic opposition to that war or to the way in which it was managed. The administration was overwhelmingly supported at the polls, and all of our generals were heroes. The rightness of American actions was so completely taken for granted that the saturation bombing of German cities and the atrocious decision to demonstrate the atom bomb on a live population went almost unnoticed.

This euphoric social confidence prevailed for about twenty-one years; that is, from the invasion of North Africa in November 1942 to the assassination of John Kennedy in November 1963. During this time, radical dissent so declined that at one point many thought that the majority of the American Communist Party membership was composed of government informers, and the slightest expression of sympathy for a foreign revolutionary movement was enough to blight a political or business career. The American predominance in military and financial power, and in science, education, and athletics, was construed to be permanent. We anticipated as a matter of course that all other countries of the world would imitate, as rapidly as possible, American machinery and methods, clothing and music, kitchens and kindergartens. That the United States should have most of the world's gold, most of its nuclear weapons, most of its college students, and most of the responsibility for the United Nations seemed only fitting and proper. The clumsy peace that settled World War II, the awkward regional alliances set up to universalize American foreign policy, the nightmare strategies of nuclear deterrence—all these were hailed as triumphs of statesmanship. The American passport, with its embossed dollar-green cover, was like the badge of Roman citizenship in Hadrian's empire. It commanded not only universal envy but a kind of immunity from the authority of inferior governments.

Social problems did not of course disappear during this fascinating era; but they seemed to become much less urgent, and efforts to solve them were given the benefit of every doubt. Most of the New Deal social programs continued in operation and a good many of them were expanded by the addition of new categories of beneficiaries or new areas of regulation. It can be called the Era of Overconfidence, and toward its end it became intellectually fashionable to identify the lack of public interest in social problems as a social problem in itself, a viewpoint expressed in Riesman's *The Lonely Crowd* and Galbraith's *The Affluent Society*. Only one domestic social problem remained salient, the problem of Negro civil rights.

The Era of Protest that extended roughly from 1964 to 1971, ending after the invasion of Cambodia, somewhat resembled the Great Depression in superficial pattern. Both eras began with a single catastrophic event which was not followed by a normal recovery of social confidence—the stock market crash in one case, the assassination of President Kennedy in the other. Neither period of crisis could be explained by its precipitating event alone; there was in each case a multiplicity of plausible causes and no reliable way of choosing among them. In each case, the federal government attempted to meet the crisis in confidence by large-scale social problem-solving, some of it highly innovative. But in neither case did such interventions end the crisis.

In both eras, there was much talk of revolution but the system survived, albeit with its institutions considerably modified. In neither case did the loss of confidence affect *all* social institutions. The Great Depression brought the survival of the economy into question and the question was answered by imposing a considerable measure of public management on the market economy. Other social institutions were scarcely challenged at all. For example, the social hierarchy of the typical American community survived intact and was perhaps even reinforced, as the Lynds reported with disappointment in their 1937 study of *Middletown in Transition* and as W. Lloyd Warner showed in detail for Yankee City in *The Status System of a New England Community* in 1942.

But in the Era of Protest, there was only a peripheral concern with economic institutions, and no important changes were made with respect to business management, government regulation of the economy, the operation of securities markets, methods of investment, tax structure, or labor-management relations. The Era of Protest was concerned with stratification rather than economics. It challenged authority but not property, and even though status rights and property rights might seem inextricably related, the sociological common sense of the public was able to draw a fairly sharp distinction between them.

During the Era of Protest, practically all non-commercial status relationships were challenged and extensively modified: the relationships between whites and blacks, parents and children, teachers and pupils, policemen and citizens, officers and soldiers, bishops and clergy, the artist and his audience, the government and its citizens, and most important of all, men and women. As the protest movement gained momentum and took new forms, some of its theorists were inevitably drawn into challenging the legitimacy of all authority, however derived, but curiously enough, the privately-owned corporation, with its powerful managerial hierarchy, its intense stratification of office and factory positions, and its heavy-handed discipline, continued to operate throughout all this excitement with only minor interference.

Every successful challenge to an accustomed status relationship generates two kinds of social problems: those associated with the *persistence* of inequality after the relationship has been reformed and those associated with the reduction of social confidence that is likely to occur whenever accustomed authority is weakened. In other words, what for some people is a step toward solution of the problem is perceived by others as an aggravation of it. This was not the case in the Great Depression, when the social problems were seen as economic; there were sharp differences about how to solve the fundamental problem of unemployment, but there was no important disagreement about the nature of the problem—or about the desired end-condition of full employment.

One reason why so many of the social projects of the Era of Protest achieved disastrous or ironical results was that, under cover of the prevailing rhetoric of social improvement, they were launched without definite end-conditions in view, and in some instances, with a firm commitment to mutually incompatible goals. I want to examine several noteworthy attempts at social problem-solving that marked the Era of Protest. But before doing so, I can most readily sketch the decline of social confidence itself during the early 1960s through consideration of some events which contributed to it. I do not say that these events "caused" the decline; most attempts to single out the causes of a large-scale historical change reveal only the biases of the analyst. But there can be no doubt that these events, among others, contributed to the social problems that dominated the Era of Protest.

In citing the American defeat in Vietnam, the black occupation of large cities, the Kennedy disasters, the introduction of oral contraceptives, the Second Vatican Council, and some aspects of environmental pollution, I am, moreover, selecting events whose effects were progressive—in the undesirable sense. That is, throughout the decade of the 1960s, as people became aware of each attendant social problem, they learned to anticipate not an early solution, but an aggravation of the problem.

The Vietnam Defeat

In relation to our domestic social problems, the American involvement in Vietnam should be seen first and foremost as a military defeat, one of the most spectacular and protracted in all history. The enemy, who was always outnumbered by the forces on our side, and outgunned on a scale beyond human imagination, managed to remain essentially invulnerable, never giving up any territory or making any important political concessions. Our defeat would have been serious, and the blow to national morale severe, if the war had been abandoned in 1965. Each succeeding year enhanced the condition which is most damaging to social confidence: collective helplessness.

The Vietnam War was the third costliest of all American wars in casualties sustained, and by far the longest in duration, but at no point did it command as much popular support as the previous wars in our history; in its latter years, it was opposed by a majority of the public and, at least *pro forma,* by many of the people conducting it. To carry on protracted war without majority support was an experiment never before attempted by the United States and seldom by other highly modernized states. Thus, there is not much historical evidence available for purposes of comparison. But theory suggests that a war without a national consensus must necessarily be inimical to social confidence, since the social and psychological mechanisms which in a normal war transform the infliction of death, suffering, and wanton damage into morally justified acts are inoperative. The American loss of confidence took a particularly acute form for those men who expected to be conscripted to fight in a war to which they did not consent. They were exposed to the double risk of becoming victims in what they regarded as a worthless cause, or being compelled without moral justification to victimize others. These risks appeared real, personal, and imminent to most of the male students in American colleges and universities between 1965 and 1970.

The demoralizing effects of defeat could also be observed in the government agencies and military commands whose projects were so often and so painfully frustrated. In the war zone itself, financial corruption, the cruel mistreatment of civilians, and the breakdown of military discipline on the battlefield undermined the self-esteem and morale of the armed forces to a degree unprecedented in American military experience. We noted in a previous chapter that the loss of a war in this century has almost invariably been followed by a revolution in the defeated country. That did not occur in this case but to a large segment of the population, and to an apparent majority of the intellectuals who produced the raw materials for the formation of public opinion, the persistence of the Vietnam War eventually came to signify that their rulers, summed up from about 1967 on as "The Establishment," were both mad and corrupt, and that perhaps they had always been so, and perhaps would always remain so.

The Kennedy Disasters

Since the beginning of the New Deal, the American president has for various reasons become more and more of an elective monarch, manifesting the nation in his person and, like a ceremonial rain king, associated in the public mind with the fluctuating fortunes of the whole society. The young, rich, handsome, and hopeful Kennedys were particularly well suited to their quasi-royal roles; the successive disasters that overtook them could scarcely have had a more jarring effect on social confidence. In that respect, the assassination in Dallas was far worse than the murder of Lincoln, with which it was so often compared, for the motives for the Kennedy assassination remained inscrutable, the process of bringing the assassin to justice was interrupted by another murder, its motives likewise inscrutable, and the massive investigation that followed shed no real light on the events, but only deepened their sinister overtones.

The assassination of Robert Kennedy and Edward Kennedy's sordid trouble at Chappaquiddick, a new sequence of enigmatic and disillusioning events, occupied the public mind intensely and for long periods of time and gave the country a sense of being politically accident-prone—a sentiment completely at variance with the American past and its pervasive conviction of special good fortune.

The Black Occupation
of Large Cities

From 1940 to 1960, the proportion of blacks in the American population increased only slightly—from 10 to 11 percent—but the geographical distribution of the races changed dramatically with the black migration from the South to the North and West, and from rural areas to the central cities. Concurrently, a massive migration of urban white families to the suburbs of these same cities took place. Thus, during the 1960s, blacks became a majority of the population in four hitherto predominantly white cities—Washington, Newark, Gary, and Atlanta—and came within measurable distance of forming the majority of the population in Baltimore, Detroit, New Orleans, Richmond, Savannah, St. Louis, and Oakland. These population ratios mask some changes even more extraordinary. Since the white families remaining in any central city were predominantly childless, by the time black parents constituted about 30 percent of a city's adult population their children became a majority of the school population, a change which occurred in Manhattan, Chicago, Cleveland, and San Francisco, among other places, before the 1960s were over. While white families were removing themselves and being replaced by black families, the total population of these cities remained relatively stable. But since, on the average, the black families had lower incomes than the white families they replaced but required more public services, many of the large cities were virtually insolvent by 1970—even after curtailments of public services and increases in property taxes; such measures further encouraged the flight of the white population.

Though it has often been suggested that black migration to the large cities was inspired by more generous welfare benefits available in these cities than in the rural South, it cannot be shown that the cities offering the most extensive welfare benefits have attracted the highest proportion of migrants; and the pattern of migration was fully established before the expansion of Aid to Families with Dependent Children made living on welfare a familiar life-style.

The black occupation of cities generated a double set of social problems in a fashion characteristic of the Era of Protest. From the black perspective, the essential problem was the continued denial of equality in communities where, as a majority or near-majority, blacks had a legitimate claim to determine public policy. From the white perspective, the cultural, economic, social, and political facilities of each metropolitan city belonged to a larger community that was overwhelmingly white, and the black claim on them was a usurpation. Not only the paranoiacs on both sides but also the serious spokesmen foresaw a long territorial struggle. Here, for example, is how a prominent white political scientist, Andrew Hacker, looked at the urban future in 1972:

Those who preoccupy themselves with the immorality and irresponsibility found in slum society would do well to turn their attention to the new generation of youngsters being spawned in our ghettos this very moment. These infants will be adolescents 15 years hence, and potential criminals, terrorists, and unemployed adults a decade thereafter. Having come into the world unwanted by their parents and unneeded by society, they stand only the slightest chance of knowing love or encouragement or even recognition of their humanity. In the process of creation right now are rioters and rapists, murderers and marauders, who will despoil society's landscape before the century has run its course.[1]

Here is an almost simultaneous view of the same situation by a black politician, Albert Cleage:

We are concerned primarily with our own black community. We are not trying to invade white communities or take over white communities. But we do insist that white people cannot enjoy the luxury of separating us into black ghettos and also enjoy the privilege of exploiting us in these ghettos that they have forced us into.

From here on in, we will take the black ghetto and make it a garden spot for ourselves. . . . White people will not live in the suburbs and come in each morning to exploit us and go home each night. We will run our own businesses. We will run our own schools. We will run our own government. We do not want the whites to *give* us anything; we want to *take* whatever our power allows us to take, because this is the only way it will become ours.[2]

One paradoxical effect of this confrontation, as we will find when we come to examine the attempted War on Poverty, was that exactly one hundred years after the end of the Civil War, the federal government and numerous private organizations controlled by whites began for the first time to campaign actively for racial integration while numerous black organizations sprang up to resist it.

The Development of
Oral Contraceptives

The institution of the family in Western Europe and the United States has proved remarkably resistant to change for the past 200 years. During the Era of Overconfidence the stability of conventional family patterns was conspicuous: the proportion of the American population married was the highest ever recorded for a modernized society, the divorce rate declined substantially from its post-war peak, home ownership increased to an unprecedented level, the birth rate rose unexpectedly, a vast program of educational expansion and improvement was carried out, and the entire society seemed to celebrate the ideal of the happy, healthy, affectionate, and prosperous middle-class family.

In 1959, after a period of mass experimentation in Puerto Rico, oral contraceptive products were first introduced to the American market. While previous types of contraception had failure rates of at least one to three percent per month of use, these had a failure rate in the neighborhood of one-thousandth of one percent per month of use. By 1964, more than four million women—a substantial proportion of them unmarried—were using oral contraceptives regularly.

Unlike most technological innovations, this one directly affected basic human relationships. Within the conjugal family, the pill decreased the dependence of wives on husbands or potential husbands by enabling any woman to decide for herself whether and when to bear children. Outside the family, it enabled unmarried women to be sexually active without the risk of pregnancy. At the same time, the pill greatly decreased the transactional value of sexual relationships outside of marriage by removing the considerable risk of an illegitimate pregnancy or a forced marriage, and thereby reducing the implicit commitments involved. The character of erotic transactions between the sexes was fundamentally modified. Changes in public morality and the patterns of family relationships were not slow to follow.

The Second Vatican Council

The impact on the Roman Catholic Church of Pope John XXIII's second great council in 1962 is largely attributable to its consensus on the obligation of the Church to become involved in social problem-solving, the desirability of limiting papal and episcopal authority, and an enthusiasm for innovation in religious ritual and dogma. For centuries the Church had opposed social change on principle and had preserved antique forms of language, architecture, costume, and social organization out of a respect for the authority of the past and a distaste for contemporary ingenuities; it was now prepared to support all sorts of changes in its own practices as well as in society at large.

The Roman Catholic Church was and is by far the largest religious denomination in the United States. With 46 million members (including infants and children) in 1965, it was two-thirds as large as all Protestant denominations combined and constituted one-quarter of the total population. Richer, more highly organized, and more tightly disciplined than any other branch of Christianity, it supported a vast network of schools, colleges, hospitals, and other semi-public institutions.

During the Era of Protest this imposing institutional structure began to disintegrate. Traditional observances that distinguished Catholics and Protestants, like fasting and confession, fell into disuse. Large numbers of the Catholic clergy rebelled against celibacy and left their vocations in order to marry. Even larger numbers repudiated their traditional poverty and demanded market wages for their services in schools and hospitals, forcing many of these institutions to close. Some clergy ran for office, or embarked on full-time careers of political activism. Severe conflicts developed between the generally conservative laity and a growing minority of radical clergy, and the laity, although conservative, became increasingly resistant to ecclesiastical authority. Nearly all of the Protestant denominations exhibited the same new interests in secular problems, together with a diminishing attachment to traditional rituals and diminishing respect for clerical authority.

Environmental Pollution

It became apparent with astonishing abruptness in the early 1960s that the natural environment was in danger of permanent damage. Among the warning signs were the disappearance of aquatic life from parts of the Great Lakes, the spread of smog up and down the coast of California, the imminent extinction of the bald and golden eagles, the accumulation of oil slicks on coastal beaches, large concentrations of mercury in seafood, high levels of radioactivity in milk, and floating trash far out at sea. These phenomena could not be adequately accounted for by the increase of population, by metropolitan concentration, by automobile traffic, or by a higher utilization of energy. The most probable explanation was that the large-scale introduction of chemical compounds and energy processes alien to the earth's natural ecological cycle was beginning to disrupt that cycle at many points.

The culpable products and processes, and their likely toll, had become public knowledge (and the subject of public protest) by the late 1960s and need not be examined here. It does remain to be said that, from whatever standpoint it was examined, environmental pollution appeared to be a failure of social policy.

I have omitted from this list some developments—the spread of

drug use, the legalization of pornography, experiments with open marriage and group sex, the formation of communes, the Jesus movement—because there was nothing about them that necessarily required
social action. While some people perceived them as problems, others
regarded them as partial solutions. The same may be said of the
counter culture as a whole.

In any event, the distinction between problems and solutions becomes academic as soon as a social system loses the confidence of a
large number of its people, because the solutions then offered by those
who want fundamental changes in the system become the priority
problems for those who want to maintain as much as possible of the
status quo. This is what happened during the Era of Protest, as we
shall see in the following chapters.

CHAPTER 11

The War on Poverty

THE national War on Poverty, a program originally outlined by the Council of Economic Advisers, was announced by President Lyndon Johnson early in 1964 and was soon afterward embodied in a series of statutes, including the Economic Opportunity Act of 1964, the Civil Rights Act of the same year, the Social Security Amendments of 1965, the Elementary and Secondary Education Act of 1965, and the Model Cities Act of 1966. With various revisions and amendments, these statutes established more than one hundred new federal programs, among them the Job Corps, the Neighborhood Youth Corps, an adult literacy program, a large number of work-experience programs, a loan program for poor rural families, a loan program for minority-owned businesses, a diversified program of social services for migrant workers, the VISTA program, Medicare for persons over 65, Medicaid for the "medically indigent," and the Community Action Program with its own thousands of community agencies, Head Start, Follow Through, legal services, comprehensive health services, Upward Bound, emergency food and medical services, family planning, a work-incentive program, several job-opportunity programs, a New Careers program, a concentrated employment program, a cooperative area-manpower planning system, diverse housing and urban development programs, and two manpower programs designated as Special Impact and Green Thumb.

This list does not begin to cover the full spectrum of the War on

Poverty, but it gives a rough picture of its multifariousness and style. As amendment followed amendment and reorganization followed reorganization through the closing years of Mr. Johnson's Administration and the early years of Mr. Nixon's, the table of organization of this vast project became too complex to be described or understood by any single mind; and its overlapping, cross-cutting, and uncoordinated functions became too intricate to be centrally administered. Each program and cluster of programs tended to become autonomous, and many worked at cross-purposes with each other.

In the beginning, the project had been drafted to eliminate income poverty by raising the incomes of all individuals and families above a fixed standard, the standard set first as $1,500 for an individual living alone and $3,000 for a family, and later modified to take account of variations in family composition and differences in living costs between farm and non-farm families. The target date most frequently mentioned for the elimination of poverty was 1980. In relation to the nation's economic capacity, the cost of the project would have been reasonable.

The War on Poverty was not, one should point out, a reaction to a crisis in income distribution as the New Deal had been a reaction to a crisis in employment and production. The War on Poverty was largely stimulated by what I have already called the black occupation of the cities and by the social problems, for blacks and whites, stemming from that. But as the Johnson Administration set out to solve these problems, there was no real agreement within it on the end-condition that was desired. One influential viewpoint within the administration was expressed in the Moynihan report of 1964 and in two presidential speeches based upon it. Briefly, the Moynihan report identified the essential urban problem as the weaknesses of the black family structure: the prevalence in the black population of families headed by women and living in poverty because of the absence of a breadwinner, with a consequent demoralization of non-supporting fathers and their inadequately educated and disciplined sons. The desired end-condition to follow from this diagnosis would be the stabilization of the black family structure. Moynihan assumed that this could be achieved in three ways: by raising the occupational status and income of black males; by reducing the education differential between white and black children so as to prevent occupational disadvantage from being carried into the next generation; and by providing existing black families with broad community services to overcome some of their cultural and material disadvantages.

But an opposing theory within the same administration, the theory which eventually prevailed, identified the urban problem as white racism, to which was ascribed the poverty of the black inner-city population, as well as that group's educational and cultural disadvantages and the high incidence of crime, illegitimacy, truancy, and drug use among black adolescents. With white racism as the problem, the desired end-condition was conceived to be school integration and the leveling of racial barriers to employment, public appointments, promotion, and union membership; and access to recreational facilities, residential neighborhoods, and private associations. A third position, increasingly identified with the Community Action Program, specified the social problem as being exploitation, rather than racism, and proposed as a desired end-condition the partition of urban territory into autonomous white and black zones controlled by their respective residents, each zone running its own schools, police, publice services, social agencies, churches, banks, and retail establishments. The costs of partition were to be carried by the "white power structure" in partial compensation for its previous exploitation of blacks.

From the outset, disagreement over the desired end-conditions interfered with the express purpose of eliminating poverty. For example, as the community-control doctrine became more influential, and as the various federal programs became better entrenched, there was a distinct tendency to abandon the goal of eliminating poverty and to substitute for it a defense of the rights of the poor—now visualized as a permanent and embattled class within the larger society. In effect, poverty ceased to be defined solely by income and therefore ceased to be curable by income-raising procedures.

If the War on Poverty differed from the New Deal in not being an essentially economic solution to an economic problem, it was also distinguished by the petty scale of many of its programs. For example, the Job Corps, whose New Deal model was the Civilian Conservation Corps, was set forth as a key measure in the Economic Opportunity Program; yet at the height of its activity in 1967 it had a peak enrollment of 41,000, less than a tenth of the CCC's peak enrollment thirty years before. VISTA, the domestic successor to the Peace Corps, never managed to accommodate 5,000 volunteers at any one time. Other programs were begun and dropped with staggering speed. Small-business loan agencies, for example, were reorganized out of existence before they had made their first loan; several vocational-training programs were discontinued before any trainees had received their certificates.

The tactical judgments of Mr. Johnson's advisers were unaccountably bad. Nearly everything that had been learned, under the New Deal and later, about how to accomplish social improvement was sedulously disregarded. The New Deal had, for example, experimented with both direct and indirect subsidies and discovered the general superiority of direct subsidies for effecting income transfers without harmful side effects. The War on Poverty shied away from direct subsidies but distributed indirect subsidies on a scale previously unseen. Thus, only trifling increases in direct public assistance were allowed to the aged, blind, and handicapped, but payments to the mothers of dependent children were sharply increased. Medicaid and Medicare provided indirect subsidies to physicians without increasing the availability of medical services, which were already in very short supply. In fact, Medicaid and Medicare increased physicians' incomes (already higher than those of any other occupational group) by an amount equivalent to about $15,000 annually for each physician in private practice; the increases were far larger, of course, for those medical entrepreneurs who fully grasped the possibilities.

Undoubtedly there was accomplished in all this some useful redistribution of medical services to poor families and aged persons. But the costs were altogether out of reason, and the benefits were counterbalanced by the decreased availability of medical care to the rest of the population; by the increased value of the doctor's working hour; by the tendency of physicians to work less and retire earlier; and by the frequency with which medical services were totally withdrawn from unprofitable districts.

The New Deal had discovered that for most purposes social insurance programs are more effective than subsidies. The systems providing unemployment compensation and insurance for old age, survivors, dependents, and bank deposits had all been operating successfully for many years when the War on Poverty began; yet no serious attempt was made to expand the coverage of these systems or to establish new forms of insurance.

As for public employment, the experience of the Works Progress Administration and the Civilian Conservation Corps, both New Deal measures, had demonstrated that such programs could succeed if they were organized around specific work to be accomplished, were adequately capitalized, and provided employment for a reasonably long term. The Job Corps and the Neighborhood Youth Corps, both measures in the War on Poverty, seem to have been deliberately designed to challenge previous experience. They were organized almost exclusively to serve or improve their workers, were more or less indifferent to the accomplishment of productive tasks, were severely undercapitalized, and offered only short-term employment.

The New Deal's experience with federally financed social services was consistently unfavorable. The War on Poverty established so extensive a network of social services that every urban slum became a cockpit of innumerable overlapping and uncoordinated agencies charged with reeducating, retraining, and reorganizing the poor. These services offered domestic management counseling, career planning, and advice and information about political participation. They also referred the poor to other social service agencies, directed them to legal and medical services, and organized groups for diverse political, cultural, and social purposes.

How much good these services did, and how much harm, is difficult to say. They were financed in a lunatic fashion, the typical local grant being very large in relation to the services to be provided, almost unrestricted with regard to the purchase of services, seldom available for permanent improvements or facilities, and always required to be spent rapidly without any assurance of renewal. Thus, many of these programs were established in great haste, and exhausted themselves in struggles for internal control. In many cases, they were phased out or by-passed by a reorganization of the granting agency before even grasping the chance to succeed or fail. The complaint of the sponsors and participants in each social service program, taken separately, had been that nobody understood what the program was supposed to do.

For example, in the program for neighborhood health centers, the ambiguity about what the program was intended to accomplish put a stop to the development of new centers long before the program had become fully national, but allowed the centers already established to continue in operation and to engage, in effect, in a quest for useful functions.

As the War on Poverty ramified in all of these interesting directions, its original, workable goal—the elimination of income poverty—was lost to view. As events turned out, poverty *was* substantially reduced in the United States between 1963 and 1970, and the reduction was fairly spectacular: from 19.5 percent of the population below the poverty guidelines of the Department of Health, Education, and Welfare in 1963 to 12.6 percent in 1970. The improvement, moreover, was relatively greater among blacks than whites. But this encouraging trend is attributed more plausibly to fiscal policy and economic growth than to the vivacious programs of the War on Poverty. Summarizing the achievements of his agency in early 1970, a former assistant director of the Office of Economic Opportunity, Joseph A. Kershaw, wrote:

". . . the outcome has been disappointing on balance, though some highly beneficial results have no doubt been achieved. The extent of poverty has continued to decline as economic growth persisted, but it is difficult to attribute much of this to the War on Poverty." [1]

Mr. Kershaw went on to suggest that the "modesty of the achievement" should be blamed on the nation's unwillingness to spend enough money on the improvement of deficient people and environments. By 1970, this viewpoint, with minor variations, was shared by many and perhaps by most of the operators of the War on Poverty. Few of them ventured to claim success for any individual program or for the project as a whole; but they most often attributed their failures to insufficient funding, not to flaws in the programs.

The empirical evidence suggests, however, that the elimination of income poverty was well within the capabilities of the federal government, in 1963. The improvement of defective people and environments was not—if only because the people considered defective were so considered precisely because they were reluctant to participate in programs of improvement, and the environments in which they lived were considered defective primarily because they contained so many people of that kind.

The atmosphere of defeat which hung over the War on Poverty as it faded away in the early 1970s was not solely generated by the failure or partial failure of some of its component programs; there was, too, some general realization that it had inflamed the racial hostility it was designed to overcome, and thus enlarged the problems presented by the black occupation of the cities. The programs centered in urban ghettos seem to have been more effective in arousing black racism than in overcoming white racism. The great upsurge of violent crime that made metropolitan life hazardous for both blacks and whites ran concurrent with the War on Poverty, and underscored the inability of its programs to reduce welfare dependency, to control narcotics, to strengthen the black family, to improve inner-city education, to modernize correctional institutions, to improve the career opportunities of high-school dropouts, or to promote social solidarity. Self-evidently, these programs had promised more than they could reasonably hope to perform. Like the Vietnam War, the War on Poverty made the world's most powerful government look ignorant, foolish, and helpless. And in both cases, the cause of misfortune was the same—the heavy investment of resources, lives, and the government's faith and credit in projects that did not even pretend to respect the requirements of social technology and seldom considered the relationship of means and ends in any serious way.

The Lessons Learned

The War on Poverty was less instructive than the New Deal had been because fewer of its projects were successful. In the field of social improvement, failure teaches us much less than success. But a few positive lessons may be drawn anyway.

1. Governmental projects of social improvement should be massive and simple, so that their results, good or bad, can be seen and so that their success, if any, will make a difference.

2. If government projects are to specify their objectives in terms of num-

bers, time, and money, some accommodation has to be worked out between the medium-term planning this requires—five to ten years in many cases— and the practice of annual appropriations. Most large-scale projects of social improvement are seriously hampered by their dependence on year-to-year budgeting.

3. Nearly every governmental project of social improvement ought to be evaluated, with regard both to the achievement of its quantitative goals and the significance of its side-effects, at regular intervals by a disinterested board of review.

4. When no promising social technology has been developed to cope with a problem, further study, and *small-scale* experimentation is the optimum course of action.

5. The federal government is extremely powerful and rich but it is not omnipotent and its resources are not infinite. Hence, its selection of projects to support ought to be guided by a list of priorities, clearly stated, publically announced, and revised from time to time. Each department and agency ought to work within the framework of a similar list, as some presently do, but most do not.

CHAPTER 12

Social Improvement
by the Courts

THE development of systematic projects of social improvement by the federal and state judiciary was one of the most striking features of the Era of Protest and might almost be said to represent a change in the American form of government.

It was of course the fact that since early in the nineteenth century, the courts had reviewed projects of social improvement and passed upon the constitutional propriety of their goals and the legality of their methods, and that on more than one occasion, a judicial decision changed the whole course of a social movement, as when the Supreme Court's decision in the Dred Scott case of 1857 virtually outlawed the abolitionist movement and removed the possibility of gradual enfranchisement as a solution to the problem of slavery.

In earlier years, the courts were generally less favorable to social innovation than the legislatures whose acts they reviewed. It is no exaggeration to say that the civil rights movement that followed the Civil War was defeated by adverse court decisions, and it was the Supreme Court's acceptance of the separate-but-equal principle in *Plessy v. Ferguson* that authorized racial discrimination by public agencies in apparent disregard of the Fourteenth Amendment. The Court interpreted the Sherman Antitrust Act very broadly to permit its use against Eugene Debs and the railroad unions in the Pullman strike of 1894, but very narrowly to prevent its use against holding companies in the Northern Securities case of 1904. The innovations of women's suffrage and of the federal income tax were enacted by constitutional amendment to escape the otherwise certain disapproval of the Supreme Court. The principle of collective bargaining was resisted much more stubbornly by state courts than by state legislatures. The 1934 decision that invalidated the National Recovery Act set strict limits to the public control of private industry. Introducing his court-packing plan in a radio address to the nation, Mr. Roosevelt accused the courts of undermining the ability of the elected Congress to protect us against catastrophe by meeting squarely our modern social and economic conditions, "and of usurping the powers of Congress by indulging in 'judicial legislation.' ''

The latter phrase was a rhetorical exaggeration. Prior to the Era of Protest, the legislative activity of the courts was confined to reviewing the constitutionality of statutes and to resolving inconsistencies between statutes or between jurisdictions. The lower courts moreover were relatively diffident with respect to constitutional questions, and the enunciation of new principles to govern what legislatures might or might not do was generally left to the Supreme Court or to the highest appeals courts of the states.

The executive activity of the courts had an even shorter reach. A court might enjoin a public official or agency to do or refrain from a particular act, but it was not likely to issue detailed orders concerning the desired performance or to supervise it directly.

In the Era of Protest, all of this changed. The courts, both federal and state, became more innovative than the Congress or the state legislatures and enacted major institutional changes without a trace of hesitation. Judicial review was applied as freely to the oldest as to the newest statutes and extended to cover the internal rules and regulations of such non-governmental associations as labor unions and nursing homes. Court orders became in some cases as comprehensive as statutes and were more readily enforceable. The execution of some important projects, like school desegregation, came under continuous judicial supervision. Other projects, like electoral redistricting, were delegated back to executive agencies for the preparation of working documents but closely supervised by courts which retained an unlimited power of revision. The promulgation of social policies ceased to be a prerogative of the highest courts. Judges at all levels legislated with unexampled freedom. A municipal judge might throw out a local ordinance and enumerate the clauses of a substitute ordinance that he would find acceptable, without even taking the trouble to prepare a written opinion.

When written opinions did emanate from lower courts they sometimes unconsciously satirized the rulings of higher judicial authorities. Thus in 1972, a Superior Court judge in Seattle [1] cited the Supreme Court's holding (in the Burstyn case) that commercial movies are a form of communication and therefore protected by the First Amendment in order to rule that nude dancing in nightclubs is a form of communication equally protected by the First Amendment and cannot be prohibited by local authorities. The whole text of the First Amendment reads as follows:

Congress shall make no law respecting an establishment of religion, or prohibiting the free exercise thereof; or abridging the freedom of speech, or of the press; or the right of the people peaceably to assemble, and to petition the Government for a redress of grievances.

It would take us far afield to try to explain the enhancement of judicial power during the Era of Protest. Its timing may have been partly coincidental, since the first full-scale project of social improvement developed by the federal judiciary—the desegregation of public schools—began with the Supreme Court's unanimous decision in *Oliver Brown et al v. Board of Education of Topeka et al.* delivered in 1954, and the extension and enlargement of judicial prerogatives in the years following occurred largely in response to the obstacles that the courts encountered and overcame in putting that decision into effect.

With continuing success, the judicial campaign against separate-but-equal schools broadened to include separate-but-equal public facilities of all kinds, then reached out for the abolition of all forms of official discrimination by race. By the end of the Era of Protest, the entire body of Jim Crow legislation had been erased by court decisions, and the courts had moved far beyond to restrict racial discrimination by private schools, churches, hospitals and charitable institutions, by threatening to withdraw their tax-exemptions; to forbid discrimination by retail establishments and commercial facilities on grounds of public policy; and by employers and trade unions under the interstate commerce clause of the Constitution. The discriminatory devices which had been worked into the fabric of American law became totally illegal in the United States, mostly by means of innumerable court decisions, although the Civil Rights Act of 1964 and its subsequent amendments had some effect also. This momentous social reform should not be underestimated. Blacks continued to be less privileged than whites because of lower incomes, occupational qualifications, and educational levels and because they possessed only a miniscule share of the country's private wealth. The great majority of whites still had some tendency to avoid blacks as neighbors and associates and to prefer white companions for their children—a disadvantage not really equalized by the increasing avoidance and distrust of whites by blacks. But if unofficial discrimination still persisted, official discrimination had been virtually abolished. Black college applicants or job applicants were not likely to be passed over anywhere in favor of equally qualified white applicants. Public agencies and employers, religious and political organizations, many large corporations, and practically all colleges and universities were more likely to practice a degree of reverse discrimination by favoring black applicants for places or jobs over equally qualified whites. Access to hotels, restaurants, public carriers and entertainment facilities was effectively unrestricted. The courts at all levels watched over these arrangements vigilantly, ready to step in at the first sign that discrimination was being practiced.

In sum, the judicial project of abolishing official discrimination by means of court action proved successful. The Fourteenth and Fifteenth Amendments, the Civil Rights Acts of 1866 and 1875 and the civil rights legislation of the 1960s, provided the necessary legal base; the active support of the executive branch provided the material resources. The end-condition could be clearly described, the methods were available and appropriate, the time schedule was reasonable, and statistical measures of progress were devised at an early stage of the project and put into continouous use.

No equivalent success attended the judicial project to abolish unplanned segregation, especially in schools. Superficially, this project resembles the feasible project of abolishing discrimination; but its underlying structure is quite different.

When the discriminating principle of separate-but-equal schools had been overthrown, many discriminatory practices still remained, for example, in the form of school districts gerrymandered to segregate whites and blacks in separate schools or track systems designed to segregate them in separate classrooms. These abuses, like other forms of official discrimination, were remediable. But some patterns of school segregation did not reflect any deliberate intent to deny equal treatment to black children (although they might gratify such sentiments), but followed from the residential distribution of black and white families. When the public schools had been cleansed of all discriminatory devices, an inner-city district was still likely to be nearly all black and a suburban school nearly all white, reflecting the composition of the surrounding populations.

At first inspection, the project of the judiciary to remove all residual segregation from the schools seems merely to extend the judicial campaign against discrimination, but on closer inspection it involves a quite different principle. Racial discrimination in pupil assignment could be done away with by compelling school officials to disregard the racial identification of the persons with whom they dealt. To do so was to reassert the original, long-lost intention of the civil rights legislation that followed the Civil War of which it was said that "hereafter there shall be no such word as 'black' or 'white' but we shall speak only of citizens and men." [2] The enforcement of color blindness on public and private authorities involved no conflict with other legal norms, but only with a set of practices whose legitimacy had always been questionable even in the South, as Myrdal discovered in his examination of *An American Dilemma* a generation before.

The project of preventing unplanned segregation involved the opposite principle. It forbade officials to be color-blind and required them to base pupil assignment on race. After the Coleman Report of 1966 it became an article of judicial faith that black children could not be effectively or fairly educated except in the presence of a substantial number of white children (although, oddly enough, the reverse was not held to be true). By one of those painful ironies that characterized the problem-solving efforts of the 1960s, the courts, once committed to

174 TOWARD SOCIAL HOPE

the project of preventing unplanned segregation in the schools, compelled local school boards to resuscitate some of the devices they had just been ordered to abandon, such as the gerrymandering of school districts to bring about a desired racial composition in particular schools and the assignment of pupils to schools or classes on the basis of their skin color alone.

Even these extreme measures were ineffective in most places where segregation persisted after the abolition of discriminatory policies. In Washington, Baltimore, Chicago, Cleveland, Detroit, Philadelphia, and St. Louis, white children, being a minority in the school population, could not possibly be distributed in any way that would prevent most of the public schools from having a majority of black pupils, but the inconveniences to which they were put as school boards pursued this futile objective under court supervision, accelerated both the flight of white families to the suburbs and the movement of white pupils into private schools, which intensified the initial problem. Spurred by this failure, some federal courts ordered the compulsory merger of inner city and suburban school districts in order to provide a larger pool of white pupils to assign to racially balanced schools while others proposed to connect widely separated schools by buses for the same purpose, but the net effect of these measures was apparently to increase the degree of *de facto* segregation.

The judicial campaign against racial segregation in the criminal justice system was much more successful. It formed only a part—albeit a significant part—of a much larger project of institutional reform. Between 1960 and 1970, judicial decisions effectively outlawed the use of force by the police in the interrogation of suspected offenders, the use of confessions obtained in the absence of the prisoner's counsel, the use of evidence obtained by illegal searches and seizures or by unauthorized surveillance, and the interrogation of suspects before arraignment. The criteria for acceptable evidence in criminal cases were generally tightened. The provision of counsel for indigent prisoners was made mandatory even in cases involving relatively trivial charges. The right of an offender to examine the prosecution's evidence before trial was extended. Several new grounds of appeal from criminal convictions were introduced and the requirements for appealing a conviction were liberalized. Police line-ups and other procedures for the identification of suspects were brought under much tighter control. The police practice of enticing an offense for the purpose of obtaining evidence was curtailed. Arrests could no longer be made for vagrancy, loitering, or merely suspicious behavior. "Drunk and disorderly" charges had to be supported by overt acts. Racial segregation of criminal offenders was effectively abolished. Appeals courts scrutinized arrest, arraignment, detention, trial, sentencing and probation procedures for any sign of racial discrimination. Discrimination in the selection of jury panels was forbidden and it became a practical rule that blacks accused of a criminal offense should not be tried by an all-white jury. The beneficial character of these measures in limiting the opportunities for injustice open to the agents of justice, and bringing the practice of law enforcement agencies into better accord with their ostensible principles, is evident. The negative consequences that followed do not suggest to me that the reforms should not have been made but only that their probable side effects should have been taken into account at the same time, something admittedly difficult to do while many courts at many levels were introducing procedural changes at a rapid rate.

One immediate effect of the judicial reform of the criminal justice system was a sharp increase in the time and labor required to dispose of a contested case, with the result that courts and detention facilities throughout the country became greatly overcrowded, and the speed and certainty of punishment for routine crime was reduced from an already unsatisfactory level. Because the new procedures were not promulgated as a single code but had to be deduced from a considerable number of disconnected decisions in various federal and state courts, it became virtually impossible to carry out a criminal prosecution from beginning to end without committing an error that might invalidate the conviction upon appeal. Since the race of a juror was explicitly recognized as effecting his eligibility to judge a particular case, it is not surprising that black jurors sometimes interpreted their task as the protection of an accused brother from white justice. As trials became more expensive and their outcome less predictable from the evidence collected in advance, the practice of plea bargaining, whereby accused offenders pleaded guilty to relatively minor offenses to avoid trial on more serious charges, became even more prevalent than before.

Police spokesmen and right-wing politicians were quick to assume that the substantial increase in urban crime during the decade of the 1960s was a direct result of the judicial campaign to reform criminal justice procedures. The theme of "law and order," with its barely disguised racial overtones, figured prominently in the 1968 and 1972 Presidential campaigns, and was often coupled with a program of reversing some of these reforms either by statute or by judicial reinterpretation. In fact, no direct connection has so far been demonstrated; the most that can be said with confidence is that the project of reforming criminal justice procedures did not reduce urban crime or enhance public confidence in the criminal justice system. Between 1960 and 1970, robbery, the prototypical street crime, increased by 224 percent,[3] as measured by offenses known to the police.[4] A staggering 98 percent of the reported robberies occurred in metropolitan areas. Only 32 percent of the robberies reported to the police in 1970 were followed by an arrest; 65 percent of those arrested were black; 34 percent were under 18 years old, and 77 percent under 25.[5] Of the persons arrested for robbery, only one in six was eventually found guilty as charged, although a considerable number were referred to juvenile courts and some were found guilty of other offenses. As far as the somewhat fragmentary statistics show, the odds in favor of escaping punishment for an urban robbery had never before been so favorable.

During the 1960s the federal and state courts, led by the Supreme Court, undertook to improve the representativeness of the state legislatures and of the lower house of Congress by compelling the several states to redraw the boundaries of electoral districts to take account of population movements and to assure that the members of each representative body were elected by constituencies of roughly equal size. It had been the previous custom to ignore constitutional and statutory provisions for redistricting after each census, so that in many states the representation granted to metropolitan areas lagged far behind the growth of metropolitan populations, with the intended effect of giving rural electors more influence than their numbers entitled them to. The reform was immediately effective in its desired purpose of removing state legislatures from the control of rural and conservative minorities. No particular difficulties attended the achievement of the project's desired end-condition. Redistricting plans were generally drawn up by officials of the executive branch of a state government but required the approval of the court which had ordered redistricting. This was likely to be withheld until several drafts of the plan had been reviewed and revised.

Another judicial project undertaken toward the end of the 1960s was the removal of state and local residence requirements for voting, welfare benefits, and access to public services. The movement initially arose from litigation which challenged residence requirements for public assistance. The courts eventually invalidated nearly all such requirements on the general ground that they interfered with the freedom of movement of indigent citizens and thereby placed them under a special disability.[6] The resisting localities found it difficult to muster sociological arguments against the free migration of welfare clients.

The situation was a little different with respect to residence requirements for voting where the unfairness of disenfranchising persons whose work or studies required them to move from place to place was balanced by the danger that the permanent residents and taxpayers of the locality might be victimized by an organized bloc of outsiders whose numbers enabled them to seize control of a local government. State courts showed more resistance to the leadership of the federal judiciary on this matter than on almost any other, but the drift of decisions appeared to be toward permitting college students, migrant workers, and other mobile persons to vote where they found themselves on election day in both local and national elections.

It should also be noted in passing that the broad prerogatives acquired by the judiciary with regard to social experimentation during the Era of Protest were limited in certain directions, and from a tactical standpoint, may have been contingent upon the observance of those limits. With respect to the most salient public issue of the period, the Vietnam War, the Supreme Court was as timorous as it was bold in its approach to other social problems. For an entire decade, it steadfastly resisted the temptation to review the constitutionality of the vast war effort which was undertaken and continued without the formality of a congressional declaration. A similar reluctance to be drawn into a direct confrontation with the executive branch characterized the judicial response to narcotic and other drug laws. Arrests under these laws increased by more than 700 percent between

1960 and 1970 [7] and this vast upsurge of law enforcement activity
inevitably raised most of the constitutional issues which figured in
concurrent projects of judicial reform—cruel and unusual punishments, the reasonableness of searches and seizures, the prosecution of
statuses rather than criminal acts, and significant patterns of racial discrimination, but all of these issues—so attractive to the judiciary in
other contexts—were generally ignored when they arose in connection
with the control of mood-changing drugs by criminal sanctions.

One of the most far-reaching social projects of the judiciary during
the Era of Protest was the legalization of pornography and the removal
of legal restrictions on erotic exhibitions and transactions of all kinds,
except for some weak provisos protecting children. The purposes of
the Supreme Court in this project are not easy to decipher. Indeed,
there are indications that the Court underestimated the effects of its
decisions in two or three critical cases and was startled by the resulting
disintegration of the machinery for regulating public morality. Unlike
most of the other judicial projects mentioned above, this one involved
very little consideration of the sociological issues. The arguments the
courts found persuasive—for example, that pornography could not be
shown to incite rape, and that it is difficult to determine the exact coverage of a moral taboo at a given place and time—were somewhat ir-
relevant to the question of whether traditionally tabooed patterns of behavior and expression ought to be placed outside the sphere of public
authority. The instantaneous, widespread appearance of establishments
specializing in pornographic films, books and magazines; the extreme
nature of some of the material; and the concomitant rise of live erotic
exhibitions eventually made the Supreme Court recoil, and in a 1973
decision, the right of localities to regulate various obscenities was
quietly restored.

Despite some oscillations of this kind, the social projects of the
courts continued to expand in scope even after the Era of Protest was
effectively over. Indeed, the several confrontations between the President and the federal judiciary in the course of the Watergate investiga-
tions demonstrated the extent to which the courts had acquired new
powers of law-making and law-enforcement, and of course reinforced
those powers by demonstration.

The three most impressive projects carried out during the judicial heyday of the early 1970s were the legalization of abortion, the abolition of capital punishment, and the enforcement of equal rights for women. In each instance, the courts preempted a controversial public issue and attempted to settle it out of hand.

In January 1973, in *Roe v. Wade* and *Doe v. Bolton,* the Supreme Court held the statutes regulating abortion in Texas and Georgia, and by implication in other states, to violate the Fourteenth Amendment by interfering with a woman's liberty without due process of law. Following its new style of active innovation, the Court's 7–2 decision proceeded in effect to lay down a national abortion statute, holding that during the first three months of pregnancy, a woman's right to have an abortion is immune from regulation by the state; that during the second three months, abortion may be mildly regulated to protect the health of the mother, and that during the final trimester of pregnancy, the state may regulate abortion as it pleases.

In the very same year, another Supreme Court decision, in the case of *Furman v. Georgia,* effectively abolished capital punishment in the United States, by holding that a statute which permitted any discretion in the application of the death penalty, left the way open for its discriminatory use. The Court had taken a long step in the same direction a little earlier by refusing to review the decision of a state court in California that capital punishment constituted cruel and unusual punishment in the light of present-day mores, and hence was prohibited by the Eighth Amendment. The desire of the Supreme Court to do away with the death penalty was clear; its choice of grounds seems to have been dictated by tactical considerations. Although it left the way apparently open for a mandatory death penalty for certain highly specific offenses like the murder of a prison guard by an inmate, the drafters of proposals to restore the death penalty, who sprang up in every state, found it remarkably difficult to devise a mandatory penalty that did not involve the exercise of discretion at some point in a given case to determine whether the mandatory penalty should apply.

The last of these great projects, the enactment of complete legal equality for women, turned into a curious race between the legislative and judicial branches. The proposed Equal Rights Amendment which read that, ''Men and Women shall have equal rights throughout the United States and every place subject to its jurisdiction. Congress

shall have power to enforce this article by appropriate legislation,''
was passed by the requisite two-thirds majority of Congress in March
1972, and sent to the legislatures of the several states for ratification.
In 1971, in the Reed case, the Supreme Court overturned an Idaho
statute which provided that of several persons claiming and equally entitled to administer an estate, males must be preferred to females, on
the ground that the arbitrary preference in favor of males violated the
equal protection clause of the Fourteenth Amendment. As this is written, 32 of the required 38 states have ratified the constitutional amendment, but various courts have meanwhile ruled that school teachers
may not be required to take maternity leaves, that the armed services
must treat women officers and officer candidates like men; that newspapers cannot classify help wanted ads by male and female preference,
that taverns cannot bar women customers, and that divorced husbands
are entitled to alimony. The amendment, if and when ratified, will be
almost supererogatory.

The Lessons Learned

1. The use of court decisions for large-scale projects of social improvement
is a constitutional innovation of enormous but enigmatic significance. The
speed, scope and efficiency of judicial projects is startling. Since lower courts
are bound to follow the rulings of higher courts, and state courts must defer to
federal courts on constitutional questions, an innovative decision by the Supreme Court takes almost immediate effect in all the multiple layers and com-
partments of government. The Court, when legislating, overrides without any
special effort the barriers between different spheres of action, and between
competing jurisdictions which ordinarily hamper the development and execution of unified national policies.

2. The courts are particularly well provided with competent agents to effect
the change from an existing condition to a desired end-condition, since all
public functionaries and many private ones can be drafted as agents of the
court by means of injunctions and other court orders, backed by the threat of
contempt penalties whenever the weight of public opinion does not suffice.

3. The judiciary is particularly effective in rooting out legitimized abuses
or obsolete practices which are so thoroughly worked into the fabric of government that no administrative policy or statute could hope to reach them all. The
abolition of official discrimination against members of racial minorities would

probably not have been feasible by any other means, if earlier experience with civil rights legislation and executive advocacy is any guide.

4. The same speed of action which figures among the advantages of judicial projects of social improvement may be counted as a disadvantage in a larger context, since it permits a decision about a controversial social issue to be made and carried out before the question has been resolved by public debate and the development of a majority consensus. The procedure, however democratic in form, is undemocratic in essence.

5. From the standpoint of project effectiveness, the characteristic defect of judicial projects of social improvement is an inability to visualize or cope with side effects and unanticipated consequences. Some side effects, like the increase of litigation which normally follows a groundbreaking decision, are intrinsic to the procedure of judicial problem-solving and may be counted as unavoidable costs, but others reflect the failure of the courts to obtain adequate feedback information in situations where it is patently called for. The history of school desegregation and legislative redistricting shows that the thing can be done, at least with respect to the direct and immediate effects of a court order. The examination of, and adjustment to, remoter consequences is hampered partly by procedural problems, but more gravely by the legal fiction whereby judges represent themselves as interpreting the existing law while engaged in making new law, and are thus self-prevented from treating their innovations as experimental, and subjecting them to empirical test.

6. However, it is relatively easy to devise ways and means of improving the effectiveness of judicial projects of social improvement, and much harder to determine the optimum limits of judicial intervention. On the basis of experience thus far, it appears that courts are most effective in achieving their goals when they strike down legislation or administrative procedures that block the way to a desired end-condition, but refrain from replacing them with detailed regulations of their own.

CHAPTER 13

Liberation Movements

WE noted earlier that what the Era of Protest protested was inequality of status rather than the inequality of wealth which had been the theme of revolutionary movements since the first stirrings of European socialism. The liberation movements of the 1960s were only peripherally concerned with stratification by wealth; when they talked about poverty, they were more likely to mean a denial of social equality than an empty purse. The inequality of occupational earnings was seldom mentioned and rarely criticized. The targets of change were those forms of status founded on personal characteristics: race, age, sex. Each sizeable racial minority developed its own liberation movement. Young people tried to shake off the authority of teachers and parents; women demanded total equality with men; and homosexuals challenged the moral superiority of heterosexuals.

Each of these liberation movements had its desired end-condition clearly in view: the removal of the status advantage enjoyed by people of one social condition vis-à-vis people of another.

In such cases, the status advantage of people in the superior category is both practical and subjective. Practically, they control social resources not available to the inferior category. Subjectively, they have higher self-esteem, based on social values which are not peculiar to themselves, but are held by people in the inferior category as well. The problem that confronts the strategists of every liberation movement is whether it is more profitable to attack the existing distribution of resources or the existing distribution of attitudes. The answer varies according to the circumstances but in the early phases of such a movement the emphasis usually falls on changing the attitudes of people in the inferior category so that they no longer acknowledge inferiority or submit to the dominance of people in the other category.

This is almost impossible to accomplish if the people in the superior category are collectively self-confident and united. When their self-confidence is shaken by ideological persuasion, or failures of collective policy, or an unfavorable shift of resources, some of them are likely to support the liberation movement in an active way, while those who resist it lack conviction.

Since liberation movements appear only when conditions are favorable, most of them enjoy considerable initial success in modifying the self-attitudes of people in the inferior category, limiting the pretensions of people in the superior category, and abolishing rituals of subordination. When it comes to equalizing resources, the results are much more uneven and depend on a variety of situational factors; in some cases, the original inequality may be reinforced rather than reduced.

The model for the liberation movements of the Era of Protest was supplied by the colonial liberation movements which arose throughout the colonial empires of the industrialized powers between the two world wars and triumphed in the wake of World War II, achieving independence for about a hundred new nations. The writings of such anti-colonial ideologists as Fanon, Senghor, and Guevara provided much of the rhetoric for Black Power, the Students for a Democratic Society, and the Women's Liberation movement. What most recommended this model was the consistent success of colonial liberation movements between 1945 and 1960. How much this success was attributable to changes in attitudes and values, and how much to military and economic developments, is difficult to determine, since the two series of events were intertwined.

The Cold War made it possible for every colonial liberation movement to obtain support from either the United States or the Soviet Union to spite the other, and sometimes from both; the shift from naval to air power diminished the value of overseas bases to the European powers; their preoccupation with economic growth at home distracted them from overseas interests at the same time that a worldwide surplus of raw materials reduced the economic value of a colony to the mother country to a negative figure. On balance, however, subjective factors were probably more important. The meaningless internecine slaughter of World War I, the period of political and economic stability which followed, the horrors of Nazi rule, the crushing defeat of the major colonial powers in the early stages of World War II, all undermined the confidence of Europeans and their descendants in the moral superiority of European civilization and in their own ability to administer the world, while the same events increased the relative self-esteem of their subjects.

The liberation movements of the Era of Protest had this same dual character. In each case, there had been a significant shift of resources in favor of the people claiming liberation—for example, the leverage that blacks acquired at the polls by virtue of their concentration in key cities; the decreased authority of academic administrators because of their new dependence on federal grants and subsidies; the autonomy conferred upon women by new types of contraception and by increased employment; the new bias of the judiciary in favor of social change; the development of a symbiotic relationship between social movements and television networks.

But in each case, the subjective factors seem at least equally important. The loss of national self-confidence which I tried to explain in a previous chapter was so extensive that it exposed every feature of American society to easy challenge, and made every social arrangement difficult to defend. The aura that normally protects the wielders of authority disappeared as if by magic, leaving them naked to their enemies. Their former followers rubbed their eyes and tried to understand why they had been so easily led.

From one perspective, the liberation movements we are going to discuss are not unique at all. Equality for blacks was certainly no new slogan. Women were demanding full parity with men a hundred years ago. Pedagogic authority has been pretty steadily eroding since the Civil War. Neither the causes nor their goals were new, and the progress they made toward equalization represented the continuation of a long-range trend but no new departure.

In certain other ways, these liberation movements *were* new (although isolated precedents can be dug up here and there). They shared a common hostility to the existing social order as a whole, which enabled them to place themselves outside it spiritually while demanding an amplification of their rights within it, just as the rebels against colonialism had denied the legitimacy of the colonial regime while working in a practical way to increase their participation in it. The tension between these two objectives made exciting political theater, which was fully exploited as long as its novelty could be sustained by the invention of new varieties of defiance, rites of protest and mock-violent confrontations. These dramatic demonstrations had an enormous impact on their audiences but could not be indefinitely prolonged, partly because it proved impossible to invent new forms of protest indefinitely, partly because the opposition absorbed the lessons of the long hot summers, the Chicago Convention, and the People's Park, and began to avoid dramatic confrontations; partly because mock violence had had a way of turning into real violence, as at Kent State; and most of all, perhaps, because the end of the Vietnam involvement removed the pin which held these diverse constituencies together and enabled them to make common cause not only with each other but with "oppressed peoples everywhere."

Another significant way in which the liberation movements of the Era of Protest differed from predecessor projects was that in addition to seeking a reduction of status inequality by claiming equality, they advanced their own counter-claims to at least a moral superiority.

The summaries of the three main types of liberation movements that follow do not do justice to their diversity, their inventiveness, nor their long-term implications. Our purpose, as usual, is to analyze them as projects of social improvement, to appraise their feasibility, and to try to find out what lessons they hold for the future.

The Liberation of
Racial Minorities

When the segregative barriers that kept them in a separate compartment began to come down in the 1950s, blacks could measure the full extent of their remaining social disadvantages. The inferior status of blacks within the larger social order was not much changed by desegregation, although the dependence of the black population was much reduced by the emergence of black majorities in the cities and the decreasing reliance of individual blacks upon the good will of individual whites for subsistence or safety.

The end-condition sought by the Black Power Movement in the United States is not easily described. For colonial liberation movements, national independence and the removal of Europeans from positions of authority solved the problem of status inferiority (without necessarily solving other social problems).

The difficulty in the American situation is that social class position is determined not only by race but also by possessions, lineage, organizational memberships, education, occupation, and income.

If all racial prejudice were suddenly to disappear, the lower average standing of the black population on each of these social indicators, would assure that blacks had lower status than whites, although nobody would then consider all blacks to be categorically inferior to all whites. Judging by the rate of progress toward equalization achieved during the Era of Protest, it is conceivable that the differences in education and occupational distribution between the two populations may be reduced to insignificance in a generation. Differences in wealth are more difficult to overcome; the existing distribution of capital, real property and personal possessions is the cumulative result of acquisitions over the past few centuries; blacks did not acquire much property in the past and have barely begun to do so now. Claims to social status based on lineage can only be equalized by a revolutionary re-evaluation of the past.

Faced with these impressive obstacles to the achievement of equal status within the American social order, black activists have explored alternative strategies but found none of them entirely satisfactory. One obvious possibility is the overthrow of the existing order by revolution. The defect in this strategy is that blacks would still constitute a relatively small and occupationally disadvantaged minority in a post-revolutionary society and might have fewer opportunities for collective self-advancement. The short-term disadvantage of a revolutionary strategy is that the white majority, being anti-revolutionary and to some extent anti-black, might welcome an opportunity to combine the two themes.

Another strategy is to embrace a new identity with a new pattern of social characteristics, as the Black Muslims have done. This is an interesting solution but it has not, for various reasons, attracted more than limited support.

Another possibility, of course, is to accept gradual status improvement as a substitute for the goal of status equality. This was the more or less successful course followed by the European immigrant populations which, at various times, stood on the lowest rung of the American status ladder. The strategy is reasonable, but not for a liberation movement. It implies a willingness to wait patiently for remote results that is not typical of the contemporary black population, who perceive the prejudice directed against them as more deep-seated and durable than the prejudices formerly directed against Irishmen, Poles, Jews, and Italians. By and large, the empirical evidence supports this perception. White respondents interviewed by the Michigan Institute for Social Research in 1970 expressed significantly less anti-Negro prejudice than a similar sample had expressed in 1964, but the magnitude of improvement during the Era of Protest was not overwhelming, the proportion of whites in favor of unqualified desegregation having increased from 27 percent in 1964 to 35 percent in 1970.[1]

Another option for the black liberation movement is to establish a separate black status order from which whites are excluded and refuse to participate as individuals in the status order of the larger society. The black liberationist who takes this course cultivates hostility toward whites and emphasizes his cultural separateness by distinctive dress, speech, and habits. An extreme version of this policy includes the establishment of armed camps whose boundaries are defended by force against white intruders. In the long run, this strategy must be self-defeating; the movement cannot hope to match the armed force available to the white majority, and the refusal to engage in peaceful relationships with whites denies blacks access to the cultural and economic resources of the larger society and penalizes them in much the same way as a system of segregation imposed from outside.

It is feasible, however, for blacks to seek access to educational and economic institutions on an individual basis and, once admitted, to form autonomous groups which engage in collective bargaining on behalf of their members. Out of context, it appears paradoxical for black students in a recently desegregated college to demand an all-black dormitory, but the underlying strategy is sound as long as collective interests take precedence over individual ambitions.

In the process of coping with these strategical choices, the participants in the black liberation movement in the Era of Protest, together with their non-black sympathizers, were faced with an apparent choice between two incompatible end-conditions: integration into the larger society on equal terms versus the creation of an autonomous black sub-society strong enough to claim a fair share of social rewards for its members. Taken separately, neither end-condition appeared really practicable, but the alternation of strategies directed toward one or the other of these end-conditions as indicated by the circumstances of a particular issue seemed, by the end of the Era of Protest, to be moving more rapidly than anyone had predicted a few years before toward equalization of blacks and whites with respect to education, occupational opportunities, health care, and legal rights. These changes had numerous consequences—anticipated and unanticipated—but none of them appeared to interfere in a serious way with the continuing trend toward equalization.

Other liberation movements arose and flourished during the Era of Protest among the Chicanos of the Southwest, the American Indians, and the Puerto Ricans of New York City.

The Chicanos, or Mexican-Americans, are estimated by the Bureau of the Census to number about five million, of whom only about seventeen percent were born in Mexico.[2] (Estimates of the same population by Chicano activists are considerably larger, ranging as high as twelve million.) Their numbers have recently increased very rapidly and they can be reasonably described as the second largest "racial" minority in the United States.

About eighty percent of this population is concentrated in the five Southwestern states of Arizona, California, Colorado, New Mexico and Texas, with the remainder scattered throughout the country. Despite their usual identification as agricultural laborers, the Chicanos appear to be somewhat more urbanized than the general population. They are also very much younger, with a median age in the neighborhood of 17. Their average family earnings, as recorded in the 1970 Census, were almost identical with those of blacks, although their average educational achievement was somewhat lower. Of Mexican-Americans over 25 in 1970, about twenty-six percent had graduated from high school, compared with thirty-five percent of blacks and fifty-six percent of whites.

Unlike blacks, Chicanos are not unambiguously identified by their fellow Americans as a racial minority. In districts where they are heavily concentrated, they have often been treated as such. In other parts of the country they have no distinct identity in the eyes of outsiders. Thus, the discrimination against which the Chicano Liberation Movement is directed has a much more local character than discrimination against blacks.

In California and Arizona, there was some formal segregation of schools and other institutions in the past, and throughout the Southwest, various devices, from voting tests to the gerrymandering of electoral districts, have been used to limit the political influence of Mexican-American voters. In addition, the Chicano Liberation Movement is strongly identified with the cause of migrant agricultural laborers, especially in California where the largest number of them are Chicanos. The strikes of the lettuce and grape pickers and their accompanying boycotts, which attracted a measure of national support during the Era of Protest, were closely associated with the Chicano movement.

The goals of the movement are economic and educational equalization, political representation proportional to their numbers, use of the Spanish language in schools and in public agencies dealing with Chicanos, and official assistance with respect to the equalization of educational, occupational, and social opportunities. Like black activists, the Chicanos oscillate between two visualized end-conditions: integration or autonomy. But in the Chicano case, the dilemma is less acute since, on the one hand, barriers to integration are much less formidable and, on the other hand, the regional concentration of the Chicano population and their proximity to Mexico make it easy for them to visualize a condition of limited autonomy based on continued attachment to Hispanic culture.

The Chicano liberation movement has a doctrine centered on the theme of *la rasa* and a picturesque ideology that sometimes includes a claim tor the independence of the Indian nation of Aztlán (an

Aztec name for the northern provinces of Montezuma's empire). More explicitly than black activists, the Chicano activists preach group solidarity, withdrawal from friendly relationships with Anglos, the assertion of a separate identity, group discipline at the polls, and collective bargaining in institutional situations. The rhetoric of the Chicano movement is so poetic that its announced hostility toward Anglos is unconvincing, and Chicano activism has not aroused nearly as much alarm in the larger society as black activism. The available evidence, although it is not thoroughly conclusive, suggests that the recent progress of Chicanos toward educational and occupational equalization has been relatively more rapid than that of blacks.

The Native American Liberation Movement is much more difficult to sum up. Between 1940 and 1970, the Indian population of the United States approximately doubled, to three quarters of a million, a number somewhat exceeding the accepted estimate of the aboriginal population at the time of the first European settlement. The Indians now identifiable are those who have retained their tribal identities and have not disappeared into the surrounding community. About half of them live on rural reservations and are appallingly poor. Most of the remainder live in the central districts of metropolitan cities to which they have migrated with the encouragement of government agencies, and where, with some notable exceptions, they have been unable to establish a secure foothold in the urban occupational structure.

Reservation housing is generally dilapidated, overcrowded and unsanitary. The educational and health levels of most reservations are relatively low, and their median family incomes are well below the poverty line in many instances. Reservation Indians, as noted in the previous chapter, are the beneficiaries of one of the oldest and least effective social service programs in the world. The program has operated for a full century without achieving any of its major goals and without being able to choose between a policy of encouraging assimilation and the contradictory policy of preserving tribal cultures.

The Red Power movement developed within this framework. Its immediate objectives have been to obtain an increase of government benefits and services, to revive old land claims, and to resist the encroachment of real estate developers in tribal areas. It rejects assimilation and advocates a return to tribalism.

Indian activists have staged a number of dramatic demonstrations, including the prolonged occupation of Alcatraz Island, the successful campaign of the Taos Indians to recover Blue Lake from the Carson National Forest, the occupation and looting of the Washington offices of the Bureau of Indian Affairs, and the 1973 seizure of the village of Wounded Knee.

Although the native American liberation movement has a superficial resemblance to the two movements previously discussed, and was partly inspired by them, its program differs surprisingly from theirs. The dilemma of integration versus cultural autonomy has a much longer history in the case of the Indians and is closely tied to questions of tribal sovereignty and land ownership which have no parallel at all in the experience of other American minorities. Between the end of the Indian wars in the 1880s, and the appearance of the Indian resistance in the 1960s, it was the federal government acting through its Bureau of Indian Affairs which took the initiative in setting long-range goals, often opting for integration as in the Dawes Act of 1887, which attempted to provide for the orderly passage of Indian lands from communal to private ownership, and became instead a vehicle for the enrichment of outside speculators; the gradual extension of full citizenship to tribal members after World War I; and the termination experiments of the 1950s, in which such prosperous tribal organizations as the Menominees and the Klamaths were dissolved; and, of course, the urban relocation programs conducted by the Bureau of Indian Affairs in the 1960s. The opposite choice, to preserve the cultural heritage of the Indian tribes by supporting and strengthening tribal organization, has been made at intervals by the same agency, although generally with less conviction. For the native American movement, the upshot of this long experience is that detribalization is a form of expropriation. Hence, the choice between integration and autonomy presents no dilemma. The desired end-condition is tribal autonomy and the restoration of lost communal lands or restitution for them. The difficulties that attend this project proceed in part from the diversity of tribes and cultures involved and the difficulty of defining any common policy to serve their myriad interests, and in part from the contradiction between the desired end-condition and the rapid urbanization of the Indian population which is under way.

The Puerto Rican liberation movement, although closely related to the black liberation movement and using parallel language and tactics with respect to local issues in New York City, centers on a very different set of problems. Puerto Rico, as everyone knows, is a densely populated Caribbean Island acquired by the United States, together with Cuba and the Philippines, as spoils of the Spanish-American War of 1898. While the other two colonies eventually obtained independence, Puerto Rico developed a special status which represented a genuinely innovative form of colonial relationship. Under this arrangement, Puerto Rico as an ''Associated Commonwealth'' is nominally sovereign. Its people have a legal (although untested) right to sever their relationship with the United States and assume national independence at any time. In the meantime, they enjoy a kind of dual citizenship which includes the obligation of military service, free access to the mainland, and participation in federal welfare programs of all types. The Commonwealth has its own organic law and its own system of economic management. It enjoys the exclusive use of its own revenues, paying no taxes to the federal government in return for the benefits and services it receives. Since 1935, when this arrangement was put into effect, Puerto Rico has modernized more rapidly than any other part of Latin America. Despite a vast increase of population, per capita income has risen much faster. Meanwhile, the culture and the language of the island have been hybridized by the addition of many non-Hispanic elements. At any given moment, nearly a million Puerto Ricans live in New York City and the immediate vicinity. Reverse immigration is so frequent and family ties are so well maintained that no sharp distinction can be drawn between the migrant and non-migrant populations.

The Puerto Rican liberation movement really involves two quite separate projects, although they are sometimes combined rhetorically. One project, which closely resembles that of the Chicanos, is directed toward the increase of political representation, the enlargement of job opportunities, a measure of control over local schools and the recognition of Spanish as an official language in the New York area, where the overwhelming majority of the Puerto Ricans in the United States are found. The goals of this project are attainable and a variety of means for pursuing them are at hand.

The other project of the Puerto Rican liberation movement has as its end-condition the political independence of Puerto Rico from the United States. It resembles other colonial independence movements in having a precisely defined end-condition, a division of the project into easily visualized stages, and an inventory of well-tested methods of getting from each stage to the next. In the Puerto Rican case, the problem of selecting a method for achieving independence is simplified by the statute establishing the Commonwealth, which provides, at least on paper, for automatic independence whenever a majority of the island's voting population so decide. Nevertheless, the project of independence has so far made very little progress because of the inability of its initiators to find any plausible solutions for the problems that independence would create for that large fraction of the Puerto Rican population who now move freely back and forth from the mainland.

The Liberation of
the Young

The student liberation movement grew out of the participation of white college students in the civil rights campaigns of the early 1960s and out of student protests against the Vietnam War. Opposition to white racism and to the Vietnam War were the cardinal points of the movement's ideology. In its most active phase, beginning with the Berkeley Free Speech demonstrations in 1965 and ending with the Kent State shootings of 1969, these two themes took precedence over all others, and the temptation to explain the movement as an expression of the political frustrations experienced by young Americans would be nearly irresistible, were it not for the puzzling fact that parallel student liberation movements appeared at about the same time in more than a dozen countries which had neither the Vietnam War nor racial injustice to answer for. In England, France, Germany, Italy and Japan the student uprisings of the late 1960s shook the social structure as profoundly as the corresponding American events and led to more drastic reorganizations of higher education. Moreover, by some unexplained historical quirk, the same years witnessed a wave of student rebellions in countries with quite different political systems and national issues—Czechoslovakia, Rumania, Spain, Colombia, and China, among others. No one, to my knowledge, has offered a plausible explanation for this concurrence. Direct imitation played some part—the Sorbonne Revolt of May 1968 was certainly inspired by the happenings at Columbia a few weeks earlier—but hardly seems to account for the whole phenomenon. The overcrowding and bureaucratization of universities are often mentioned, but it is not clear why these factors became critical at the same time in countries at varying levels of educational development.

Considered in its narrowest sense, that is, solely in relation to academic authority, the student liberation movement in the United States presented five basic demands: that college and university administrators abdicate their authority over the personal lives and extracurricular conduct of students, that the same authorities abandon any claim to restrict or censor the political activities of students but submit instead to some degree of political restriction and censorship by students, that students participate in decisions about the content and form of instruction and the requirements for degrees, that students participate in the administrative evaluation of individual students and faculty members at various points in their careers, and finally, that the testing and grading of student performance be reduced or eliminated.

From a tactical standpoint, the most striking feature of the student liberation movement was that although it was a rebellion against both administrative and faculty authority, it enjoyed widespread faculty support and, in many places, profited from active faculty leadership. Some of these elder brothers were able to discover student grievances that students had never perceived:

Where a hotel or motel, for example, provides in its budget for normal wear and tear and a reasonable level of theft of linens and equipment and quietly covers itself with liability insurance, the school—though it may actually do the same thing—pompously indoctrinates its students with "respect for public property," "good health habits," and so forth before it lets them near the swimming pool.[3]

Faculty support for the student liberation movement was not entirely disinterested. Professors are no better disposed towards their administrative superiors than other bureaucratic employees, and the student revolts weakened the authority of deans and presidents over faculties much more than the authority of teachers over students. In many institutions, radical students played the role of *sans-culottes* tearing down the Bastille of administrative authority for the eventual benefit of a rising middle class.

The results achieved by the student liberation movement had a coherent pattern although they varied in detail from one place to another. The demand for a lessening of administrative authority over students was uniformly successful. The parietal rules whereby residential colleges and universities had formerly separated the living accommodations of men and women students, prohibited sexual intercourse in dormitories and forbidden the cohabitation of unmarried students, were weakened or abolished. The power of educational administrators to punish students for deviant conduct was greatly reduced although some vestigial authority was retained with respect to cheating, vandalism, and other strictly intramural matters. Students gained a nearly unrestricted right to join political organizations, to engage in political activities on and off the campus and to express dissident views in speech or writing. Censorship of college newspapers became impracticable except in the most remote and parochial institutions. At the same time, the quasi-political activities of educational administrators were placed under a measure of student control; some institutions were persuaded to liquidate their investments in corporations disapproved of by students, to refuse a platform to lecturers of rightist views, to terminate the training of reserve officers, to prohibit research related to military purposes and to turn away personnel recruiters from certain companies and public agencies. The freedom of action of administrators with respect to admissions policies, employee relations, the conduct of public ceremonies, collaboration with the civil authorities, institutional expansion, physical planning, and a variety of routine matters was considerably curtailed by student demands.

With respect to the reduction of faculty authority, the student liberation movement was much less successful. Grading systems were somewhat liberalized in most institutions, and curricular requirements were softened in various ways. There was a great vogue for experimental and informal courses and a perceptible trend away from mass lectures, but these innovations did not have any decisive effect on student-faculty relationships. Some of them had the unintended result of increasing the individual student's dependence on faculty good will. For example, students who graduate from a college which does not issue grades must rely on letters of recommendation from former teachers when they apply for admission to graduate or professional schools. With respect to the evaluation of student applicants for promotion and honors and of faculty candidates at various levels, most faculties were able to maintain their prerogatives.

The overwhelming success of the student liberation movement with respect to administrative authority left little room for further achievement in that sector; the problems of academic governance in the 1970s had much more to do with administrative helplessness than with administrative tyranny. In the faculty-student relationship the collective authority of the faculty in relation to the student body appears stronger than before, now that the powers of governing boards, presidents, deans and business managers have been so sharply circumscribed.

Closely associated with the student liberation movement was the project of achieving a new social order by adopting new ways of perceiving and reacting to the external world and one's own experience. The elements of this new consciousness were enumerated in the project's most influential manifesto, Charles Reich's *The Greening of America*. Included in these were the liberation of the individual from automatic acceptance of the imperatives of society; recognition of the individual self as the only true reality; a refusal to compete with others or to evaluate them by general standards; a view of the whole world as a community; the rejection of coercion, authority and fixed roles; the substitution of honesty and impulse for duties and contractual relations; antagonism to social institutions; a personal commitment to the welfare of the community and to social change; openness to any and all experience; and adherence to a style of behavior (often called the counterculture) which included identifying styles of hair and dress, a distinctive vocabulary, rock music, and a variety of euphoriant drugs. In a chapter entitled "Revolution by Consciousness" Reich argued that social problem-solving by legal and political means had failed, that civil liberties had declined, that projects of social reform had brought the country to the brink of fascism, and that the corporate state was too powerful to be opposed by conventional means. But, he

went on to say, the road to the perfect society was open nevertheless:

Consciousness is capable of changing and of destroying the Corporate State,
without violence, without seizure of political power, without overthrow of any
existing people . . . Should Consciousness III sweep the country, the Federal
government could simply be ignored until it became completely isolated from
the people of the nation and had no choice but to change. At that point, the
President would have to don bell-bottoms and a dirty T-shirt and go looking
for his constituents.[4]

Another advocate of consciousness-changing wrote:

Youth demands that basic needs be met without toil, that the patriarchal family be abandoned as authoritarian, that 'junk' production stop, that private
property be abolished, and that formal education be either revised or dumped.
Youth opposes the entire way of thinking that has served as a vehicle for
scientific and technical achievement in the West.[5]

And here is the version of a very sophisticated but unsympathetic observer:

In Russia and America alike, the alterationists would plead, men study physics and build the bomb, worship the ego and fear their own bodies, ban heroin
and drink alcohol, so what is there to choose? The world apparently cannot be
changed by fiat or force of arms, by understanding or revolution, but what can
be altered is the range of our perception and its mode. We can *see* a different
world without firing a shot or framing a syllogism merely by altering our consciousness and the ways to alter it are at hand: drugs, on one hand, the techniques of oriental adepts on the other. . . .[6]

As a style of behavior, the counterculture evolved gradually. Its
prototype was the existentialist style of the Parisian quarter of St.-Ger-
main-des-Prés in the late 1940s although two central elements, hallucinogens and rock music, were not introduced until much later. In lieu
of an ideology, the young people who embraced the counterculture
during the Era of Protest held certain obligatory opinions—obligatory
in the sense that agreement with them was taken for granted throughout their vast informal fellowship. These opinions included beliefs in
the absolute wickedness of the Vietnam War, the moral superiority of
the young, the existence of an oppressive Establishment, racial equality and spontaneous self-expression, a prejudice against any form of
sexual regulation, and the certainty that magic, astrology, Eastern

mysticism and organic foods ought to be taken seriously. These odds and ends of opinion reflected the products that were successfully marketed to the followers of the counterculture and the ideological promoters who succeeded in engaging their attention: Marcuse and his ambiguous call to violence, Norman O. Brown with the message of polymorphous sexuality, homosexual proselytizers like Ginsberg and Burroughs, the advertising agents of hallucinogens and hashish, theologians specializing in blasphemy, and professors of education calling for the abolition of schools. The middle-aged entrepreneurs of the counterculture often seemed to be having more fun than their youthful audience.

A full-blown change of consciousness implies disaffiliation from organizations involved in the social division of labor and a refusal of obedience to the norms of such organizations. The individual may continue to participate in the organization so long as he repudiates its moral authority. For example, he may continue to live with his parents or to be supported by them, but ought not to offer them any special respect. He may live peaceably with a woman who bears his child provided that their relationship is not regarded as a permanent bond. He may work at a job but not with any commitment to his employer's purposes. He attends church for an experience of communality or ecstasy but never to support the institution by his presence. He prides himself on his honesty and kindness and at the same time, on his unwillingness to make a binding promise or fulfill the expectation of others.

These mannerisms are sustained by a conviction that social institutions are inherently bad and that truth, goodness and beauty are properties of the presocial human animal which can only be realized in unorganized forms of social interaction. The virtues of the natural human are held to be corrupted by any form of specialization, even specialization by sex or by age, and by any form of compulsion derived from the assignment of tasks in a division of labor or from the occupancy of positions in a status hierarchy. Man is good; society perverts him and the more advanced and intricate the society, the greater the perversion. Civilization is a mistake; the individual has a duty to undo it. Rationality itself may be viewed as a social problem. ''We may therefore entertain the hypothesis,'' writes Brown, ''that formal logic and the law of contradiction are the rules whereby the mind sub-mits to operate under general conditions of repression.'' [7]

The perfect society of the counterculture's vision turns out to be a society without social institutions, the same dreamlike end-condition to which the young Marx alluded in *The German Ideology* and which a modern commentator on that work summarizes as follows:

> Socialized humanity is humanity brought back into total harmony with itself by the abolition of the antagonism inherent in the social division of labor. All subordinate expressions of the division of labor and the antagonisms inherent in it vanish along with the basic one. Socialized humanity is not only a class-less but also a stateless, lawless, family-less, religion-less and generally structureless collectivity of complete individuals who live in harmony with themselves, with each other, and with the anthropological nature outside them. [8]

Earlier in this book, we traced the discouraging evolution of Marxist doctrine from this happy vision of perfection to the practical project of combining all the productive enterprises of a country into one giant firm wherein the worker's good behavior is assured by a combination of continuous indoctrination and iron discipline. The pathos is too fa-miliar to need any underscoring. The promise of perfect freedom in a perfect society leads inexorably to the insensitive tyranny that becomes possible when the dismantling of every other institution gives the state unlimited authority.

The counterculture is not so much a symptom of the Era of Protest; it is the thing itself—the public rejection of social institutions that have lost their sacred character because of their apparent inefficacy. Not all the damage done to these symbols is likely to be restored. Flag etiquette, filial respect, the restriction of obscenity, clerical celibacy, and the alma mater spirit are unlikely to return in their 1960 forms in the foreseeable future. On the other hand, new pious sentiments, in the best sense, have been springing up at the same time—respect for the environment, sexual democracy, an activist religion, a passionate egalitarianism in politics and a new set of ethnic loyalties. The proj-ect of revolution by consciousness-changing is absurd if the end-condi-tion of an institutionless society is taken seriously; it is less absurd if it compels institutions to acknowledge the failure of some of their major projects so that new and sounder projects can be undertaken.

The Liberation
of Women

The women's liberation movement came relatively late in the Era
of Protest, not really beginning until 1969, and the organizations supporting it were weak and ephemeral. It was more a fashion in popular
literature than an organized social movement. Nevertheless, its short-
term effects were far reaching and its long-term effects are incalculable, if only because of the size of the constituency and the fundamental character of the issues. It represents the culmination of a
trend described in the first chapter of this book, whereby features of
human existence once regarded as part of nature and outside the sphere
of human control have come to be regarded as subject to human manipulation. The ideologists of the movement widened the sphere of
social problems by criticizing aspects of social life that had almost
always in the past been ascribed to human nature rather than to the
social order—sexual love, childbearing and the lesser aggressivity of
women compared to men. As a literary fashion, the movement exhausted itself by excess. Its program, originally announced as the removal of the economic and social disabilities imposed on women
because of their sex, came to include the dissolution of the nuclear
family, and eventually, the abolition of mating and natural gestation.
Between the publication of Betty Friedan's *Feminine Mystique* [9] in
1963 and Shulamith Firestone's *The Dialectic of Sex* [10] in 1970, the
goals become increasingly ambitious, until "Feminists have to question not just all of Western culture, but the organization of culture itself and further, even the very organization of nature. For we are
dealing with an oppression that goes back beyond recorded history to
the animal kingdom itself."

But if the end-condition to be achieved grew hazier with the
progress of the movement, the immediate goals became more definite.
They included increased opportunities for women in professional,
managerial, and official occupations; the removal of income differen-
tials between men and women workers; proportional representation of
women in legislatures, political parties, governing boards and other
authoritative bodies; the suppression of laws and customs interfering

with the ability of women to determine when and if to bear children; the removal of the social disabilities of unmarried and divorced women by forbidding employers and officials to inquire about marital status, and by the use of the neutral title, Ms.; the provision of public day-care facilities to give women with small children full access to employment and recreation; the abolition of legal and customary restrictions on the sexual activities of women and of all forms of obligatory segregation by sex.

Long before women's liberation had played out as a literary fashion, the realization of the foregoing program was well underway. Between 1967 and 1972, nearly every important institution of higher education formerly segregated by sex began to admit students of the opposite sex. Publicly supported institutions were compelled to do so by court orders which invoked the ban on separate-but-equal accommodations against institutions which excluded women. Women began to apply for and obtain appointment as officer cadets; the first female general officers were named; the Navy announced a plan to send women to sea on its ships. Women obtained injunctions admitting them to all-male taverns and clubs. The guidelines for the selection of political delegates were revised to give women equal representation among the Democrats and a vast increase in representation among the Republicans. Abortion was legalized in a few key states and, soon after, nationally; federal agencies began to plan for a vast network of publicly supported daycare centers. Employers of all kinds were required to demonstrate that they were not discriminating against women in hiring and promotion. Women applied for and obtained licenses as jockeys. Local ordinances against prostitution were challenged in the courts and became inoperative. Women orators and entertainers used obscene language in public as freely as their male colleagues and were less subject to censure for it.

The long-term significances of these changes could not be so easily gauged. With respect to occupational equalization, the gains made by women during this period were perhaps more symbolic than real, but given the lapse of time required for any major shift of occupational distribution, this was unsurprising. With respect to coeducation, the elimination of segregation by sex in schools and colleges completed a process that had been underway for a hundred years. The availability of abortion complemented the infallible contraceptives that had become available a decade before and further equalized the situation of men and women with respect to their sexual involvements. The disengagement of the law from the enforcement of sanctions against prostitution and promiscuity was part of a much larger decline in moral consensus.

There was virtually no overt opposition to the program described above. Public officials were understandably reluctant to alienate half of their constituencies, or to offend their wives and daughters by taking an anti-feminist position. But men continued to oppose a clandestine resistance to the acceptance of women as occupational equals or superiors and this might be expected to persist into the foreseeable future. The other factor that tended to set limits to the liberation of women was the apparent satisfaction of large numbers of married women with the status quo and their apparent unwillingness to modify their domestic roles. The appeals of the movement were largely directed to college-educated women with career ambitions, the working mothers of small children and older women without husbands. These categories taken together, although impressively numerous, do not add up to a majority of adult women and are not likely to do so as long as present trends in marriage, divorce and labor force participation persist.

The Lessons Learned

1. Liberation movements, like other projects of social improvement, succeed or fail according to their ability to assemble the essential elements of a feasible project. None of the liberation movements just reviewed succeeded completely in reducing the status inequalities against which they were directed, but all of them made appreciable progress in that direction. Each of them was stopped considerably short of its desired end-condition either because of the falling away of participants when they felt their other interests to be jeopardized or because of stiffening resistance from outsiders whose interests were indirectly challenged, or from both causes at once.

2. To the extent that every institutionalized pattern of social status inequality is tied to the division of labor and the management of social institutions, as both cause and effect, it is probably not possible for an established condition

of status inequality between large groups to be totally removed in the short-run unless the institutions in which they are jointly involved are totally destroyed. But when that happens, new institutions must be created to carry on the business of society, and with those new institutions some new forms of status inequality, as well as the reinstatement of some old forms, must be expected.

3. Although it is surprisingly difficult to abolish status inequality, it has proved surprisingly easy to reduce it significantly whenever the people in the disadvantaged group can be sufficiently aroused by rhetorical appeals to unite, if only briefly, behind a set of specific and plausible demands for measures of equalization.

4. The members of the privileged group are induced to accede to such demands partly to avoid the institutional breakdown that might occur if the disadvantaged group withdrew its cooperation altogether; partly because they themselves find the rhetoric of protest at least partly persuasive. The latter factor is particularly important at low points in the cycle of social confidence when the managers of social institutions are assailed by self-doubt and there appears to be a real and imminent danger of institutional collapse.

5. A liberation movement necessarily secures its results by means of dramatic and highly symbolized confrontation. Such episodes are short and sharp and tend to fall into series of first ascending and then descending intensity. Neither the episode nor the series can be indefinitely prolonged. Whether its scale is as small as a cafeteria strike or as large as a national revolution, a liberation movement has only a few moments of opportunity and its ultimate results are determined by what is done or not done at those critical points.

6. As devices of social problem-solving, liberation movements have an ambiguous character because the solutions offered by those who want to remove existing inequalities become problems for those who want to maintain them. Urban blacks, responding collectively to the problems created for them by whites, create new problems for whites in their turn. The most interesting feature of this opposition is that it does not preclude the successful collaboration of two such factions in the development of feasible projects—like the improvement of urban education—which both factions can support for different reasons.

CHAPTER 14

The Good Society

WE have been suggesting all along that the perfect society is a mirage. A society can only be perfect (that is, free of recognized social problems) if it is not a real society at all *or* if it prohibits complaints or criticisms by its members. The perennial dream of a post-revolutionary society without any division of labor is an example of the first alternative. Plato's vision of a society in which the governing myths are composed once and for all by philosophers and never questioned thereafter illustrates the second alternative, as do the China of Chairman Mao and the Haiti of Sonny Duvalier. As we have seen, the quest for the first type of perfect society—the society without any institutions or constraints—has frequently led to the second type of perfect society—the state which punishes all dissent. The pursuit of absolute freedom, when embodied in a social movement and translated into political action, seems to lead almost inevitably to tyranny, either because the believers in perfection triumph and find themselves surrounded by non-believers who must be suppressed or because the defenders of established institutions use the threat of a perfectionist rebellion as an excuse for establishing a patchwork perfectionism of their own, with the usual thought control and secret police.

The project of a perfect society purports to bring out the essential goodness in all men. It takes no account of their essential evil because it blames evil on defective social institutions such as Christianity, private property, or the conjugal family. In one form or another the proposition that man is basically good until corrupted by society has been found plausible by millions of people in the past two centuries and it has repeatedly shaken to their foundations the social institutions of both modernized and unmodernized countries. In terms of the sociological evidence, it was a dubious proposition from the beginning and the numerous efforts made to put it into practice have not provided any confirmation whatever. The social systems and social movements framed in accordance with the doctrine of original virtue exhibit the characteristic forms of aggression just as abundantly as conventional social systems, together with an extra supply of hypocrisy.

By hypocrisy, I mean the habit of evaluating one's own behavior or the behavior of one's own group more favorably than one evaluates similar behavior by others. By aggression, I mean the habit of obtaining satisfaction by inflicting injury. Aggression is a widespread mammalian trait and appears to be universal among subhuman primates. Hypocrisy is an exclusively human trait, arising from our ability to represent and misrepresent reality by means of symbols. Every working social system exhibits both aggression and hypocrisy, and to survive must regulate and harness them, rewarding those patterns of aggressive and hypocritical behavior that contribute to collective purposes.

Aggression is regulated by a variety of devices, for example, by organized contests that permit intensely aggressive conduct but limit its consequences, or by the division of the social universe into near and far sectors with respect to which different degrees of aggression are permitted. The most fundamental device for containing aggression appears to be the establishment of a social hierarchy in which the expression of aggression is channeled and supports the achievement of collective tasks.

Hypocrisy is likewise controlled by a gamut of basic devices that are as old as human society and that transcend particular cultures. Hypocrisy is formalized and made socially useful by ceremonies wherein the participants express sentiments which fit the occasion but do not necessarily correspond to their subjective feelings; by rituals in which people pretend to be animals or personages that they are not; by creeds which require the believer to express knowledge of things not in his own experience, and by the encouragement of self-aggrandizement in the service of collective interests.

A project which proposes to purify human nature of aggression and hypocrisy is not feasible in the present state of knowledge. We cannot abandon our organic heritage to the point of becoming consistently nonaggressive. Aggression is too closely linked with sexuality and feeding, territory and the reflex avoidance of dangers, to be permanently abandoned by any sizeable population. (The abandonment of aggressive behavior by certain morally gifted individuals is admired as a prodigious and rare achievement.) Likewise, we cannot eliminate hypocrisy from an organized social system because all social systems require a selective revelation of the individual's subjective experience to his fellows.

The mass of ordinary people caught up in ordinary social systems are continuously aware of these constraints but cannot articulate them clearly and they react with fear and fascination to the perfectionists' claim to be better than they themselves can possibly become and the perfectionists' offer to break down the barriers which hold in check their own aggressive impulses and those of others.

The new hypocrites have a clear advantage over the old hypocrites because, in principle, they are opposed to hypocrisy itself and adherence to this principle gives them a conviction of moral superiority that is difficult to overcome. With respect to aggression, the perfectionists figure as victims in the early stages of a perfectionist movement when their means of reprisal are limited; but are very likely to be oppressors when the movement becomes more successful and the overriding importance attached to its goals justifies a degree of ruthlessness in the extirpation of opponents from which the less confident agents of a conventional society might shrink.

If the dream of a perfect society is a snare and delusion, the hope of a good society is not. The perfect society, when attempted, solves its social problems by refusing to hear any complaints. A good society, by contrast, has many unsolved problems, since its members are permitted to criticize institutions and to set about changing them. Many, or most, of the criticisms cancel each other out. Relatively few of the myriad proposals for social improvement that are launched in such a society come to command a majority, and those that do may not be pushed to completion for various reasons.

In a good society, synergy—as Ruth Benedict named the convergence of private and collective interests—is high. The individual who pursues his own interests generally does so with the conviction that he is pursuing the good of his fellows at the same time. Aggressive contests are conducted with reasonable adherence to the rules. Relationships of superiority and subordination are based on familiar and workable assumptions. The suffering of individuals is relieved by spontaneous collective action. Coercion is used sparingly in the enforcement of norms because the norms are largely self-enforcing. The larger social system is compartmented into many small systems which operate more or less autonomously and provide most people with a wide variety of social relationships and considerable opportunity to change roles. The present is attributed—with some satisfaction—to the successful projects of the past and the future is expected—with some satisfaction—to emerge from the ongoing projects of the present.

It is not by chance that many perfectionist movements, like Marxism and the counterculture, begin with a theory of historical inevitability which says in effect that history is the outcome of blind forces and not the result of deliberate human projects, and that it follows a sequence of stages which must necessarily culminate in the perfect society.

The theme of this book has been exactly the reverse, that history can only be understood as the outcome of deliberate human projects, an outcome that includes both the intended consequences of such projects and their accidental and unanticipated results. In this picture, there are many imponderables but few blind forces and there is no way of reducing all social problems to a single social problem whose solution would put a stop to all our troubles. Likewise, I have tried to demonstrate that when an important project fails, the failure can usually be explained by flaws in the project design without recourse to historical inevitability.

When we reviewed the history of social improvement in the United States, we saw how a good society is not something to be achieved once and for all—like a perfect society—but something which can be found and lost and found again. We must not tire of repeating that social problems are statements about the real world in relation to subjective preferences. The inequality of income is an empirically verifiable fact but it only becomes a social problem when a large number of us make it so by wanting income equality and it ceases again to be a social problem when we lose interest in the question or are content with a particular distribution of income.

The cycle of social confidence has not been studied nearly as much as the business cycle and its operation is much less well understood. We do not know, for example, whether there are elements in any peak of confidence that generate a subsequent decline or if the cycle merely reflects the impossibility of maintaining a constant adaptation between a social system and an unstable environment.

Social confidence is a collective sentiment, not a technical condition. The attachment of individuals to a social system is influenced but not determined by the system's performance. Some societies are able to maintain and even increase confidence while their measurable effectiveness declines, while other societies suffer substantial losses of confidence as their levels of achievement rise.

Anomalies of this kind may be explained in two different ways. Acting rationally, the participants in a social system evaluate its success by comparing its performance with some expectation they have formed. If their expectation remains unchanged and the performance improves or deteriorates, their confidence in the system will rise and fall accordingly. If, however, their expectations rise while the performance of the system remains more or less constant, their confidence will fall. If the system's performance and the expectations of its members change simultaneously, the effects are more complex, but not inscrutable.

It may be objected that this explanation only isolates the question further by compelling us to ask why the expectations held by the members of a given social system changed during a particular period of time. But this further question may be readily answerable in a given case. Expectations are readily changed by exhortation and example. More often than not, it is possible to identify some of the particular exhorters or examples that made the difference.[1]

The other way of explaining peaks and troughs of social confidence that are not adequately accounted for by fluctuations in a system's performance, is to bring the irrational elements of social confidence into the picture. All social systems are held together by sacred symbols, which embody the collective life of the organized group. The sacredness of the symbol is experienced, not inferred. The individual in the presence of the sacred symbol has a direct sensation of the power and moral force of the organized group and it is this sensation, rather than any objective evaluation of the group's collective performance, that accounts for his initial confidence. In order for confidence in a social system to increase, according to this explanation, the sacredness of its symbols must be enhanced by an increase in their number or quality, or by new proofs of their efficacy. Any successful sacrilege reduces social confidence and thereby imperils the continued existence of the social system in which it occurs. Sacrileges may be performed deliberately for this very purpose, to demonstrate that the sacred symbols do not have the power attributed to them and that their protective taboos can be violated with impunity. Or sacrilege may occur by accident, when the sacred symbols are damaged or spoiled or made ridiculous by uncontrollable events.

These alternatives explanations of the cycle of social confidence are not contradictory. In exceptional cases, an affiliation with a social system may be based exclusively on rational or on sentimental motives, but most affiliations involve a mixture of both.

The loss of national solidarity is both an effect and a cause of a rapid decline of social confidence. Every social system has its own way of coming apart at the seams. European nations, in times of trouble, seem to dissolve into a cacophony of non-communicating groups. Latin American nations turn to guerrilla activity and civil war. China and India fragment into isolated provinces. The United States polarizes into two camps. This occurred in the prolonged political crisis of the 1790s, the years of the slavery issue, the Civil War and Reconstruction; in the confrontation of industrialism and agrarianism in the 1890s, of wets and the dries in the Prohibition era, of the New Deal and its enemies, of the New Left and the Silent Majority.

Such splits are painful for all concerned. They have some of the peculiar bitterness we associate with conflict among intimates. The lines of division run through families, friendships, peer groups, and local associations. Each side has moments of paranoid panic because the other side appears to be strong, hostile, and gaining strength. (The impression on each side that the other side is gaining strength is quite accurate during the rising phase of a crisis; it results from the recruitment of formerly neutral or indifferent persons to one faction or the other.) Thus, men of reasonably good will see a police state as imminent while their neighbors are complaining that the police have been made helpless by judicial interference, and both find evidence to confirm their apprehensions.

The dominating social problem in a social system that has split into mutually distrustful factions is to recover collective confidence in the system as a whole. This cannot be accomplished by exhortation or by the victory of one faction. It requires a renewal of societal success, that is, the development of projects which command widespread support (even if for contradictory reasons) and the successful completion of such projects. A society only loses the confidence of its members when its collective efforts are frustrated, when the linkage between sacred symbols and practical activities is broken, and when projects do not make sense to the people who are called on to carry them out. These ills can be cured by designing and carrying out projects that command support from both factions and that *succeed*.

All of this is part and parcel of our daily experience in social systems smaller than the nation. One of the most important things that can be learned from the sociological study of social systems is that the behavior of large and small systems is the same in many respects, indeed that each of the component systems of which a large social system is composed has the same set of functional requirements and is subject to the same types of external and internal influence as the larger system taken as a whole. Cycles of confidence do not affect large social systems only. They occur in families and chess clubs, municipal governments and shoe factories, labor unions and boarding schools.

In these smaller social systems which account for so large a part of our everyday experience, we take for granted much that we must painfully learn to apply to larger social systems. We know without exhaustive analysis that a family which launches a house-building project will be greatly strengthened as a social system if the house is built in accordance with the plan at about the expected cost in about the expected time and turns out to be pretty and comfortable. We do not need much sociological apparatus to predict that a total failure of the house-building project may threaten the continuity of the family. If we are at all sane and serious about such a venture we shall take care to see that the plans are drawn in such a way as to give the project a reasonable chance of success, and we will not embark on the construction without some assurance that the members of the family want this kind of house and can find the labor and the money to complete it before their expectations turn to discouragement and disgust.

To what extent confidence in a component organization, like a union local or a branch office or a county political party, is affected by confidence in the larger organizations of which it is a part, is a complicated question to which no general answer can be given. In the usual case, the level of confidence in a component organization is more likely than not to rise and fall with the level of confidence in the larger system to which it belongs, but there are so many exceptions to this principle that it cannot be taken for granted in any given case. The decline of national confidence in the Era of Protest had an apparently disruptive effect on the armed forces, on colleges and universities, on the Catholic church and some Protestant churches. It had little observable impact on the solidarity of state and local governments, business corporations, or recreational associations. Some professional organizations were disrupted but others had their solidarity reinforced; labor unions were not much affected one way or the other.

If we examine the whole roster of American social organizations after a decade of almost-revolutionary discontent, some have been drastically changed, many have been changed to some extent, and some have been quite unaffected by either the loss of national confidence or the efforts that have been made to regain it. What is more interesting perhaps is that many of the churches, universities, military units, and municipal agencies most heavily affected by the troubles of the larger system have regained their equilibrium much more rapidly than the nation as a whole, thanks to projects of institutional improvement that succeeded well enough to restore their collective confidence. Needless to say, there are negative instances too—colleges heading for bankruptcy and dissolution, churches whose congregations have fled, military and political organizations that have ceased to perform their functions—but on the whole, the prolonged social experimentation of recent years has demonstrated the resilience of these smaller social systems when faced with the same kind of challenge that threatens to overwhelm the government of the larger society to which they belong. There are several reasons for lack of resilience in the national government:

First, the managers of that government cherish delusions of omnipotence and are committed—at least rhetorically—to the impossible task of solving all problems at once instead of a few problems at a time.

Second, the national government suffers from its failure to recognize the social problem of war or to experiment with serious projects for the prevention of a nuclear holocaust. Since this problem would claim a very high priority in any rational evaluation of contemporary social problems, the refusal to accord it priority makes every other national project of social improvement somewhat implausible, as if a family were to occupy itself in arranging piano lessons for the children while its house was burning down.

Third, the sheer variety and complexity of government programs of social improvement renders them nearly invisible to the public. Only a handful of experts—less than a dozen persons I would guess—are capable of describing the national welfare program in a comprehensive way; none of these are likely to be familiar with agricultural price supports or arms control negotiations. Because of this opacity, ineffective programs do not arouse as much opposition as they should.

Fourth, and perhaps most important, the agencies of government have not actively encouraged social inventors until very recently, and then only with respect to such specialized problems as criminal justice, school administration, and tax collection. With respect to problems of larger scope, there has been no real effort to stimulate social invention.

The Importance of
Social Invention

The argument of this essay has been that it is quite possible to shape the social system according to our desires if the project is framed according to the elementary logic of technology and takes account of what is already known about social systems and methods of changing them. The experience of a great variety of successful and unsuccessful projects, as traced in the foregoing pages, seems to me to support this thesis convincingly, but as usually happens in any close study of social reality, the initial hypothesis, even if verified, turns out to be much less than the whole story. In this case, the critical role of the social inventor in social problem solving was not at first understood, but became increasingly evident in the course of analysis.

Social inventors are people who identify social problems and design feasible projects for solving them. Whatever else they may be, they are writers addressing a particular set of readers whom they incite to action. Some social inventors have been private men who never held an official position—Rousseau, Locke, Fourier, Riis, Harrington, Reich, for example. Some began as private commentators but followed their ideas into the arena of political action—St. Simon, Marx, Bellamy, Woodrow Wilson, Malcolm X, and Ralph Nader, among others. A number of them were political leaders whose books were written for the instruction of followers—Lenin, Hitler, Che Guevara, and Mao Tse-tung, for example.

The social inventor defines a social problem and proposes an apparently feasible project for solving it, both within the same frame-of-reference. He sets out, in other words, to describe an existing social condition in terms of his own choosing, to persuade his readers to find the condition intolerable, and to show them what they can do to change it. For a social invention to take effect, all three parts of the presentation must be believable—the description of the existing condition, the reasons for not tolerating it, and the project of changing it. But note how these components differ in logical structure. The description of the existing condition may be highly colored but is usually subject to some degree of verification, although it may be a sloppy kind of verification if the facts alleged are remote from the immediate experience of those to whom the presentation is directed. The second component of the presentation, the reasons for not tolerating the existing condition, are not subject to verification at all, being purely subjective. Any situation whatever may become intolerable if it is successfully represented to the audience as dangerous to them or degrading and, at the same time, unnecessary. The third component of the presentation, the project for transforming the existing situation into something different and better is not, strictly speaking, verifiable in advance but, as we have repeatedly shown in the course of this book, such projects can be evaluated as to their feasibility. Indeed, even an unsophisticated audience can often recognize a feasible project although its details are a little hazy.

Nothing is easier than to describe some existing social condition and to complain about it. The right to criticize is perhaps the distinguishing trait of a good, as contrasted to, a would-be perfect society. Even in periods of high social confidence, the volume of social complaint in the United States remains very high; in periods of low confidence, like the 1890s or the 1960s, its volume is beyond all reckoning. Moreover, it tends to expand with the general expansion of print and other forms of mass communication. A comprehensive bibliography on the Prohibition movement would contain about 5,000 titles; a similar bibliography on the regulation of drugs would have to be very much larger. Most of these works do not greatly illuminate the problem to which they are addressed, and their effects on public opinion are imperceptible.

The case is very different for those rare manifestos that combine a passionate description of a social problem with a novel and apparently feasible proposal for solving it. The impact of such a manifesto is often all out of proportion to the author's credentials. So rare is the gift of social invention that even the clumsiest and craziest inventors— a Fourier or a Gobineau or a Germaine Greer—are likely to attract large and respectful followings.

To understand this phenomenon we must go back and examine the basic components of such a manifesto: the description of an existing condition, the rationale for changing it, and the apparently feasible program of change. The first and the last terms of this formula are objective; the middle term is wholly subjective. That is to say, the description of an existing condition identified as a social problem must be at least partly grounded on demonstrable facts within the experience of readers in order to convince them, although of course, some other facts in the same description may be invented or distorted. The feasibility of the action program is also subject to objective demonstration, at least with regard to its earliest stages, although the attainment of its ultimate goals may have to be taken on faith. By contrast, the middle term, the rationale for change, has a purely subjective character, no matter how logical it may seem. It rests, finally, upon an arbitrary preference for certain values over other values, a voluntary allegiance to one sacred symbol rather than another.[2]

Because the decision that a given social condition is intolerable and ought to be changed is not subject to empirical proof or disproof, it is likely to be made in response to the possibility of change, whenever that possibility is clearly offered. For humans are game-playing, habitat-improving animals and no games are more exciting than those which promise social improvement. Anyone who formulates a plausible program of social improvement is almost certain to discover that he has founded a social movement, ready or not.

It follows from this that every social invention is potentially dangerous, as the rulers of totalitarian societies understand so well. At the same time, we must recognize that unless the evolution of physical technology is interrupted in some unforeseen way, it will continue to cause frequent and unpredictable dislocations in existing social arrangements, in addition to the spontaneous troubles which social institutions develop even in the absence of technological progress. In other words, we can count on a large and increasing number of social problems for the foreseeable future. Solving them within the framework of a good society calls for more social inventors and better social inventions than we have had in the recent past. The increased number of social inventors is certain to appear as it becomes increasingly obvious how the lone inventor can move the social world, given an ideology on which to stand and a long-term project to use ar lever. It is less certain that the quality of social inventions will be generally improved. It cannot be done by exhortation. It can be done by example. What we need, in other words, are more projects of social improvement which include an accurate description of the condition to be changed; a careful and honest description of the end-condition to be achieved; a division of the project into successive stages, and descriptions of the conditions to be achieved at each stage; practicable methods for getting from each stage to the next; estimates of the time, personnel, material resources and information required to get from each stage to the next; procedures for measuring goal attainment at each stage; and procedures for detecting unanticipated results at each stage. Plus a measure of humility, an awareness of mortality, and abundant good will.

Notes

Chapter 2

1. Perez Zagorin, "Thomas Hobbes" *International Encyclopedia of the Social Sciences,* Vol. 6, p. 485.

2. John Locke, *An Essay Concerning the True Original Extent of Civil Government,* 1690. Chapter 1, p. 1.

3. Ibid., Chapter 8, p. 99.

4. Thomas Jefferson, *A Declaration by the Representatives of the United States of America in Congress Assembled,* July 4, 1776.

5. In 1792, the Revolutionary Convention declared Rousseau a national hero and ordered his body transferred from a country churchyard to the Pantheon of Paris.

6. Jean-Jacques Rousseau, *The Social Contract,* 1792.

7. Ibid.

8. Thomas Jefferson to James Madison, from Paris, September 6, 1789. Quoted in Philip S. Foner, *Basic Writings of Thomas Jefferson* (Garden City, New York: Halcyon House, 1950) p. 588.

9. Lewis Namier, *Vanished Supremacies: Essays on European History, 1812–1918* (New York: Harper Torchbooks, 1963) pp. 13–14.

10. Charles Seignobos, *Histoire Sincère de la Nation Française* (Paris: Presses Universitaires de France, 1946) Chapter 18.

11. Quoted by Reinhard Bendix (in Cahnman and Boskoff's *Sociology and History*) from Baron von Haxthausen, *The Russian Empire, Its Peoples, Institutions and Resources,* (London, Chapman and Hall, 1856) Vol. 1, p. 335.

12. Quoted in Claude G. Bowers, *Jefferson and Hamilton: The Struggle for Democracy in America* (Boston: Houghton Mifflin Company, 1966) pp. 321–322.

13. For evidence of this see Herman R. Lantz, Eloise C. Snyder, Margaret Britton and Raymond Schmitt, "Pre-Industrial Patterns in the Colonial Family in America: A Content Analysis of Colonial Magazines," *American Sociological Review,* Vol. 33, No. 3 (June 1968) pp. 413–426.

14. Daniel Boorstin, *The Lost World of Thomas Jefferson* (Boston, Beacon Press, 1948) p. 7.

15. Locke, *Civil Government,* Chapter 9, p. 124.

Chapter 3

1. Joseph Needham, *Science and Civilization in China* (London: Blackwell, 1954–74) Vol. 1, p. 74.
2. Indeed with hindsight, we can now see its beginnings in the fifteenth century and even earlier.
3. Jean Fourastiê, *Machinisme et Bien-Etre* (Paris, 1951).
4. See, among other sources: *Demographic Yearbook of the United Nations, 1967,* Table 6; Warren S. Thompson and David T. Lewis, *Population Problems* (New York: McGraw-Hill, 1965) Table 6-2; Kingsley Davis, "The Origins and Growth of Urbanization in the World" *American Journal of Sociology* (March 1955). Adna Ferrin Weber, *The Growth of Population in the Nineteenth Century,* originally published in 1899 (Ithaca: Cornell University Press, 1963).
5. Henry Watterson, quoted in John P. Davis, *Corporations, a Study of the Origin and Development of Great Business Corporations and Their Relation to the Authority of the State* [originally published 1905] (New York: Capricorn Books, 1961) p. 4.
6. The resurgence of despotic government in twentieth-century Europe was apparently not anticipated by anybody.
7. Pitmin Sorokin, *Social and Cultural Dynamics,* Vol. 3 *Fluctuations of Social Relationships, War and Revolution* (New York: Bedminster Press, 1962) Tables 15 and 17.
8. The same cannot be said of the peripheral areas, like Turkey or India, where Western personality models were often adapted along with European clothing and furniture.

Chapter 4

1. Edward Bellamy, *Looking Backward* (New York: D. Appleton and Company, 1888) *Equality* (New York: D. Appleton and Company, 1897).
2. Ibid., *Looking Backward,* p. 345.
3. Karl Kautsky, *The Class-Struggle,* originally published in 1892. (New York: The Norton Library, 1971).
In 1892, Marx had been dead nine years. Friedrich Engels was still working on the manuscript of Volume III of *Das Kapital,* which Marx had left unfinished. He had already appointed Kautsky, who was only 32, to succeed himself as Marx's literary executor and had introduced him to the material intended for Volume IV, which Kautsky eventually published under Marx's name as a separate work called *Theories of Surplus Value.* Kautsky, then, was no marginal commentator on Marxist doctrine but the lineal successor of its founder. When he sat down in 1892 to prepare a fuller explanation of the Erfurt Program adopted by the German Social Democratic Party the previous year, he wrote with authority and what he wrote left an indelible imprint on the future course of Marxism.
4. Quoted in Robert Tucker, *Philosophy and Myth in Karl Marx* (Cambridge: The University Press, 1971) p. 201.
5. Karl Marx and Friedrich Engels, *The Communist Manifesto,* 1848 (New York: Washington Square Press, 1965).
6. Ibid., Chapter 2.
7. Tucker, *Philosophy and Myth in Karl Marx.*
8. Karl Marx, *Selected Writings in Sociology and Social Philosophy,* eds. T. B. Bottomore and Maximilien Rubel (New York: McGraw-Hill, 1956) p. 238.
9. For an ingenious attempt to reconstruct their opinions about how the classless society would be administered, see John Plamenatz, "The Paris Commune and the Soviets," *Man and Society* (New York: McGraw-Hill, 1963) Vol. II, pp. 381–386.

10. Karl Kautsky, *The Class Struggle*, p. 27.
11. Ibid, p. 138.
12. Ibid., p. 152.
13. Ibid., p. 156.
14. See Chapter V of *The Rules of Sociological Method.*
15. For contrasting interpretations of Durkheim's political orientation, see the papers by Joseph Neyer, Melvin Richter, and Lewis A. Coser in Kurt H. Wolff, ed., *Emile Durkheim, 1858–1917.* (Columbus: Ohio State University Press, 1960) p. 26.
16. Ibid., p. 22.
17. Ibid., p. 119.
18. Emile Durkheim, *Suicide,* pp. 373–374.

Chapter 5

1. Adolph Hitler, *Mein Kampf* (New York: Stackpole Sons, 1938) p. 153.
2. Even the toy nations of Europe, preserved as tax shelters and tourist attractions— Monaco, Liechtenstein, Andorra, San Marino—have most of these features.
3. Quincy Wright, "The Study of War" *International Encyclopedia of the Social Sciences,* 1968, Vol. 16, pp. 453–468; *A Study of War* (Chicago: University of Chicago Press, 2nd ed., 1965).
4. Lewis F. Richardson, *Statistics of Deadly Quarrels,* eds., Quincy Wright and C. C. Lienau (Pittsburgh: Boxwood Press, 1960).

Chapter 6

1. Niccolò Machiavelli, *The Prince,* (1513) (New York: Modern Library, 1936).
2. Karl Marx and Friedrich Engels, *The Communist Manifesto,* (1848) (New York: Washington Square Press, 1965).
3. About 1908. See W. I. Thomas and Florian Znaniecki, *The Polish Peasant in Europe and America, 1918–1920.* 4 Vols.
4. Marx and Engels, *The Communist Manifesto,* p. 3.
5. Some idea of the scale of the movement can be gotten from Samuel Eliot Morison, *The European Discovery of America: The Northern Voyages* A.D. *500–1600* (New York: Oxford University Press, 1971).

Chapter 7

1. The classic analysis of the similarities of these two revolutions may be found in Crane Brinton's *Anatomy of Revolution,* 1938.
2. There were several slightly different versions of the Fourteen Points presented at various times.
3. James MacGregor Burns, *Roosevelt: the Soldier of Freedom,* (New York: Harcourt, Brace, Jovanovich, 1970) pp. 129–130.
4. Alexander Hamilton, *Federalist Paper* No. 15.
5. There are some variants of these arguments that would have to be considered in a more extended discussion of such a project. They have to do, for example, with the difficulty of extending personal rights of citizenship in a confederation to the subjects of autocratic governments and the danger that a successful *coup d'état* against the central authority might accomplish world conquest by a single stroke, particularly if the conspirators obtained access to a stock of nuclear weapons. Objections of this kind are serious but not as fundamental as the two major points above.

6. Alexander Hamilton and James Madison, *Federalist Paper,* No. 18.

7. For a rather feeble but well-meaning attempt to provide one, see Grenville Clark and Louis Sohn, *Introduction to World Peace Through World Law,* (Cambridge: Harvard University Press) successive editions, 1958, 1960, 1966, 1973.

8. For example, a resolution submitted to the fifth World Peace Through Law in Conference in Belgrade in 1970 proposed a "broad revision of the United Nations Charter to provide for compulsory adjudication of disputes by the International Court of Justice; a new European Equity Tribunal; the transformation of the General Assembly into a world parliament with legislative powers; a world executive council unrestricted by the veto to enforce law made and judgments rendered by the United Nations organs; UN revenue raising authority; universality of membership without the right of succession; general and complete disarmament; and human rights safeguards." *New Jersey Law Journal,* October 21, 1971.

9. The almost single-handed achievement of Jean Monnet in describing a European Union so convincingly that organized support for the project eventually developed in a dozen countries within the framework of their existing political structures, is a good model of how this might come about.

10. Alexander DeConde, *A History of American Foreign Policy* (New York: Charles Scribner & Sons, 1963) pp. 508–509.

Chapter 8

1. Reproduced in Henry Steele Commager, *Documents of American History,* (New York: Appleton-Century Crofts, 1949) pp. 278–281.

2. Letter to Horace Greeley, August 22, 1862.

3. *Historical Statistics of the United States 1957,* Series A, pp. 181–94.

4. Ibid., Series C, pp. 88–114.

5. Jane Addams, *Twenty Years at Hull House, with Autobiographical Notes,* (New York: Macmillan, 1910) pp. 120–126.

6. Jane Addams, *The Second Twenty Years at Hull House: With a Record of a Growing World Consciousness* (New York: Macmillan, 1930).

7. Addams, *Twenty Years at Hull House,* p. 85.

8. As was alcoholic consumption in general. See *Historical Statistics of the United States: Colonial Times to 1957,* Series G, 249 and 288.

9. Clark Warburton, *The Economic Results of Prohibition* (New York: Columbia University Press, 1932) E. M. Jellinek, "Recent trends in alcoholism and in alcohol consumption," *Quarterly Journal of Studies on Alcohol,* Vol. 8 (July 1947).

10. Joseph R. Gusfield, *Symbolic Crusade: Status Politics and the American Temperance Movement.* (Urbana: University of Illinois Press, 1963).

11. Ibid., p. 121.

12. Mayor Dever of Chicago told a congressional committee in 1926 that at least 60 percent of Chicago policemen were in the liquor business. For further details on the relation between law enforcement and bootlegging, see Herbert Asbury, *The Great Illusion: An Informal History of Prohibition,* (Garden City, N.Y.: Doubleday, 1950).

13. Robert S. Lynd and Helen Merrill Lynd, *Middletown: A Study in American Culture* (New York: Harcourt Brace, 1929).

Chapter 9

1. *Historical Statistics of the United States 1957,* Bureau of the Census, Series D, 741–745.

2. *Statistical Abstract of the United States,* 1971. Table No. 442.

3. Ibid., Number 440.
4. *Statistical Abstract of the United States,* 1970. Table No. 451.
5. *Statistical Abstract of the United States,* 1970. Table No. 463 and the President's Commission on Income Maintenance Programs, *Background Papers,* 1970, p. 235.
6. Ibid.
7. *Statistical Abstract of the United States,* 1971. Table No. 1108.
8. For a full exposition of these problems, see Jane Jacobs, *The Life and Death of Great American Cities* (New York: Random House, 1961).
9. A fascinating account of the operations of one such office during this period by a close observer can be found in Peter Blau's *The Dynamics of Democracy: A Study of Interpersonal Relations in Two Government Agencies* (Chicago: University of Chicago Press, 1955).
10. *Statistical Abstract of the United States,* 1971. Table No. 469.
11. An account of one of these projects, and an explanation of its early decline, may be found in Edward C. Banfield's *Government Project* (Glencoe, Illinois: The Free Press, 1951).
12. With the exception that the project soon lost its original populist inclination and aligned itself with local interests. See Philip A. Selznick, *TVA, The Grass Roots* (Berkeley: University of California Press, 1949).

Chapter 10

1. Andrew Hacker, "The Violent Black Minority," in Guthrie and Barnes, eds. *Man and Society: Focus on Reality,* 1972 p. 85.
2. Albert Cleage, "Transfer of Power" in Horowitz, ed., *The Troubled Conscience: American Social Issues,* 1971, pp. 208–09.

Chapter 11

1. Joseph A. Kershaw, *Government Against Poverty,* (Chicago: Markham, 1970) p. 2.

Chapter 12

1. *New York Times,* July 7, 1972, p. 39m.
2. Charles Sumner, *Congressional Record 948,* 1874.
3. *Statistical Abstract of the United States,* 1972. Tables No. 223 and 224.
4. Although survey data covering 1965–1966 suggests that about one third of all robberies went unreported at that time. President's Commission on Law Enforcement and the Administration of Justice, *The Challenge of Crime in a Free Society,* (Washington, D.C.: United States Government Printing Office, 1967), Chapter 2.
5. According to uniform crime reports as summarized in Tables No. 237, 230, 240, and 241 of the *Statistical Abstract,* 1972.
6. For a summary of the legal issues see Bernard Evans Harvith, "The Constitutionality of Residence Tests for General and Categorical Assistance Programs, in Jacobus Ten Broek and the editors of *California Law Review, The Law of the Poor* (San Francisco: Chandler Publishing Company, 1966) pp. 243–317.
7. *Statistical Abstract of the United States,* 1972, Table No. 239.

Chapter 13

1. Angus Campbell, *White Attitudes Toward Black People* (Ann Arbor: Institute for Social Research, 1971) Chapter 7.
2. *Statistical Abstract of the United States,* 1971, Table No. 30.
3. Edgar Z. Friedenberg, *Coming of Age in America* (New York: Random House, 1965) p. 45.
4. Charles A. Reich, *The Greening of America* (New York: Bantam, 1971) pp. 327–331.
5. Evan Stark, "Up from Underground: Notes on Youth Culture" in Feldman and Thielbar, eds., *Life Styles: Diversity in American Society,* (Boston: Little, Brown and Company, 1972).
6. Leslie A. Fiedler, *Waiting for the End,* (New York: Stein and Day, 1964) pp. 167–168.
7. Norman O. Brown, "The Resurrection of the Body," in Theodore Roszak, ed., *Forces,* (New York: Harper and Row, 1972) p. 129.
8. Robert Tucker, *Philosophy and Myth in Karl Marx* (Cambridge: The University Press, 1971) p. 201.
9. Betty Friedan, *The Feminine Mystique* (New York: Norton, 1963).
10. Shulamith Firestone, *The Dialectic of Sex* (New York: William Morrow, 1970).

Chapter 14

1. For a full-scale case history of changing expectations in a traditional society, in which both the exhorters and the examples are fully identified, see Margaret Mead, *New Lives for Old: Cultural Transformation in Manus—1928–1953.* (New York: William Morrow, 1956).
2. These observations apply to the solution of social problems where, by definition, there is a conflict of values. Social technology may also be applied to certain types of organizational problems, in which the goals to be realized are given in advance and accepted by all participants. In such cases, of course, the rationale for changing an existing situation may be objectively verifiable.

Index

224

Index

Child-welfare services (*continued*)
activities of, 142-143; expansion of, 141;
use of funds in, 141-142, 143
Citizen, role of (1848-1970), 62-63
Civilian Conservation Corps (CCC), 16,
138, 139
Civil Rights Act (1964), 161, 172
Civil rights movement, judicial decisions
on, 169
Class Struggle (Kautsky), 49, 51-54
Cleage, Albert, on urban social problems,
156-157
Cold War: and colonial liberation move-
ments, 183-184; international relations
in, 64-67
Collective bargaining, 129; judicial deci-
sions on, 169-170
College students. (*See* Student liberation
movement)
Colonization, 29, 39
Community development, as social im-
provement project (during New Deal),
144, 148
Congress of Vienna, 34, 35
Communist Manifesto, The, program of,
49, 50
Communist revolutions, successful, 92-93
Confederations, historical perspective on,
104-105
Cost, of defective projects, 7
Counterculture, 197-199
Criminal justice system, judicial reform of,
174-176
Critique of the Gotha Program (Marx), 50

Dawes Act (1887), provisions of, 191
Declaration of Independence, and social
contract theory, 22
Declaration of Sentiments, 112
Demonstrations, and liberation movements
of 1960s, 185, 191
Dialectic of Sex, The (Firestone), 200
Dictatorships, forms of (during 1900s), 72,
73
Direct subsidies, as social improvement
projects (during New Deal), 133-136,
146-147
Disarmament projects: historical perspec-
tive on, 107-108; problems of, 108-109

Division of Labor, The (Durkheim), 54, 56,
58
Dix, Dorothea, and exposé technique, 111
Doe v. Bolton (1973), 179
Durkheim, Emile, 54-59

*Economic and Philosophical Manuscripts
of 1844* (Marx), 51
Economic Opportunity Act (1964), 161
Education: impact of women's liberation
movement on, 201; trends in (during
1800s), 34-35. (*See also* Student liberation movement)
Elementary and Secondary Education Act
(1965), 161
End-condition(s): of abolition movement,
112, 113, 115; of Black liberation
movement, 186, 188; of Chicano liberation movement, 189-190; of defective
projects, 7; of direct subsidy projects,
133-134; of good society, 206-207; of
liberation movements (during Era of
Protest), 182-183; of Native American
liberation movement, 190-191; of public
housing projects, 137-138; of Puerto
Rican liberation movement, 192-193; of
regulatory commission (during New
Deal), 127, 128; of settlement house,
118-119; of student counterculture,
198-199; of War on Poverty, 162-163,
166, 167; of women's liberation movement, 200-201; in world revolution
project, 94
Environmental effects, of war (during
1900's), 70
Environmental pollution, public awareness
of (during Era of Protest), 159
Equality (Bellamy), 45, 46
Era of Protest, 16: characteristics of,
151-153; liberation movements during,
182-202; social improvement by
judiciary during, 169-181
Essay on Civil Government (Locke), 21
Exposé technique, in American social
movements, 111
Eighteenth Amendment, provisions of,
120. (*See also* Prohibition experiment)
English Garden City movement, 144
Executive Order No. 9 (1941), 145